LAWYER NATION

Lawyer Nation

*The Past, Present, and Future of
the American Legal Profession*

Ray Brescia

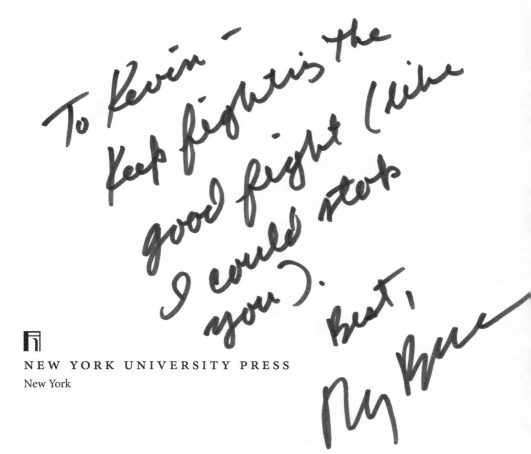

To Kevin —
Keep fighting the
good fight (like
I could stop
you).
Best,
Ry Bre

NEW YORK UNIVERSITY PRESS
New York

NEW YORK UNIVERSITY PRESS
New York
www.nyupress.org

© 2024 by New York University
All rights reserved

Please contact the Library of Congress for Cataloging-in-Publication data.
ISBN: 9781479823680 (hardback)
ISBN: 9781479823703 (library ebook)
ISBN: 9781479823697 (consumer ebook)

Manufactured in the United States of America

10 9 8 7 6 5 4 3 2 1

Also available as an ebook

To my parents

CONTENTS

1

A Janus-Faced Profession

Hired cunning. That is what the president of the United States called lawyers, particularly the "most highly remunerated members of the bar" whose "bold and ingenious schemes" enable their rich clients to evade the laws designed to "regulate in the interests of the public the use of great wealth." When such lawyers employ their talent and learning "in the highly remunerative task of enabling a very wealthy client to override or circumvent the law," they encourage "a spirit of dumb anger against all laws and of disbelief in their efficacy."[1]

Another prominent critic at the time—a successful corporate lawyer who would later become a U.S. Supreme Court Justice despite religious and ethnic affiliations that made him an outsider in the legal profession's exclusive upper echelons—noted that the general public no longer held the practicing bar in high esteem. His reasons echoed the president's: "Instead of holding a position of independence, between the wealthy and the people, prepared to curb the excesses of either," lawyers had "become adjuncts of great corporations and have neglected their obligation to use their powers for the protection of the people." He complained that we "hear much of the 'corporation lawyer,' and far too little of the 'people's lawyer.'" If the excesses of wealth are not curbed, he warned, "[t]here will come a revolt of the people against the capitalists unless the aspirations of the people are given some adequate legal expression."[2] As a result, the people "are beginning to doubt whether in the long run democracy and absolutism can co-exist in the same community" and whether "there is a justification for the great inequalities in the distribution of wealth." This has resulted in the people beginning to "think" and showing signs "on all sides of a tendency to act."[3]

These criticisms arose at a time of great change. A dynamic economy, new technologies, changing population demographics due to an influx of immigrants, new social movements, and growing income inequality were all having a dramatic effect on life in the United States. An American legal profession—proud of its role in the founding of the republic, the adoption of the U.S. Constitution, and the defense of democracy and the rule of law—was having its prominence in society called into question. More and more Americans saw law, lawyers, and the legal system as standing in the way of reform, democracy, civil rights, workers' rights, and political progress—whether it was elites of the bar securing the interests of their wealthy clients in opposition to those of consumers and the working class, or judges determined to thwart efforts to expand basic rights and regulate businesses in even their most basic functions. A profession steeped in tradition, one that cultivated collegiality and practiced the dark art of exclusivity, soon found its structure and institutions ill-suited for a modernizing economy and a diversifying populace. A clubby, exclusive, elitist, and gendered legal profession reflected the more homogeneous, hierarchical, insular communities that dominated American culture in prior eras. Formed to serve a very different nation, lawyers found themselves poorly suited to operate effectively in a new age.

One could raise many of these critiques of American lawyers at various times throughout U.S. history. Lawyers defended slave owners and robber barons, Japanese internment during World War II, and the destruction of Indigenous lands and lives. They constructed the Jim Crow system. They have been central to political and economic crises, like Watergate, the savings and loan crisis of the 1980s, and the financial crisis of 2008. Indeed, members of the legal profession have often played significant roles in some of the darkest moments of American history.

But like the mythical two-faced Janus, the American legal profession has also played more noble roles. Lawyers have been at the center of efforts to advance democracy, civil rights, political freedom, and the rule of law. Starting even before the American Revolution, colonial lawyers defended a free press in the trial of John Peter Zenger in the 1730s, and others, like James Otis and John Adams, helped to frame the arguments in favor of independence. Thomas Jefferson and other lawyers embedded those arguments in the Declaration of Independence. At the nation's birth, some of the country's most prominent lawyers crafted its constitution and advocated for that document's adoption. In the early part of the nineteenth century, in a nation established as one of laws and not men, lawyers played a prominent role in the expansion of the United States (with some facilitating the decimation of Indigenous populations and native possession of those lands). They served, as Alexis de Tocqueville observed, as the closest thing America had to an aristocracy, playing a significant role in balancing the interests of society's different sectors to promote a functioning community. Later, although some lawyers created and defended the institutions of white supremacy, others like Thurgood Marshall, Constance Baker Motley, Moorefield Storey, and Jack Greenberg worked to dismantle them. Today, some lawyers continue to advance democracy, voting rights, and civil rights; others are working to undermine them.

In a nation that has relied so heavily on its lawyers and legal system to structure society, define rights, and maintain peace and order through lawful dispute resolution, it is hardly a surprise that members of the legal profession have played a prominent role in American culture, government, and history since even before the nation's founding. Of course, members of the legal profession have not always operated in an honorable way, choosing instead to use their skills and knowledge for personal gain and to advance the interests of their clients or themselves at the expense of the community and the nation. Throughout U.S. history, when this predatory behavior has become particularly misaligned with what should be the profession's core functions—promoting the rule of law, the institutions of democracy, and civil rights—the American legal profession has found its role in society called into question. When its members have abused their role within the system that, in many ways, lawyers themselves created, it has sparked periods of introspection from within and elicited calls for reform from without. Today, some members of the legal profession are engaged in just the type of behavior that has brought it into disrepute for centuries.

Lawyers have opposed the peaceful transition of power and are engaged in concerted efforts to roll back significant rights. The profession is still predominantly white and male, especially in its upper ranks. Due to the high cost of legal representation, the profession is failing to serve far too many American families. This failure has created a market opportunity for those who would provide services at a more affordable price. Often such affordable services are the product of technological advances, which are shaping and enhancing the way lawyers practice while also presenting threats to the lawyers' monopoly power over the practice of law.

The introduction of new technologies into the practice of law, as in many other economic sectors, raises questions about the potential for professional obsolescence. Some of these technologies helped to transform the practice of law virtually overnight in the face of pandemic protocols, changing law practice dramatically. Finally, and perhaps as a function of these other phenomena, today's lawyers experience high rates of depression, anxiety, and substance abuse, leading some to question their career choice and likely discouraging others from joining the profession in the first place. These six forces—*the pandemic, a racial and gender justice reckoning, an insurrection, the legal services market failure, technology, and lawyer disaffection*—not only pose a significant threat to the future of the legal profession but also present an opportunity for real change. If the American legal profession does not respond to these forces in an effective way, it would certainly change American culture significantly. What is more, should those lawyers undermining the rule of law and engineering the rollback of well-established rights actually succeed in their efforts, this may result in the end of the United States as a functioning, multiracial, constitutional democracy, creating a nation in which law has no role. Legal scholar Roscoe Pound once said that "there is no law without lawyers."[4] The corollary is that there is not much need for lawyers where there is no law. Indeed, lawyers become little more than handmaidens for authoritarian rulers where the rule of law does not exist.

This book is about the state of the American legal profession and the fact that it faces what may be nothing short of an existential crisis. And the American democratic experiment hinges on resolving that crisis in an effective and meaningful way. Are there lessons to be learned from prior periods in American history when the profession faced similar crises and emerged from them largely intact?

The American legal profession has faced several different crises over the roughly three centuries of its existence. One deserves special attention when we consider the fate of the American legal profession today. The particularly pointed critiques that started this chapter arose at the turn of the nineteenth to the twentieth century. The U.S. president who criticized the legal profession was Theodore Roosevelt. The future Supreme Court Justice? Louis Brandeis. The profession at that time faced a series of crises: changing national demographics; innovations in technology that changed how and where people lived and worked; and the fact that many Americans could not afford legal representation. The final crisis represented threats to the rule of law, which included the profession's failure to serve the needs of most Americans as well as its fealty to economic hierarchy.[5] President Roosevelt, Justice Brandeis, and others criticized a legal profession that had remained largely unchanged in its demographics and practices over a hundred years, even while the nation evolved all around it. In the late nineteenth century, lawyers still practiced largely on their own or in loose partnerships with one or two others. There were few effective bar associations and no rules of ethics to guide behavior except in a handful of states. Most lawyers had never attended a law school. Many had never even obtained a college degree. There were no meaningful bar examinations. Because there were few barriers to enter the profession, and no formal ethical guardrails once a lawyer started practicing, lawyer behavior was practically unregulated. This sometimes led to a race to the bottom in terms of sharp practices. Meanwhile, aspiring lawyers who were women and from minoritized groups found their path to the profession all but blocked and leadership roles within the profession nonexistent. The profession at that time had faced few changes in its structures or practices over nearly a century. As a result, it found itself ill-suited to the changes afoot in the nation and needed to modernize to meet the needs of the American people.

The critiques of the profession raised at the time might ring true even now: that too many lawyers work primarily to gain advantages for their wealthy clients and fail to meet the legal needs of many American families. Some even engage in practices that undermine the rule of law and weaken civil rights. Because those criticisms of the profession at the turn of the nineteenth to the twentieth century might resemble critiques of the profession today, there is some value to revisiting those critiques from that prior era and the legal profession's response at that time to learn what reforms the profession should consider now. While the profession's past and present challenges do not repeat themselves, they do seem, like history itself, to rhyme.

A global pandemic hastened the adoption of new technology in legal practice. There are calls for greater diversity in the profession and fears that an unmoored Supreme Court is poised to undermine even more previously established rights than it already has. Authoritarianism is on the rise, throughout the world and even, perhaps, in the United States, and lawyers are playing a critical role in its re-emergence. Since these forces are similar to those faced by the profession a hundred years ago, the changes adopted to modernize the profession then might help inform its response today.

The profession adopted several reforms to address the challenges it faced at the turn of the nineteenth to the twentieth century. First, many lawyers, especially in large cities, began to organize formally into law firms for the first time and established bar associations, where few had enjoyed much staying power before then.[6] They also adopted formal codes of ethics where few had existed before. Admission to the bar had been fairly easy for a century—if the applicant was a white male, native born and Christian. Elites of the profession were concerned that weak barriers to entry to the profession permitted those who would diminish the professionalism of the bar join its ranks. To address this fear, they raised the profile of law schools in the education of lawyers and instituted bar exams and other requirements for admission in an effort to make it harder to become a lawyer, even though, throughout American history to that point, many men of impoverished backgrounds— like John Adams, Andrew Jackson, Millard Fillmore, and Abraham Lincoln—found a way to apprentice with a practicing lawyer and gain the ability to practice. At this time, some lawyers created fledgling public interest legal organizations in a modest attempt to address economic inequality. Lawyers did all of this in response to the core crisis of the day: the profession of the early twentieth century, created for the most part in the early days of the republic, was failing to meet the challenges and needs of a changing nation. But in looking at these reforms for insights into the reforms needed today, it is important to ask whether they did, in fact, solve the problems associated with the legal profession at the time.

Some of the institutional responses were designed to improve professionalism. The imposition of new accreditation requirements on law schools had the effect of shutting down many of the schools that were educating women and African Americans for law practice.[7] The organization of the bar into law firms, coupled with exclusionary practices of those firms, meant those who were not white, Christian, and male had a hard time finding employment with established firms, let alone advancing professionally within those firms.[8] Similarly, a national organization of lawyers, the American Bar Association (ABA), created a model national code of ethics that institutionalized prohibitions on what elite lawyers perceived as questionable tactics carried out by lawyers serving working-class Americans. Specifically, the code imposed restrictions on lawyer advertising, limiting how such lawyers found their clients, and constrained the use of contingency fee arrangements that made representation of low-income people possible.[9] Although legal aid organizations emerged at this time to address the bar's failure to serve the working class, such organizations never had enough resources to serve their clients; there were also strict limits on the types of cases such organizations could bring, the manner in which they could bring them, and the relief they could seek.[10] While these efforts made it harder to serve working class clients, especially those from immigrant and minoritized communities, they also mollified demands for more comprehensive reforms to increase access to legal representation. In sum, through institutions of its own creation, the profession often masked the problems it claims it was trying to solve and sometimes even made matters worse.

An analysis of the crises that shaped the legal profession at the turn of the nineteenth to the twentieth century and the profession's responses to them reveals three critical insights that will animate this book. *First*, the weaknesses inherent in the institutional response at that time meant the profession has struggled, and still struggles, with issues that plagued the profession over a century ago. These weaknesses have, in turn, led to crisis after crisis in the profession, including the political crises of the early 1970s and the economic crises of the 1980s and 2000s. At the center of many of these crises were lawyers who either failed to prevent their clients' illegal conduct or tacitly (or explicitly) approved it. These crises caused many to ask: "[W]here were the lawyers?"[11] The legal profession's core function is ensuring compliance with the law and preserving the rule of law; clearly it failed its clients and their communities by failing to prevent these crises.

Such crises have often been the impetus for those both inside and outside the profession to ring the alarm bells and demand reform. In the wake of the Watergate scandal, there were calls for law schools to mandate that all students receive training in legal ethics.[12] After the Enron scandal and similar events, the ethics rules around reporting corporate malfeasance were strengthened, albeit modestly.[13] Many of the same concerns raised at the turn of the nineteenth to the twentieth century have echoed over the last hundred years and, many would say, still linger with us today when it comes to the shortcomings of the American legal profession. This suggests that those legacy institutions were not adequate to address the profession's core challenges, leaving those challenges to reemerge over and over again. The failure to adopt meaningful reform that addressed those issues at the time ensures they continue to emerge, in crisis after crisis. It is also no surprise that, soon after each of these crises, when the profession has largely gone back to business as usual, a new crisis soon follows, restarting the cycle.

This time might be different. Indeed, the *second* core insight animating this analysis is that the American legal profession is at an inflection point every bit as critical as the one faced at the turn of the nineteenth to the twentieth century. Then, a profession largely unchanged for over one hundred years found itself a poor match for an evolving nation. Today's profession still so closely resembles the profession of a century ago in terms of its core institutions, like its rules of ethics, bar associations, and admissions criteria, even as the nation has changed around it once again. As a result, there is another mismatch between the needs of the community and the structure and functions of the profession. The well-worn crisis-response cycle—lather, rinse, repeat, embedded in these one-hundred-year-old institutions—is unlikely to ensure the profession emerges with continued relevance and a central role in the preservation of American democracy.

This observation leads to a *third* important insight about the institutions put in place at the turn of the nineteenth to the twentieth century also emerges: the institutions created by the legal profession at the beginning of the twentieth century remain the core components of the legal profession to this day—law firms, bar associations, codes of ethics, law schools, barriers to entry to the profession, and a public interest bar. Indeed, these institutions of the legal profession as they exist today more closely resemble those in existence in 1923 than those of 1923 resembled the profession's institutions in 1903. Thus, a deep analysis of these institutions is important now because they provide a logic and structure to the legal profession today. Indeed, the contemporary institutions of the legal profession, forged at a critical inflection point in the history of the American legal profession, have cast a century-long shadow over the profession, continuing to serve to structure it even as it exists today.

The following chapters will provide a deeper and more comprehensive assessment of the measures, structures, and organizations that the bar's elites put in place to respond to the perceived professional crises of the early twentieth century. Their actions reflect a distinctly *institutional* response. Any attempt to assess the effectiveness of this institutional response, and to determine whether legacy institutions are adequate to address today's challenges, requires a review of the reforms and the profession itself through an institutional lens.

Assessing the Institutions of the Legal Profession

In this book, I will assess the origins and the relative successes of the legal profession's institutions and examine what changes are necessary to those institutions to rise to the professional challenges of today. As a result, I will take an explicitly institutional perspective. I will not merely explore how the institutions *of* the profession do or do not serve desired policy goals; I will also ask whether the profession, *as an institution itself*, embedded in a multiracial democracy that purports to promote the rule of law, civil rights, and individual liberty, is effectively serving its institutional role within American society of today and the one we hope to have tomorrow.

At the outset, it is important to understand how I will use the term "institution." When most people think of an institution, they think of an organization like a company, university, or government agency. When scholars of institutions talk about institutions, they sometimes mean an organization and sometimes mean the norms, practices, rules, and laws that govern behavior within a particular system. The field in which institutional norms operate could be an organization, a family, a profession, an entire market, or society as a whole. Norms become *institutionalized* when they guide behavior within a particular system. My use of "institution" in this book, explored in greater depth in chapter 5, will encompass both meanings: that is, institutions are both organizations *and* patterns of behavior.

The legal profession and the institutions it created, enhanced, or expanded in the early twentieth century—for example, the ABA and state bar groups, law schools, law firms, and the public interest bar—exhibited tangible qualities. But these institutions also adopted norms and rules— like the 1908 Canons of Professional Ethics and more rigorous entry requirements for law schools and the bar—that ordered behavior within them. Because the profession embedded these norms into organizations and the practices of those who functioned within them, the norms became institutionalized.

To examine whether the existing institutions of the American legal profession in their current forms are suited to address the current challenges the profession faces—and to assess whether the profession is in a position to fulfill an appropriate and beneficial institutional role with the larger American political, social, and cultural landscape—my analysis will utilize the concept of *institutional fit*. Such an analytical approach facilitates an examination as to whether institutions embedded in a particular ecosystem are appropriate to fulfill their intended purposes.[14] I will also utilize the institutional typology championed by economist Daron Acemoglu and economist and political scientist James Robinson, who identify those institutions that contribute positively to society and those that leech benefits from it, what they call, respectively, "inclusive" and "extractive" institutions.[15] A legal profession that contributes constructively to the functioning of American democracy and community is one that is inclusive and not extractive.

In the end, I will argue that the institutional role of the American legal profession within the United States is primarily to defend democracy, promote the rule of law, advance civil rights within a multiracial community, further economic development within a market economy, and preserve individual liberties—all within an adversarial system of justice. I will attempt to measure the historical success of the profession in fulfilling this role and ask what institutional changes, if any, are necessary for the profession to adapt to the six forces it faces at present. Knowledge of the origins of institutions that constitute and shape the legal profession, a deep analysis of them, and an appreciation for the role the legal profession should play in a multiracial democracy will aid in assessing the effectiveness of these institutions, determining what reforms are necessary, and considering whether new institutions are needed. In the end, this will require the application of the concept identified above: institutional fit. It will also require an appreciation for how institutions change.

If the past is any guide, the six forces identified here will provoke a period of reflection—even soul-searching—within the legal profession, as they should. They should also prompt an appreciation that the profession's institutions established over the previous century are no longer capable of ensuring the profession plays its appropriate institutional role in society. This awareness should prompt calls for change—institutional change. It is entirely possible, if not likely, that the legal profession will respond to these forces the way it has to past crises: by adopting changes that fail to address the root problems before it, some of which have plagued the profession for over a century, if not since the founding of the republic. If so, the profession—and society as a whole—will not be better for it. But it does not have to be this way. As the legal profession faces a new series of challenges, are the profession's legacy institutions capable of addressing them? And what role can a more robust and meaningful embrace of reform play in that effort? It is to these questions that the remainder of this book is dedicated. Returning to the metaphor of the Roman god Janus, he was the god not only of duality but also transitions, and his two faces reflected his ability to look both backward and forward.[16] This book attempts to do just that.

The Plan of the Book

The first few chapters of this work will focus on the history of the legal profession leading up to the crisis situation that emerged at the end of the nineteenth century, when the institutions of the modern legal profession were forged. This history is important to understand, not only the critical role the profession has played in the American experience but also the challenges the elite members of the bar faced when they put these institutions in place. Specifically, chapter 2 will describe the profession of the colonial period and the first decades of the republic. Chapter 3 will provide the history of the legal profession from the first decades of the nineteenth century through to the post–Civil War era, when the crises that would spark the creation of the modern institutions of the legal profession emerged. Following that, chapter 4 will describe not only these crises as the public and the profession saw them at the turn of the nineteenth to the twentieth century but also the adoption of the institutions described above. It will also examine the values the bar's elites tried to institutionalize, and the institutions they ultimately created, in an effort to address those crises. Chapter 5 takes a more theoretical approach in analyzing the institutions of the profession. It also assesses the legal profession itself as an institution within a larger institutional framework and identifies the ways in which the institutional values should shape the profession moving forward, what I identify as *professionalism*, *access*, and *inclusion*. This institutional lens will provide a framework for the remainder of the book, which will analyze the six forces that the profession faces at present and then will offer suggestions for a course forward for the profession to rise to meet these challenges.

Indeed, in the remaining chapters, this work will discuss the six forces that the legal profession faces today. It will address some of them together, in single chapters, where they represent similar phenomena and the appropriate response to them might also appear closely connected. Specifically, the issues of the pandemic response and the racial- and gender-justice reckoning are assessed together in chapter 6 for reasons that will become apparent. Chapter 7 addresses the rule-of-law crisis made manifest in efforts to overturn the results of the 2020 election. Chapter 8 discusses the failure of the market for legal services and the growing threat that technology poses to the practice of law. Chapter 9 will conclude with strategies centered around the three institutional values that could help animate meaningful and lasting change for the legal profession. Implementing such strategies, this book will argue, will not only strengthen the profession but also likely address the last force affecting the profession: the problem of lawyer disaffection.

As the legal profession—and American democracy itself—face the series of challenges described here, this book will argue that a turn to what should be the profession's core values within that multiracial democracy will help to chart a course through these challenges and ensure the profession will not merely survive them but will thrive within a changed and ever-changing world and preserve and advance core democratic principles. More than a century after the legal profession faced a series of crises and created the institutions that would shape the profession for a hundred years, we hear the echoes of the features of those crises in the challenges the profession faces today. What is more, the profession created flawed institutions a century ago to respond to what it perceived as crises; those institutions and their flaws have meant the profession has faced the same crises, in different forms, with different names, in the intervening century. A clear-eyed view and deep reform of the profession are both necessary.

This book argues for an embrace of the three core values of professionalism, access, and inclusion to offer the American legal profession its best chance of moving past the current challenges it faces and those it will confront in the future. A commitment to these values will enable the profession to fulfill its rightful and historical role in preserving American democracy and the core principles that should animate it. If the legal profession is going to serve any role in the maintenance of democracy and the American system of justice, as it must—indeed, if those pillars of American society are even to survive—the profession must institute significant reforms and break its all-too-commonly invoked and weak crisis-response cycle.

There is still time to ensure the profession continues to serve critical functions in our economy and democracy. This book is a call to the profession—even as we are still in the midst of these six forces in many ways—to take a different approach than what it has done in the past in response to crises. It can, instead, seize the opportunity to advance real, lasting, and meaningful change and recommit to the central role the legal profession must play in promoting racial justice, meeting human needs, confronting inequality, and defending the rule of law and democracy. This book attempts not only to predict the legal profession's future but also to invent it. Not only to describe how current crises are shaping the profession but also to imagine how the profession can respond effectively and in ways that fully meet community needs. It strives not only to understand the critical role lawyers have played and should play in a democracy but also to reaffirm it, ensuring that the profession defends democracy and the rule of law, advances civil rights, protects individual liberty, and promotes equality. This exploration begins with the origins of the American legal profession. It is to that history that I now turn.

2

An Index to the Character of the People

His name and life story have been memorialized in song and his face adorns the ten-dollar bill. Alexander Hamilton, the immigrant striver, rose from an impoverished upbringing to the highest echelons of American power in the early days of the republic. After serving as a lieutenant colonel in the Continental Army, he participated in a media campaign in New York that was designed to ultimately lead to the adoption of the U.S. Constitution and then organized the new nation's finances in the Washington administration. He also became one of its most prominent and sought-after lawyers from the late 1780s until his death in 1804, representing clients in high-profile litigation and lucrative real estate transactions. In many ways, he was probably one of the first Americans to enter what today we call the "revolving door" between government service and private law practice. While he has been portrayed as both brilliant and petty, virtuous and selfish, the core principle upon which he and his revolutionary generation strove to create a new nation was the concept of *republicanism*: that is, the idea that disinterested patriots would place the common good above personal gain. When the liberty and relative equality among white men engendered by independence did not produce a nation of virtuous citizens, national leaders worked to create a system that would place in leadership positions those individuals who would hold to the republican ideal—who would embody this notion of public-spirited disinterestedness. In their eyes, this system, one that would be constructed mostly *by* lawyers and enshrined *in* law, would also end up with lawyers at its center because of their rhetorical skills and their assumption of political roles in the new republic. In this chapter, I will explore the emergence of the professional bar in colonial America as well as the critical role lawyers played in the American Revolution. I will also examine the first days of independence through to the drafting and ratification of the U.S. Constitution. As part of this analysis, I will describe the ways in which the American legal profession became a central institution in the emerging American republic, serving, as one commentator at the time would assert, as an "index to the character of the people."[1]

While lawyers may have played a prominent role in the American Revolution, the forming of the new nation, and the adoption of the U.S. Constitution, in colonial times lawyers were not always welcome in local communities. In some of the colonies, particularly those that had been founded on concepts of religious—even utopian—principles, religious leaders held prominent positions both within their church and in society at large and did not cede power to other professionals.[2] To these religious leaders, the lawyer's role represented a turn to material precepts over religious order and communitarian goodwill.[3] In the first years after the founding of New England, many civil disputes were resolved within religious congregations, with references to passages of the Bible often controlling their outcome.[4] In the seventeenth century, there was no formal and professional bar, and laypeople mostly represented themselves in the courts, which had an informal quality to them.[5] In those colonies formed in an effort to gain religious independence from England, English law was explicitly rejected.[6] Generally speaking, though, the law as followed in the colonies was but a pale imitation of English common law. Local judges and magistrates, many of them without formal legal training, often tailored their decisions to fit local conditions based on what they considered to be the practical wisdom of the community.[7]

In the oldest colonies—Plymouth and Massachusetts Bay, founded in 1620 and 1630, respectively—the General Court and county courts created in those colonies' earliest days did not resemble our courts of today. They would mete out punishment for what we might consider criminal offenses, or settle land disputes, but they also passed laws binding in the community, even those related to setting up new courts.[8] A single magistrate played the roles of judge and lawyers, and the parties had no independent legal representation.[9] Some of the earliest settlements prohibited representatives-for-hire in the courts.[10] In addition, even those who practiced in the colonies in the 1600s found that learning the law to apply in a given situation, if there was any, was also nearly impossible. Throughout the colonies, legal sources like law books were rare. Although some of the early colonies codified and published their early statutes, law libraries were almost nonexistent.[11]

In several of the colonies, prior to the Revolution, the number of lawyers was in the single digits: New Hampshire had one lawyer in the seventeenth century and just three by the Revolution; the admittedly sparsely populated Maine territories had a total of six.[12] In Connecticut, where many of the colony's more prominent lawyers were educated at Yale, each court would determine which lawyers could practice before it. A statute passed in 1730 provided that there could be no more than eleven lawyers admitted to practice in the entire colony at one time.[13] Given the small number of practicing lawyers, litigants could represent themselves or have a family member assist them.[14]

By the mid-eighteenth century—as the population in the colonies grew, trade expanded, and small, religiously homogeneous communities became more diverse—the outright prohibitions on the practice of law largely disappeared. Still, in order to prevent lawyers from taking advantage of clients, many colonies instituted the first regulations on the practice of law: mandatory fee schedules that set forth the amount of compensation a lawyer could receive for handling a matter for a client.[15] When Virginia tried to regulate admission to practice, all its legislature could muster was a limit on legal fees. Lawyers practicing in the local courts could charge fifteen shillings or 150 pounds of tobacco to take on a case. Lawyers practicing in the General Court—a sort of supreme court that included the colonial governor and his closest advisers as jurists—could charge fifty shillings or 500 pounds of the leaf.[16]

With the growing complexity of communal life, the courts and the lawyers who practiced in them started to embrace complexity and formality within the law and the pleading of claims before those courts. This embrace would serve to entrench the role of lawyers not only within the functioning of the courts but also in society itself.[17] Furthermore, as British officials sought to centralize and strengthen legal control in the colonies, the courts became more formal, with even more sophisticated pleading requirements.[18] As those pleading requirements became more complicated and specialized, a professional bar began to emerge, made up of lawyers competent to deal with these developments.[19] Lawyers became, as legal historian Lawrence Friedman has described them, "a necessary evil."[20] While few colonial courts and jurisdictions adopted the formal divisions between barristers and solicitors found within the British bar,[21] many of the colonies' higher courts adopted the practice of having jurists and lawyers wear wigs and gowns like their British counterparts.[22]

Apart from elevating their physical appearance, lawyers also tried to raise standards of practice to improve their own position in the community. While the lawyer might have enjoyed "a marked measure of honorable distinction" at the time, they were sometimes seen as "a character of sharpness, pettifogging, and greedy manipulation of technicality to oppress the weak and ignorant."[23] Lawyers strove to create a more professionalized bar and judiciary to ensure the practice of law was more than a "groveling, mercenary trade," as one commentator from Virginia explained.[24] The manner in which most lawyers could gain the ability to practice law was through an apprenticeship with a practicing lawyer for whom the apprentice would engage in a great deal of menial work for a period of years, often paying for the privilege of doing so.[25] Some colonies would reduce the number of hours an apprentice needed to serve if he had some college training.[26] This apprenticeship served a gatekeeping function: in the words of historian Lawrence Friedman, it "kept the bar small" and "kept older lawyers in firm command" of the means of entry to the profession.[27]

Many of the first lawyers during the colonial era were either immigrants themselves who had studied in Great Britain, such as James Wilson, who helped author the U.S. Constitution and signed it, served on the U.S. Supreme Court, and studied law in Edinburgh;[28] or the sons of wealthy landowners, who sometimes went to England to study,[29] like John Dickinson, who also signed the Constitution and studied in London in the 1750s.[30] Indeed, those who could afford the cross-Atlantic trip, or who could dedicate a number of years to an apprenticeship within the colonies, often at a low wage, tended to be the wealthier members of the community in the first place.[31] For these reasons, as Friedman explained: "Many aristocrats, of mind and money, were lawyers. Politically, too, many lawyers were conservatives."[32]

From what we can surmise of the legal profession in the second half of the eighteenth century, many lawyers were drawn from the economic elite of society, either by blood, marriage, or ambition. Prominent lawyer John Jay married the daughter of one of the richest families in New York.[33] Alexander Hamilton joined the profession because of his ambition but also married into one of the wealthiest families in North

America, the Schuylers, with massive real estate holdings in upstate New York.[34] But not all lawyers came from wealth: John Adams of Massachusetts and Patrick Henry of Virginia emerged from modest backgrounds to join the profession. As James Willard Hurst wrote, one of the characteristics of the bar at the time was its "continuing role as one of the main roads of self-advancement for ambitious young men."[35] For Lawrence Friedman, the legal profession was a "ladder to success, financially and politically."[36] Still, bar membership was also exclusively white and male. Perhaps because there was this possibility of financial reward that attended legal practice, by the 1750s, given the loose practices regarding admission and the increasing complexities of the law that made self-representation more challenging, the courts were soon filled with those with little formal legal training that nevertheless sought to advance their own careers. The situation in Massachusetts at the time led a then-young John Adams, himself educated at Harvard like many of his legal brethren practicing in the area at the time, to rail against the "deputy sheriffs, petit justices, and pettifogging meddlers" who would "attempt to draw writs and draw them wrong more oftener that they do right." These objects of his derision would "receive[] the fees established for lawyers and stir[] up unnecessary suits" while doing so.[37] In the ensuing decades, the members of the Massachusetts bar would take it upon themselves to set requirements for admission in the courts, raise the educational standards to practice, and insist that candidates for admission receive the endorsement of current members of the bar before those apprentices could enter the profession.[38]

Given the insular and conservative nature of the bar at the time of the Revolution, there was no small measure of devotion to the Crown due to class sympathies many lawyers likely harbored toward the British aristocracy or even what lawyers perceived to be their duty to adhere to the rule of law.[39] In fact, many practicing lawyers remained loyal to George III at the outbreak of hostilities in the colonies and ultimately fled to England or Canada at their conclusion.[40] That is not to say that all lawyers, even those educated in England, were Tories; in fact, some of the most prominent lawyer-revolutionaries received their legal training in London like John Dickinson, including John Rutledge, Charles Pinckney, and Thomas Heyward, Jr. By one estimate, thirty of the original fifty-six individuals who signed the Declaration of Independence were lawyers, and nine of them had received their legal training in England.[41] Regardless of where they were educated, colonial lawyers played a central role in the emerging resistance to English rule. Indeed, in the early 1760s, lawyers devised a legal framework for responding to actions of the Crown that captured the imagination of those who sought freedom from royal oppression and set the wheels in motion for revolution.

In the colonial era, one of the British government's primary means to raise funds was through the imposition of tariffs on goods entering the colonies. Tariff evasion among the colonists became fairly commonplace. Around the turn of the seventeenth to the eighteenth century, Parliament enabled the issuance of what were called "writs of assistance"—documents, like a warrant, that provided British officials with the authority to search homes and warehouses to determine whether goods had passed into the colonies without their owner having paid the tariff.[42] For more than half a century, these writs were one of the principal means by which British officials enforced and collected the tariffs.[43]

The death of King George II in 1760 meant that, according to the law, existing writs were no longer enforceable and new writs had to be issued by the new monarch, George III.[44] A group of Boston merchants objected to the issuance of writs to the local tariff merchant in that port city and filed suit in the local court to challenge them. A local lawyer, James Otis, agreed to take on the case, resigning his official position within the colonial government to do so.[45] He argued not only that the writs had expired but also that the writs themselves were contrary to the fundamental rights of the colonists and a tool of oppression against the colonies. As John Adams, present in the courtroom when James Otis gave his arguments against the writs, would later declare: "Then and there was the first scene of the first act of opposition to the arbitrary claims of Great Britain. Then and there the child Independence was born. In fifteen years, namely in 1776, he grew up to manhood, and declared himself free."[46]

Beyond framing the legal arguments for why British rule was oppressive, some lawyers themselves became radicalized because their very livelihoods were the object of British attention. Indeed, apart from the challenges to the writs of assistance, the second great legal event of the 1760s that would have profound geopolitical consequences was the passage of the Stamp Act of 1765. Eager to raise funds to pay off the debt from the Seven Years' War against France, Parliament imposed a tax on different classes of printed materials, including many forms of legal pleadings.[47] This had a direct impact on the livelihoods of not only printing press operators but also lawyers themselves. The most expensive tax under the Stamp Act applied to documents central to the lawyer's practice, including land conveyances and even a single law license, which carried the highest tax of ten pounds sterling, or nearly $2,500 today,[48] and had to be paid in British, and not colonial, currency.[49] As legal historian Edwin Surrency explained: "Certainly, no act could have been better conceived to affect adversely the interests of the members of the two most influential professions that molded public opinion, namely, lawyers and journalists."[50]

In what was possibly the first "statewide" bar meeting, held before the nation was formed in the colony of New Jersey, lawyers practicing there gathered in Perth Amboy to develop a strategy as to how they would respond to the passage of the Act.[51] Many lawyers throughout the colonies unified against the tax, either suspending their practice or simply refusing to pay. Some of the more radical elements among the profession pressed the colonial courts to refuse to follow the requirements of the law. Few colonial courts agreed to such a dramatic step, choosing instead to close or to carry out only those procedures where the Stamp Act did not apply.[52]

Among lawyers as a class, resistance to the Stamp Act was broad. For some, it helped to galvanize their opposition to continued British rule of the colonies.[53] But for others, their conservative leanings and a devotion to legal process over extralegal means likely drove them away from the cause of independence a decade later.[54] Still, between the inspirational legal arguments made against the writs and the legal community's opposition to the Stamp Act, it is not a coincidence that no colonial profession had as much representation among the signers of the Declaration of Independence. The committee responsible for drafting the Declaration was mostly made up of lawyers, including Thomas Jefferson, John Adams, Robert Livingston, and Roger Sherman, with the only nonlawyer of the group Benjamin Franklin.[55] What is more, the legal arguments against the Stamp Act and the writs of assistance became the rhetorical spine around which the committee would construct the Declaration—if not the Revolution itself.

Indeed, the arguments for independence were often couched in terms of combating the mercurial nature of rule from a monarch, which was inconsistent with the rights of the colonists. The arguments often went beyond that, however. The leading theorists of independence, not just content to say King George III was acting arbitrarily, asserted that acts of the Crown and of Parliament were void insofar as they were contrary to a higher law,[56] a natural law that, in the words of the Declaration of Independence, "endowed" men, even when in the colonies, with certain "unalienable rights." These were fundamentally legal arguments, couched in language about the rule of law.[57] They struck a chord not only with the lawyers but also with communities across the colonies, where many white men were literate, and helped to build a national consciousness around such concepts.

Edmund Burke, staunch conservative and member of the British Parliament, recognized the role of lawyers in stoking separatist discontent in the American colonies. For Burke, it was in the colonies, as in "no country perhaps in the world," where the law was "so general a study." In the colonies, he argued, "all who read (and most do)[] endeavor to obtain some smattering" of knowledge in the law, which led colonial booksellers to print law books on their own. He asserted that residents of the American colonies possessed as many copies of the leading treatise on British law, Blackstone's *Commentaries*, as did residents of England.[58] In those colonies, "[t]he [legal] profession itself is so numerous and powerful[] and in most provinces it takes the lead."[59] Although clearly exaggerating the size of the American legal profession at the time, Burke recognized that the Continental Congress was made up mostly of lawyers, and he posited it was the study of law that "renders men acute, inquisitive, dexterous, prompt in attack, ready in defense, full of resources" and led them to "snuff the approach of tyranny in every tainted breeze."[60] Similarly, the commander of British forces in the colonies, General Thomas Gage, lamented the role of lawyers in stirring up the American masses. As he would say a full decade before the first shots rang out in Lexington and Concord: "The Lawyers are the Source from whence the clamors have flowed in every Province."[61]

Although Thomas Paine had no formal legal training, his pamphlet *Common Sense* displayed just the sort of legalistic approach that both concerned and impressed Burke:

> But where says some is the King of America? I'll tell you Friend, he reigns above, and doth not make havoc of mankind like the Royal Brute of Britain. Yet that we may not appear to be defective even in earthly honors, let a day be solemnly set apart for proclaiming the charter; let it be brought forth placed on the divine law, the word of God; let a crown be placed thereon, by which the world may know, that so far as we approve of monarchy, that in America THE LAW IS KING. For as in absolute governments the King is law, so in free countries the law ought to be King; and there ought to be no other.[62]

What is more, lawyers, in addition to serving as the most common of the "learned professions" (that is, lawyers, physicians, and religious ministers) among the signers of the Declaration, they also played significant roles in the quest for independence itself. As one Massachusetts politician and revolutionary, Jonathan Jackson, would argue, when it came to lawyers, "more than to any other class of men in the community, have been owing the spirit and conduct of our revolution, so far as it has been well conducted."[63] He would continue:

> [L]ook into all our publick assemblies, more or less of them will be found; look through the lists of congressional members, a greater proportion of gentlemen have been bred to the law, will be there seen, than of any other class whatever; and in my opinion less confusion has taken place in our councils, in consequence of their good judgment and better information, than from of most others.[64]

In addition, the legal profession—which shaped the laws and legal system that would emerge after the Declaration of Independence, framed the arguments for independence, and assumed leadership roles in the Continental Congress—may have also helped to ensure that the American Revolution would not devolve into lawless chaos and terror. As legal scholar Robert F. Boden has argued: "The quest for liberty never became a thirst for license; the dedication to law never became a lust for power."[65] A system where "law is king," as Paine put it, would necessarily vault lawyers to prominence.

This notion that law would be king—that is, law would take the place of hierarchy to protect liberty and, by extension, a degree of individual equality—was perhaps the most radical thing about the American Revolution. Indeed, as historian Gordon Wood has noted, the American Revolution was "as radical and revolutionary as any in history" because of the transformation it brought about "in the relationships that bound people to each other."[66] It made "the interests and prosperity of ordinary people—their pursuit of happiness—the goal of society and government."[67] In colonial times, authority and liberty flowed from the "social relationships" in the community.[68] The new Massachusetts constitution, which John Adams would help draft, implemented legal and structural checks and balances between the branches of government. The purpose of those checks and balances, famously, was for Massachusetts to "be a government of laws[] and not of men."[69] Adams would assist many of the colonies in organizing their state governments during the last years of the 1770s with this notion in mind.[70]

But it was not just the newfound independence that enabled an expanded role for lawyers. Many forces transformed this new nation from a colonial one to one that was free and founded on principles of equality and liberty, at least for some. Between 1750 and 1770, the population of the colonies doubled. Then it doubled again between 1770 and 1790. It was in this changed and changing environment that the former revolutionaries sought to make a society in which equality and liberty, not hierarchy and status, would be the touchstones. These leaders would introduce the concept of republicanism—not a new idea by any stretch of the imagination but one that would take on a particularly American cast.

Thomas Paine explained that the word "republic" stands for "the public good, or the good of the whole, in contradistinction to the despotic form, which makes the good of the sovereign, or of one man, the only object of the government."[71] Indeed, as eighteenth-century historian David Ramsay wrote: "In monarchies, favor is the source of preferment; but, in our new forms of government, no one can command the suffrages of the people unless by his superior merit and capacity."[72] According to Gordon Wood, with the success of the American Revolution a dramatic political shift occurred: "Far from remaining monarchical, hierarchy-ridden subjects on the margin of civilization, Americans had become, almost overnight, the most liberal, the most democratic, the most commercially minded, and the most modern people in the world."[73] (These developments did not include enslaved peoples, women, and the Indigenous population, of course.)

While British society had its share of Whig politics, which espoused a more hierarchical form of republicanism and had done so for at least a century,[74] the American take on republicanism proved revolutionary for the time. As Wood explains, the American form of republicanism was "as radical for the eighteenth century as Marxism was to be for the nineteenth century" because it "challenged the primary assumptions and practices of monarchy—its hierarchy, its inequality, its devotion to kinship, its patriarchy, its patronage, and its dependency." This form of republicanism "offered nothing less than new ways of organizing society." It "defied and dissolved the older monarchical connections and presented people with alternative kinds of attachments [and] new sorts of social relationships" and "transformed monarchical culture and prepared the way for the revolutionary upheavals at the end of the eighteenth century."[75] At the center of this form of republicanism were the values that it would champion: integrity, virtue, and disinterestedness.[76] With these principles, the revolutionaries hoped to "destroy the bonds holding together the older monarchical society—kinship, patriarchy, and patronage"[77]—and to replace them with "new social bonds of love, respect, and consent."[78] In the eyes of the founders, it was not just the laws that would accomplish this task; it was also the lawyers themselves.

One of these lawyers was Alexander Hamilton. Looking back on his life and career, we see the ways in which a member of the legal profession could serve as a reflection of these republican ideals. While early in his life Hamilton might have hoped for a war so that he might show his mettle, bring attention to himself, and satisfy his ambition,[79] he would ultimately conclude that joining the legal profession was a route to acclaim and wealth. And while popular culture has identified Hamilton as serving as an American icon, he was also a lawyer, and his story also serves as a symbol of the role lawyers played in the early days of the republic.

After the Revolution, the courts had largely taken over the task of determining who could be admitted to practice, no longer leaving it completely in the hands of the practicing bar.[80] To gain admittance, an individual who had served as an apprentice would be sponsored by his host to come before a judge for questioning. This judge would consider whether the apprentice seemed to have learned enough about the law to earn the ability to appear before the court as an advocate. The exodus of as many as 200 loyalist lawyers after the Revolution,[81] what Roscoe Pound would characterize as the decimation of the profession following the war,[82] however, meant that there was opportunity for young, ambitious men to pursue this line of work, which is exactly what Alexander Hamilton did even before the formal conclusion of the war.

At the Battle of Yorktown in 1781, the last major battle of the Revolution, Hamilton led a critical and successful assault on the British outer defenses of their garrison.[83] This field command was his first major combat role since early in the hostilities, when he served as an artillery captain in the failed defense of New York City in 1776.[84] It was during the fighting over New York City that George Washington observed Hamilton's organizational acumen as the young captain supervised the construction of defenses in northern Manhattan.[85] Soon thereafter, Washington asked Hamilton to serve as one of his aides-de-camp, a relationship that would sometimes prove tense but was beneficial to Hamilton's ambitions. His service under Washington resulted in close personal and professional ties the two would maintain during and throughout the remainder of Washington's life and career.[86]

Following the Battle of Yorktown, and before the execution of the Treaty of Paris that formally ended the war two years later, Hamilton moved to the estate of his wife's prominent family, the Schuylers of Albany, New York.[87] There he prepared to seek admission to the bar. As legal historian Paul Finkelman has explained: "In 1782, Hamilton had ambition, a liberal education, and sought a profession that would give him status, a decent income, personal autonomy, and intellectual stimulation."[88] In a new nation that would eschew hereditary titles, the honorific "Esquire" would accompany Hamilton's name upon admission. This title "connoted nobility and legitimacy."[89] Hamilton, as Finkelman explains, "who valued order and authority above democracy itself, as his admiration for the British monarchy suggests, and who wished to be an aristocrat, came naturally to his profession."[90]

A student of King's College (which would change its name to Columbia University after the Revolution), Hamilton followed the path of many who had some college training at the time. As historian Samuel Haber has noted, in the last half of the eighteenth century "[n]ot only did the law overtake and surpass the ministry as the calling of the graduates of Harvard, Yale, and Princeton, but in the often expressed opinion of the day it was the brightest students who chose the law."[91] This, Haber points out, "owed much to the growing profitability of legal practice in America, where increasing wealth and lucrative suits probably went together, and also to the informing example of the mother country, where legal learning and ability could lead notoriously to sizable fortunes."[92] But Haber notes that this explanation is incomplete: the movement away from the ministry and into law for these individuals was likely also a result, in part, of a drift from the centrality of religion in daily life to one in which "liberty, happiness, and rights" were increasingly the "commanding ideas" of the era.[93] These concepts, "with all their built-in and ineradicable ambiguity, were characteristically translated into rules." And since "rules were the lawyer's business," the legal profession found a sense of honor and a prominence in the late colonial era.[94]

Hamilton—famously described as someone who wrote so much and so quickly it was as if he was "running out of time"[95]—could not abide the typical delay of the apprenticeship period for aspiring lawyers in New York. The highest court in New York had temporarily suspended this requirement for men who had spent time in military service, but Hamilton failed to apply before the expiration of the waiver period. He petitioned the court for permission to seek the waiver after the deadline, and the request was granted.[96] He then set himself to preparing for the examination requirement, which was still in force. Since he seems to have been someone who learned things by writing about them, Hamilton proceeded to draft an outline of procedures in the New York courts. Such a compendium had not been assembled in any of the colonies before.[97] For several decades after, those who could obtain a copy used it to study for admission in New York and prepare to practice,[98] just as law students purchase study aids and bar preparation materials today.

Hamilton would seem to embody, to a degree, the republican ideal of public-minded virtue. In addition to his military service, his role in advocating ratification of the Constitution stands as one of his crowning feats of public service. As the tumultuous 1780s unfolded, the leading figures of the nation, who had imagined a country founded on virtue and a disinterestedness through which the common good would prevail over self-interest, came to believe, in the words of Gordon Wood, that the "American people seemed incapable of the degree of virtue needed for republicanism."[99] Republican leaders would turn not only to law but also to lawyers, to preserve a nation founded on the principles of liberty and equality, at least for some. As a result, by embodying such principles in the legal system, it made it easier for those with intelligence and some legal training and acumen to advance through various channels. In a nation where law was "king," then the legal profession became a path toward personal and, obviously, professional advancement. And when law became the lever of power, it is not surprising that those who knew how to operate that lever assumed leadership roles, and those who could afford to do so would hire those who knew how to operate such levers.

It is also not surprising that as those who sought to create a more perfect union—one purportedly founded on equal rights but also one that advanced the republican spirit—would also seek to strengthen and place at the head of the national government what Jefferson called a "natural aristocracy," one that was founded on "virtue and talents."[100] While there is "an artificial aristocracy founded on wealth and birth, without either virtue or talents," Jefferson argued that the natural aristocracy is "the most precious gift of nature for the instruction, the trusts, and government of society."[101] Thus, "that form of government is the best which provides the most effectually for a pure selection of these natural aristoi into the offices of government."[102] The problem, as those who would come to be known as federalists saw it, was this: the independent nation that emerged victorious from the American Revolution, as established through the Articles of Confederation, was not much of a nation.[103] The relative political equality and liberty that its white inhabitants enjoyed were threatened by what some would see as the potential excesses of democracy and the relative weakness of the central government. Once again, though, we see law as one of the main drivers of the challenges the new nation faced.

The Revolution's lofty goals of freedom and equality led to real gains, like in the Northern states, where lawyers like Hamilton, John Jay (who owned slaves), and John Adams would all work to outlaw slavery in many such states. By Hamilton's death in 1804, most Northern states had abolished slavery or had plans to do so.[104] In the wake of the war, a newfound liberty and a greater degree of equality than had ever been experienced before occurred in the market, the legislatures, and the courts. Domestic trade expanded greatly and access to capital increased. The people's appetite for commercial and even what would be considered luxury goods led to increases in business and personal debts.[105] At the same time, the nation also experienced a deep economic recession in the 1780s, which not only helped to spark Shays' Rebellion but also led to the passage of different legislation in many state legislatures designed to ease the burdens on debtors, often at the expense of creditors.[106] Such legislative efforts tended to stoke class divisions and raise fears of a tyranny by the masses, even within the newly "equal" society.[107] According to Gordon Wood, many of the founders "had a glimpse of what America was to become—a scrambling business society dominated by pecuniary interests of ordinary people—and they did not like what they saw."[108]

In response, some leaders turned to law as a remedy in the form of a national constitution. In the 1780s, across the new nation, there existed a mishmash of statutes and judicial decisions carried over from the colonial period: American local laws and customs mixed with the residue of British common law and statutes.[109] And just as thirty years earlier, when it was perceived that charlatans were taking advantage of the state of the law to press their own interests, the solution was not less law but rather the direction of energies toward reform—and legal reform at that. Thomas Jefferson, speaking of the laws of Virginia at the time, expressed the desire to "reform the style of the later British statutes, and of our own acts of assembly, which from their verbosity, their endless tautologies, their involutions of case within case, and parenthesis within parenthesis, and their multiplied efforts of certainty by saids and aforesaids, by ors and by ands, to make them more plain, do really render them more perplexed and incomprehensible, not only to common readers, but to the lawyers themselves."[110] Jefferson pointed out that he could "easily correct [a] bill to the taste of my brother lawyers, by making every other word a said or aforesaid, and saying everything over two or three times, so that nobody but we of the craft can untwist the diction, and find out what it means; and that, too, not so plainly but that we may conscientiously divide one half on each side."[111]

James Madison described the situation affecting the new nation as follows:

> Among the evils then of our situation may well be ranked the multiplicity of laws from which no State is exempt. As far as laws are necessary, to mark with precision the duties of those who are to obey them, and to take from those who are to administer them a discretion, which might be abused, their number is the price of liberty. As far as the laws exceed this limit, they are a nusance: a nusance of the most pestilent kind. Try the Codes of the several States by this test, and what a luxuriancy of legislation do they present. The short period of independency has filled as many pages as the century which preceded it.[112]

He added that laws are "repealed or superseded, before any trial can have been made of their merits" and even before "the remoter districts within which they were to operate" even learn of their passage. This "instability" of the law was "a snare not only to our citizens but to foreigners also."[113] Jefferson's law reform efforts in the state of Virginia, completed by the "unwearied exertions" of James Madison in the statehouse while Jefferson was serving as ambassador to France, succeeded despite the "endless quibbles, chicaneries, perversions, vexations and delays of lawyers and demi-lawyers."[114]

The complicated mix of American and British statutes and common law gave lawyers a distinct advantage in the post-Revolutionary legal environment. Indeed, the ability of skilled lawyers to work within these complex systems enabled them to advance their clients' interests, both in the courts and the legislatures. Many attacked lawyers and the legal system, demanding the removal of British law from the books and "the codification and simplification of American Law."[115] As Jonathan Jackson, a federalist politician from Massachusetts, stated, however, while lawyers were the subject of "almost universal prejudice, among the common people of this country . . . and even men of higher class," they serve as "the middle men between the parties and the courts, and counsellors to the many who want direction, when injured or insulted."[116] He added that "no country without lawyers . . . has shared any great degree of liberty."[117] As a result, "we may determine such to be necessary in every free country." What is more, he would add, and which I quoted at the start of this chapter: "The character and conduct of this class of men, has been said to be an index to the character of the people."[118]

James Madison would decry what he thought of as new populist legislation that pitted debtors against creditors, with legislatures generally attempting to put their thumbs on the scale in support of debtors.[119] For Madison, this was an example of the tyranny of the majority and highlighted the risk that, in a representative democracy, a particular faction could dominate a small legislative body such as a state legislature. Madison argued for a strong central government that would transcend the petty interests arising in local assemblies by drawing representatives from a larger pool of voters and having as its charge the management of national affairs. As he wrote to George Washington:

> The great desideratum which has not yet been found for Republican Governments, seems to be some disinterested & dispassionate umpire in disputes between different passions & interests in the State. The majority who alone have the right of decision, have frequently an interest real or supposed in abusing it. In Monarchies the sovereign is more neutral to the interests and views of different parties; but unfortunately he too often forms interests of his own repugnant to those of the whole. Might not the national prerogative here suggested be found sufficiently disinterested for the decision of local questions of policy, whilst it would itself be sufficiently restrained from the pursuit of interests adverse to those of the whole Society?[120]

Ultimately what would emerge from this tumultuous time was a stronger central government, one that sought to address the tensions created by competing interests and different sources of power, limit the damage that could come from factional competition, reduce the friction of internal commercial activity, prepare for national defense, and rein in the potential of despotic forces. A core aspect of the U.S. Constitution is the different checks and balances found within it designed to pursue these goals: that which exist between the bicameral national legislature, among the three branches of the federal government, and between the federal and state governments.[121] Yet a deeper investigation into this institutional *structure* reveals that at the center of this system designed to smooth out local differences and weaken factions was a critical *actor*: the virtuous elected official. Critical to the federalists' system was the idea that the nation's best men would assume roles in not just the legislature but also the executive and judicial branches. As Madison wrote in *Federalist No. 57*: "The aim of every political constitution is, or ought to be, first to obtain for rulers men who possess most wisdom to discern, and most virtue to pursue, the common good of the society; and in the next place, to take the most effectual precautions for keeping them virtuous whilst they continue to hold their public trust."[122] For Madison, then, the "first" aim of the Constitution should be to create a structure through which individuals could be chosen to serve in those institutions who could "discern" and "pursue" the common good.

The structure of the new legislature was conceived to ensure, to the greatest extent possible, that the voters would select just this type of virtuous representative: one who could rise above their own petty interests to keep the good of the community—indeed, the nation—in mind.[123] The Constitution would accomplish this by broadening the number of voters, to between five and six thousand, who would select each member of the House of Representatives. This was in contrast to state legislators' districts, which would typically contain a much smaller number of voters. From the larger pool, Madison imagined "a fit representative would be most likely to be found, so the choice would be less likely to be diverted from him by the intrigues of the ambitious or the bribes of the rich."[124] Lawyer-federalist James Wilson would echo these sentiments during the constitutional debates.[125]

Jefferson also had a vision for this kind of legislature. Decades after the ratification of the Constitution, he wrote of his belief that it was not necessary to pack the wealthy into an upper chamber of the legislature, like in England, and hope the other institutions within the government would be able to check them, because "to give them power in order to prevent them from doing mischief, is arming them for it, and increasing instead of remedying the evil." He believed no explicit designation was necessary within the legislature for the wealthier members of society who may have assumed their political roles by inheritance or other means that did not reflect talent or merit. There was no need to protect against the incursion of the wealthy into the legislature, nor was there fear that their interests would not be protected, because enough of them would be elected to the legislature to prevent unjust laws, but not so many that it would perpetuate or extend inequality.[126]

The size of these new legislative bodies would also differ from the larger state and local institutions, and this would serve to encourage those elected to them to pursue the common good. As Jonathan Jackson argued: "A small number of men are more easily observed, and in fact better kept under publick eye, than a numerous assembly."[127] With "human nature as it is, a consciousness of the publick eye being always open upon men entrusted with the publick weal, is a great security to the political honesty of the publick servants."[128] He continued: "We have found indecision and roguery enough in large assemblies, let us now try small ones." Even those who are "roguishly disposed" when "narrowly watched" within a small assembly, which is not "so good a theatre for them to practice on," will be "under more restraint."[129] Fixed, regularly scheduled elections would also serve as an appropriate check on the legislature. Writing in the early days of the Revolution, Samuel Adams said to his cousin John Adams that frequent elections alone can ensure the security of the people due to the "Spirit of Jealousy & Strict Inquiry" that they engender.[130]

While these structural controls would likely curb some of what the federalists saw as excesses of democracy by sending the most virtuous men to serve in the legislature, an additional check was required on factions that might emerge within the legislature. Interested groups of voters—for example, merchants and landowners—might elect representatives to pursue the groups' selfish interests. The prominent lawyers who advocated for the Constitution, however, envisioned a disinterested class of professionals who could balance out the various economic groups that might seek to dominate the legislature. "With regard to the learned professions," Hamilton argued in *Federalist No. 35*, "little need be observed; they truly form no distinct interest in society, and according to their situation and talents, will be indiscriminately the objects of the confidence and choice of each other, and of other parts of the community."[131] He added:

> Will not the landholder know and feel whatever will promote or insure
> the interest of landed property? And will he not, from his own interest
> in that species of property, be sufficiently prone to resist every attempt to

prejudice or encumber it? Will not the merchant understand and be disposed to cultivate, as far as may be proper, the interests of the mechanic and manufacturing arts, to which his commerce is so nearly allied? *Will not the man of the learned profession*, who will feel a neutrality to the rivalships between the different branches of industry, be likely to prove an impartial arbiter between them, ready to promote either, so far as it shall appear to him conducive to the general interests of the society?[132]

To at least two of the authors of *The Federalist Papers*—prominent lawyers Hamilton and Jay—this disinterested class would likely consist largely of lawyers.[133] Given the prominent roles law and, by extension, lawyers were expected to fill in the new government, it is perhaps no accident that, by century's end, many of the brightest students in the nation's leading institutions of higher education would start to pursue the law.[134]

But it was not just elected officials who needed to be men of virtue. Since the judiciary served as a critical check on the legislature and executive, judges also needed to be men of virtue—as well as skilled and knowledgeable lawyers. As Hamilton wrote in *Federalist No. 78*:

> Hence it is, that there can be but few men in the society who will have sufficient skill in the laws to qualify them for the stations of judges. And making the proper deductions for the ordinary depravity of human nature, the number must be still smaller of those who unite the requisite integrity with the requisite knowledge. These considerations apprise us, that the government can have no great option between fit character; and that a temporary duration in office, which would naturally discourage such characters from quitting a lucrative line of practice to accept a seat on the bench, would have a tendency to throw the administration of justice into hands less able, and less well qualified, to conduct it with utility and dignity.[135]

Returning to the career of Alexander Hamilton as a window into the legal profession at the turn of the eighteenth to the nineteenth century: he served for six years in Washington's cabinet as secretary of the Treasury, where he would draft lawyerly documents, like his "Opinion on the Constitutionality of the Bank of the United States" in 1791. After leaving cabinet service, he would spend most of the last decade of his life as a practicing attorney. Hamilton certainly played a significant role in promoting ratification of the Constitution, writing the lion's share of *The Federalist Papers*. During the constitutional convention and the period leading up to ratification, however, he was still in private practice, handling a range of cases and holding a place of prominence within the New York bar.[136] Many of the cases he took on—including matters involving land conveyances and the arcane subject of marine insurance—proved quite lucrative in the last years of the eighteenth century.[137] He also appears to have handled transactions involving the sale and purchase of enslaved persons, despite his public opposition to slavery and the slave trade.[138] On top of his law practice, and even when out of government toward the end of his life, he kept his hand in electoral politics. In the critical election of 1800, his somewhat feeble attempt to coordinate and promote a slate of electors from New York failed.[139] In this effort, he was outorganized by Aaron Burr, with whom he crossed paths early in their legal careers in Albany[140] (and who would, of course, take Hamilton's life in a duel several years later). Through his years in private practice, we see in Hamilton the interplay between the public ideals he espoused and quite literally fought for—a desire for political equality, national independence, a strong central government, and viable and effective democratic institutions—and his willingness to put his ample rhetorical skills and indominable work ethic to use in the service of his personal ambition and in pursuit of the financial rewards, and to gain the social status available to him because of his unique gifts. The path Hamilton blazed in the new nation stands as a metaphor for the role lawyers have played throughout the nation's history. Others also stand out and, like Hamilton, possess mixed records. Burr, known for heroics during the Revolutionary War, would reach the position of vice president of the United States but also faced trial for treason for allegedly hatching a plot to sever off the western territories from the country, combine them with Mexico, and become regent of the newly formed nation.[141] Similarly, John Marshall, the fourth Chief Justice of the United States, purchased, owned, and passed down to his relatives upon his death hundreds of slaves.[142] What is more, in the words of historian Paul Finkelman, "[o]n the bench Marshall always supported slavery, even when statutes and precedent were on the side of freedom."[143]

Since the founding, important members of the American legal profession have, at times, distinguished themselves by serving as critical guardians of the rule of law, democracy, and political equality. Its members have often assumed leadership roles in local communities and served in the highest echelons of the federal and state governments. Many have come from modest beginnings to assume these great political and professional heights. Many have also earned more than a satisfactory living by doing so—even when it meant taking on less-than-glamorous clients and matters, sometimes even controversial ones. In many ways, the practices of lawyers in the first days of the nation show that the profession proved capable of combining a degree of civic virtue (and, at times, vice) with personal profit, all while holding a position of prominence within the community. In fact, several decades after Hamilton's death, lawyers would be called the de facto American aristocracy.

In chapter 3, I will explore the role of lawyers in the nineteenth century and show how the tensions over equality, democracy, and aristocracy mounted in a nation that struggled to define what it meant to be a nation of laws and not of men and women. At the same time, it would appear that the nation was quickly becoming, if not a nation *of* lawyers, then one that was certainly made *by* them in no small part.

3

An Independent Bar and an Honest Judiciary

French aristocrat Alexis de Tocqueville visited the United States several decades after Alexander Hamilton's death, ostensibly to review the American penal system. His two-volume text, *Democracy in America*, which describes the young republic in the first half of the nineteenth century, provides a remarkable view into the social, political, and legal systems of the United States at that time. France's experience with revolution and its aftermath informed his views on the fledgling democracy in America, and his observations from his journeys also provide insights into the critical role of law and lawyers in England, France, and the United States at the time.

One of Tocqueville's most striking observations about American society then was what he called the apparent "equality of conditions": that is, the notion that the United States had less of a social hierarchy than did historically monarchical societies.[1] At the same time, while decrying the persistence of slavery in the United States,[2] he also noted that one group—the American legal profession—held a prominent role in the functioning of American society and its democratic system and institutions. He argued that, as a class, lawyers in other nations tended to side either with the aristocracy (as in England) or with the masses (as in France). Their choice depended on a number of factors, most importantly the role law itself played in those societies. When the law was necessary to restrain the excesses of the aristocracy, Tocqueville opined that lawyers would ally with commoners to serve as a counterweight to aristocratic power. When excesses came from below, Tocqueville believed a legal regime managed by lawyers was needed to cool passions and restrain violence.[3] And this was precisely how Tocqueville saw lawyers in the United States. Restraining the excesses of the masses was a role, Tocqueville argued, that Americans "have entrusted to members of the legal profession." This type of authority, "and the influence these individuals exercise in the Government," he would assert, are "the most powerful existing security against the excesses of democracy."[4]

The United States had no aristocracy to speak of—at least, not an official one. Roughly a half-century earlier, Thomas Paine said the law was "king" in the fledgling democracy. So perhaps it is no surprise that Tocqueville saw lawyers as a de facto American aristocracy: "If I were asked where I place the American aristocracy, I should reply without hesitation that it is not composed of the rich, who are united together by no common tie, but that it occupies the judicial bench and the bar."[5] The legal profession's position in society as the "only aristocratic element" therein meant the profession could "be amalgamated without violence with the natural elements of democracy, and which can be advantageously and permanently combined with them."[6] Indeed, according to Tocqueville, "[l]awyers belong to the people by birth and interest, to the aristocracy by habit and by taste, and they may be looked upon as the natural bond and connecting link of the two great classes of society."[7] Without a formal aristocracy, lawyers in the United States were "sure to occupy the highest stations" in society because "they are the only men of information and sagacity, beyond the sphere of the people, who can be the object of the popular choice."[8] At the same time, those who "devote[] themselves to legal pursuits derive" from them "certain habits of order, a taste for formalities, and a kind of instinctive regard for the regular connection of ideas, which naturally render them hostile to the revolutionary spirit and the unreflecting passions of the multitude."[9]

In France, Tocqueville argued, the law was mostly derived from the legislative codes, which were "often difficult of comprehension, but they [could] be read by every one."[10] In contrast, in the United States and England at that time, the law was mostly derived from the common law, which required the development of legal principles from judicial precedents and arguments from concepts like natural law. This approach necessarily favored those knowledgeable about such bodies of information. What is more, both England and the United States "retained the law of precedents; that is to say, they continue to found their legal opinions on the decisions of their forefathers."[11] The predominance of the common law in these two nations meant that "the indispensable want of legal assistance which is felt in England and in the United States, and the high opinion which is generally entertained of the ability of the legal profession, tend to separate it more and more from the people[] and to place it in a distinct class."[12] Because of this, in the minds of English and American lawyers, there is "a taste and reverence for what is old," which "is almost always united to a love of regular and lawful proceedings."[13] As "masters of a science which is necessary but which is not generally known," they ultimately "serve as arbiters between citizens; and . . . direct[] the blind passions of parties in litigation" so that "their purpose inspires them with a certain contempt for the judgment of the multitude."[14] For Tocqueville, the legal profession constituted "the only enlightened class which the people does not mistrust," and, as a result, lawyers were "naturally called upon to occupy most of the public stations, . . . fill the legislative assemblies, and . . . conduct the administration."[15] Indeed, as is true today, the highest ranks of government were often filled by men who were lawyers—notably, twelve of the first sixteen U.S. presidents (all except George Washington, James Madison [who studied some law but never sought admission to a bar], William Henry Harrison, and Zachary Taylor). Because lawyers held positions of authority within the community, Tocqueville observed that they "exercise a powerful influence upon the formation of the law[] and upon its execution."[16] Moreover, because of the pervasiveness of the law influencing all social relations within the new nation at the time, Tocqueville explained that "[s]carcely any question arises in the United States which does not become, sooner or later, a subject of judicial debate."[17] Further, because "most public men are, or have been, legal practitioners, they introduce the customs and technicalities of their profession into the affairs of the country."[18]

The Tocquevillian view—that lawyers as a class stood *between* the elites and the masses, moderating both—was not seen as a positive by everyone, however. Across the political spectrum, many saw lawyers as aristocrats. Some believed that was their appropriate role, while others excoriated it. One prominent Baltimore lawyer, who held a position teaching law at the University of Maryland, probably shared Tocqueville's view. Writing under a pseudonym,[19] David Hoffman, whose work I will return to shortly, asserted that the aristocracy was "patriotic, enlightened, and mainly virtuous" as compared to the masses, which were "selfish, crude, and mainly unprincipled."[20]

The pervasiveness of law in the United States, and the role that lawyers played in creating and extending its dominance, was something

Tocqueville observed and more recent commentators have validated. Legal historian Morton Horwitz has described how American lawyers in the late eighteenth century took pains to channel legal disputes into venues where lawyers held more sway—for example, resisting efforts to resolve commercial disputes through arbitration because arbitration was less formal than judicial proceedings and thus more accessible to the nonlawyers involved in such disputes.[21] Lawyers also sought to minimize the role of juries, first wresting the decision to interpret the law from such nonprofessional bodies and then limiting altogether the types of disputes juries could resolve.[22] These actions echo those of lawyers in the middle of the eighteenth century, when they worked to consolidate their authority and raise their prominence by making legal processes more opaque and formal—and, as a result, less accessible to nonlawyers.

What is more, law practice itself was tightly controlled and fairly inaccessible, unless one was white and male. The process of gaining admission to the bar was still fairly simple in the first quarter of the nineteenth century to those privileged to have the opportunity to pursue the field. An aspiring lawyer would apprentice with an established practitioner for a brief period, sometimes paying a fee for the privilege.[23] He would handle office tasks; write and copy, by hand, legal documents; learn procedure; and read the legal treatises of the day.[24] The duration of such apprenticeships varied by jurisdiction, from one to as many as five years, with the length sometimes dependent on the apprentice's prior schooling.[25] After an apprenticeship, the aspiring lawyer would then face an examination by a sitting judge. The rigor or formality of this process was inconsistent to say the least. Accounts of such interviews reveal a process that might include a series of withering questions over several hours, a chat over lunch or during a stroll around the courthouse that lasted a few moments, or even a conversation while the interrogator was sitting in a bathtub (as Abraham Lincoln appears to have done when screening at least one aspiring lawyer to determine whether he was ready to appear before the court for admission).[26] But if the practicing bar and members of the judiciary could control entry to the profession, they could also exclude anyone they wanted, and often did, for many reasons, like the desire to limit the number of lawyers in a community or because of the applicant's race or gender. Thus, the practices of the courts became more complex and inaccessible to nonlawyers, while the legal profession itself, like an aristocracy, was tightly controlled and self-perpetuating as well, reserved for only those professionals approved for membership.

Critiques of the New American Aristocracy

Almost as soon as Tocqueville proclaimed lawyers as the American aristocracy, a new force would emerge, one that sought to strip away many of the aristocratic elements that might have existed in society.[27] That force, Jacksonian democracy, sought to promote the notion of equality for all white men, and at least equality of opportunity.[28] Consistent with this view, the period between Tocqueville's American journeys and the outset of the Civil War was notable as one in which access to the profession would become fairly open.[29] The law and legal processes were generally becoming more complex and less accessible to nonlawyers, even as efforts began to take hold to try to simplify the law, as described below. At the same time, as the nation spread westward, the legal systems that organized life and commerce at the time bore little relation to the complexity of law today.[30] Consistent with Jacksonian principles, even the modest barriers to entry to the profession that might have existed earlier in the nineteenth century began to fall by the mid-1800s.[31] Indeed, in one state, Indiana, the state constitution provided that any voter of good moral character had the right to practice law; of course, since only white men could vote, those characteristics served as a bar-admission requirement as well.[32]

Historian Lawrence Friedman explained that American society at the time "needed a large, amorphous, open-ended profession." And while "Jacksonian democracy did not make every man a lawyer," it did seem to "encourage a scrambling bar of shrewd entrepreneurs."[33] As historian Douglas Miller explained, speaking of the public's views of equality and inequality more broadly during the Jacksonian era: "Almost no one wanted to rid the nation of inequality by taking from the rich and giving to the poor; instead, people wanted the right to become rich themselves."[34] The vision of equality was not that everyone should be equal, however. As the words of one manual of etiquette from the time proclaimed: "True republicanism requires that every man shall be free to become as unequal as he can."[35] (Of course, this sentiment did not apply to enslaved peoples, disfavored religious groups, and women.)

For those seeking greater equality, particularly for the working class, any monopoly the lawyer-aristocrat might have on the practice of law was seen as antidemocratic, with one prominent Jacksonian arguing that the doors to the courthouse should be flung open even wider. Labor leader Frederick Robinson was challenged by Rufus Choate, a leading Boston lawyer, when Robinson attempted to appear in court as an attorney on behalf of a litigant. In Robinson's account, Choate gathered the "brotherhood of the bar" to oppose Robinson's appearance in court and "put [him] down."[36] For his part, Robinson said he did not fear Choate, "'nor all [his] secret fraternity," because Robinson was "standing on broad constitutional ground, and no power on earth should put [him] down," until it put him "in the grave."[37] When Choate claimed that a statute prevented anyone from practicing as a lawyer in Massachusetts who had not been admitted by the courts, Robinson declared that "if there be any laws, which contravene the rights of my appearing as an attorney, on terms of equality with other men," then such laws were "unconstitutional and void."[38] These types of prohibitions, Robinson continued, could easily be manipulated by the bar and the courts to secure "to themselves a patent right of establishing and exercising an oppressive monopoly in the practice of the law." And what security did the public have "that this monopoly shall not become still more exclusive?"[39] He continued:

> If you have a right to decide, that no one shall practice law, without a degree and a title from college, and without subsequently devoting at least three years, at the expense of five hundred dollars under the nominal instruction of a member of the bar, and if the judges, as members of the bar, have a right to enforce this decision, what is then to prevent a majority of your fraternity, at any time, in compliance with their own interests, and in order to render their monopoly still more advantageous to themselves, to decide that no one shall by admitted to participate in your monopoly, unless he devote ten years and five thousand dollars to the acquisition of the qualifications required?[40]

For Robinson, it was not just the barrier of the admission process that preserved this monopoly on legal practice, however. It was also the adoption of the common law of England, "whose principles of government are totally abhorrent to our own, customs contained in ten thousand different books, so intricate, so ambiguous, so contradictory, that no man ever yet understood them, and which it is the height of hypocrisy to pretend to understand."[41] What is more, by the use of, among other things, "verifications; by pleading generally, by pleadings specially, by pleading double, by pleading in abatement; by replications, by rejoinders, by surrejoinders, by rebutters, by surrebutters, by joining issue; by hard words, in the Saxon, in the Norman, in the French, in the Latin languages, by having the judges also members of your fraternity and interested in your monopoly," lawyers "contrived to exclude every one who would not submit to all of your offensive exactions" and keep them from the "important right of doing business" in the "public courts" because the practice of law had become "such a dark maze of uncertainty as to render it impossible for any one to practice law without a previous understanding with every other practitioner."[42] Instead of this complex maze, and having Americans "living under British laws," Robinson believed the nation should have "republican laws, enacted in one code, written with the greatest simplicity and conciseness, alphabetically arranged in a single book, so that every man could read and understand them for himself."[43] While Robinson would not succeed, the spirit of simplification of the law as an equalizing force would begin to take hold with some strength.

The complexity of the law and the mechanisms through which one might vindicate one's rights privileged the lawyer's role and also meant that the more experienced, skilled, and knowledgeable lawyers would have the upper hand in the courts. Their clients would thus operate at an advantage over those represented by less-experienced or less-knowledgeable counsel or those facing a lawsuit without representation at all. In the landmark case *Marbury v. Madison*, decided in the first years of the nineteenth century, Chief Justice John Marshall wrote that the province of the judiciary was to "say what the law is."[44] By the middle of that century, however, it was at times difficult for anyone, even lawyers and judges, to say what law governed a particular situation at a particular time and in a particular jurisdiction, especially as the nation's march westward expanded the geographic reach of the country—and the law itself.

The American system was still mostly based in the common law, even as the sources and digests that catalogued the law expanded and became more widely available and accessible.[45] A knowledge of the body of judicial decisions from which common law was derived, and through which it might evolve, was essential—not only to understand one's legal rights and obligations but also to vindicate them in court. One had to have a knowledge of and facility with common law pleading—the intricate incantations that must be recited in arguments before a court. One could advance a suit in *either* a court of law *or* equity; knowing which to choose, and the proper court in which to pursue which claim, was critical. One also had to select among one of dozens of "forms"—"fifty-nine in all," as reformer David Dudley Field explained[46]—in which to present one's case and to carefully select which factual allegations to present and what relief to seek. Such forms could, as Field argued, "be traced as far back as Henry the Second[] and were probably derived from the customs of Normandy."[47] Failure to choose the right forum or the proper form, to set forth the appropriate allegations to match that form, or to seek the right remedy to match forms and facts would prove fatal to the action. As Field proclaimed: "Justice is entangled in the net of forms."[48]

Finally, if the common law was the product of what judges said the law is, as the critics claimed, it was impossible to know what the law was before a judge pronounced it. Worse still, one's rights were completely dependent not on the elected legislature acting to realize the will of the people but on judges—even elected ones—who might be perceived as acting on little more than whim.[49] What is more, lawyers and courts were engaged in a "constant struggle . . . to evade the rules which [they] have framed."[50] The lawyers and the judges before whom the lawyers practiced "made the rules and they defend them, as a means of eliciting the precise point of fact in dispute between the parties; and they contrive every means in their power to conceal it, under forms the most general and unmeaning that can be imagined."[51] Reformers like Field often drew inspiration from the theories of English utilitarian Jeremy Bentham, who saw in the common law the clutches of formalism that failed to adapt to economic and political change.[52] For the critics, in sum, adherence to an unknown and at times unknowable body of law mostly generated by judges, based on ancient and inherited principles or judicial whim,[53] was hardly consistent with the democratic spirit. Nor was it an appropriate mode for a dynamic market economy within a democratic republic.[54]

The Birth of Law Reform

Concerns like those expressed by the labor advocate Frederick Robinson would animate advocacy to reform not only the legal profession but also the law and the entire legal system. And the Jacksonian ethos carried over into law reform itself, including both greater codification and simplification.[55] In New York in the early 1840s, for example, land speculation led to a growing divide between landowners and their tenants. The "Anti-Rent" movement emerged, with renters of farmlands expressing growing dissatisfaction with the laws; courts that seemed to favor the landed class; and a legal profession that tended to side with the landowners and was itself harder to access by those who could not afford to serve as an apprentice, a prerequisite to bar admission in the state at the time.[56] Populist agitation led to a state constitutional convention in the mid-1840s, and the result was a new state constitution that called for the codification of civil pleading rules; the popular and direct election of judges; a reorganization of the courts to merge the courts of law and equity; and a lowering of the requirements for admission to the bar.[57] The Jacksonian spirit continued to animate these efforts in New York and elsewhere, and bar admission requirements would be relaxed in other states as well during this period. But other developments in the law in New York would also have profound implications, not just for the legal profession but for the law itself.

The reformer David Dudley Field would help to spearhead this effort. Born at the start of the nineteenth century and educated at Williams College, he apprenticed in Albany and began practice as a lawyer in New York City.[58] His brother, Stephen, would become a Justice of the Supreme Court, as would a nephew, David Brewer.[59] Field, while not attaining such professional heights, nevertheless had a profound influence on the direction of the law and the legal profession itself for the next hundred years, much more than his close relatives who would serve on the Supreme Court itself. Indeed, his career spanned much of the nineteenth century, and he played a critical role in several developments that would shape the procedural rules governing the practice of law. He also helped to build some of the institutions that still structure and shape the legal profession to this day.

Field began practicing law in the midst of a growing consensus that the legal system needed reform. In all but one state, common law dominated both substantive law and procedure. The exception was Louisiana, which in 1825 had adopted a civil code modeled on the French Napoleonic Code, although it tended to have a mixed code and common-law system by the middle of the century. The common law, in contrast, distinctly British and arguably aristocratic in its origins, which privileged those knowledgeable of its complexities, could be viewed in stark contrast to a code-based system. Such systems, inspired in part by the French Revolution (like the Roman code system of laws before it), were intended to democratize the law itself, to make it clear and accessible even to those not versed in the law.[60] As legal scholar Roscoe Pound later explained, during this era many "not only distrusted all things English but . . . [were] sentimentally inclined to things French, including French law."[61]

Field studied not just the Louisiana code but also the laws of other nations. He believed that codification of procedural law as well as all bodies of substantive law would ensure that American laws and the American legal system were more democratic and republican in nature by limiting complexity, increasing accessibility, and breaking the power of cunning lawyers and capricious judges. He asserted that "[t]he more perfect is the civilization, the more complete the law," and "[t]he latter is, in many respects, both the cause and the consequence of the former."[62] For Field, "a system of rules and conformity to them are the essential conditions of all free government[] and of republican government above all others."[63] If, however, the law was dependent on the "will of the Judge or upon his notions of what was just, our property and our lives would be at the mercy of a fluctuating judgment[] or of caprice."[64] He argued that "[w]here there is no law, there can be no order, since order is but another name for regularity, or conformity to rule. Without order, society would relapse into barbarism."[65] Thus, Field echoed the sentiments of Paine and Tocqueville in his reverence for the law as ordering democratic society: "The law is our only sovereign. We have enthroned it."[66] For Field, the law was the "guardian and guide at once of the weak and the strong." And "even when invisible to the common eye," it serves as "the measure of our daily life, . . . covers us with its shield, restrains us by its power, and . . . goes with us wherever we go, by the side of every carriage on the loneliest road, on the deck of every ship even to the farthest sea."[67]

Field also recognized that, in a democratic republic, the legal profession plays a critical role in maintaining justice and preserving individual rights. While the judiciary also has a role to play, "the office of the advocate begins and rises at once to dignity and power, as the means of communication between the magistrate and the suitor, and as assessor or aid to the magistrate."[68] What is more, "[w]here there is arbitrary power, there is no occasion to study the law; when the law begins to reign, its teachers and practices come forth; the law and the lawyer go together all the world over."[69] It is the legal profession that gives the law its "life and vigor," holding it as a "shield before the weak and a sword against the strong."[70] In the end, the need of a civilized society, for Field, was "good laws well administered, or, which comes to the same thing, a written code of all useful law which all may read and be able to understand, together with a learned and conscientious bench and bar that nobody can frighten."[71] Several decades later, he summarized his philosophy about simplification and codification as follows: "The Americans are a practical people, and they want something they can understand and live by."[72]

Even relatively early in his career, Field developed a reputation as an outspoken advocate for reform, one he did not resist. He even advocated for what he called "radical reform," which required a movement "to go back to first principles, break up the present system, and reconstruct a simple and natural scheme of legal procedure."[73] When voters approved a new constitution in New York in 1846, that document called for the creation of a commission to rewrite the practice codes for the state's civil and criminal courts. At first, Field was perceived as too radical to serve as one of three commissioners on that new body.[74] But when one of the original commissioners determined that the other two shared Field's appetite for radical changes to the law, that commissioner withdrew. Field was named soon thereafter to fill that void.[75]

Field described the commission's challenge as one of amending the law. He saw that body of laws as a "cumbrous thing—three hundred years old and more—ill adapted to our present circumstances, unequal to our present wants, and so altered and mended, that scarce any two parts seem of a piece."[76] He added that the "technicality and the drudgery of legal proceedings are discreditable to our profession."[77] He assumed his responsibilities on the commission with vigor, recommending dramatic reforms and urging his brethren at the bar to embrace change lest they have it thrust upon them by others: "None can reform so well as we, as none would be benefited so much."[78] Furthermore, lawyers needed to "either take part in the changes, or set ourselves in opposition to them, and then, as I think, be overwhelmed by them."[79] Reform was on its way whether or not lawyers liked it, and it was "no longer possible to resist the current, which sets so strongly in that direction."[80] Indeed, as he would add, "[r]adical reform will come sooner or later, with us or without us."[81] Even though not a first choice for the commission, the force of Field's influence on the commission's process was so impactful that its work product, a new procedural code for civil lawsuits, became known simply as the "Field Code."[82]

After quick work, the commission presented its recommendations to the New York State Legislature. Those recommendations were adopted in 1850 and took effect soon thereafter. Other states would soon follow, and the codification of the rules of civil practice became widespread. Field continued to study and pursue broader codification of all laws, and he proposed an approach to codification of New York's criminal procedure and substantive law in its entirety. What he would develop in these areas would become models for many states, although they would mostly be rejected by Field's home state of New York.[83] Roscoe Pound would later reflect on Field's impact, and the reasons behind the rejection of some of his more ambitious codification efforts, as follows: "With procedure simplified, a conservative profession was unwilling to go further in what, to the common-law lawyer, was an untrodden path."[84]

Still, the reforms to the laws of procedure, Field's greatest contribution to the codification movement, were not insignificant. As one commentator explained of the conservative legal profession, "historical continuity was thought of as a duty, such things as fusion of law and equity in procedure, equitable relief and legal remedy in one proceeding, and doing away with forms of action seemed to go counter to the legal order of nature."[85] Nevertheless, Field's reforms to the procedures in civil cases took root in New York, across the nation, and even internationally. Field himself would spend much of his later years spreading the gospel of reform of the common law through codification, and through the next century international bodies embraced codification in such wide-ranging areas as maritime law, international trade, and human rights.[86]

Field would also play a significant role, both famous and infamous, in the creation of formal organizations that would represent the legal profession itself, which would begin in the second half of the nineteenth century. But the events that led to the creation of those institutions in particular would emerge only after a profound existential crisis affected the nation as a whole. Once again, not just the law, but lawyers themselves, would play critical roles in these events.

Lawyers and the Civil War

In the decades preceding the Civil War and during it, debates around slavery often hinged on questions of law: the rights of current and former enslaved persons, the supposed rights of slave owners, the rights of states to control internal relations between people and property, the war powers of the executive branch, et cetera.[87] Abolitionist lawyers played critical roles in pressing for the rights of enslaved and formerly enslaved people prior to the Civil War, like Salmon P. Chase[88] (who would also serve in Lincoln's cabinet, among other political posts); John Quincy Adams; and Roger Sherman Baldwin.[89] At the same time, laws and judicial decisions, advanced by white supremacist lawyers and judges, like Chief Justice Roger Taney,[90] and a predecessor, Chief Justice John Marshall, protected and preserved the institution of slavery time and time again.[91] Similarly, whether it was the Lincoln–Douglas debates, the advocacy of Frederick Douglass, the grounds for the trial and execution of John Brown, the contours of the Missouri Compromise, or the role and power of courts and juries in the enforcement of the Fugitive Slave Act, many of the arguments about the future of the Union, the Constitution, and slavery were often legalistic in nature. The abolitionists themselves argued internally over whether the Constitution itself was "pro-slavery," neutral on the issue, or could be read to promote equality before the law.[92]

Once the war commenced, another critical legal question emerged: What were the rights of formerly enslaved persons who had been able to flee Confederate-held territory to make their way behind Union army lines? Benjamin Butler, a lawyer before the war, would earn a commission as a general in the Union army and found himself at the command of a fortress in northern Virginia. In that role, he had to decide what to do with a group of formerly enslaved persons who had previously been forced to help Confederate forces build their own fortifications, slipped their captors, and made their way into the Union garrison under Butler's command.

The question for Butler, ever the lawyer, was whether the Fugitive Slave Act covered the situation before him.[93] According to his reading of the law, it authorized an enslaver residing *in a state* that permitted slavery to enlist federal authorities in securing the return of an escaped and former enslaved person.[94] Butler took the position that Virginia, because it had seceded from the Union, was no longer a state;[95] and if it was no longer a state, the Fugitive Slave Act did not apply to the situation.[96]

Moreover, Butler argued that the escaped and former enslaved persons who had sought his protection had aided the Confederacy when they were forced to build rebel fortifications. If he had come across Confederate munitions, Butler argued, he would not have been expected to return such contraband to his opponent. He claimed that the formerly enslaved persons were similarly contraband of war and thus he was under no obligation to return them to the enemy.[97] According to his autobiography, when a Confederate emissary appeared under a flag of truce for the return of the escapees, Butler responded: "'I mean to take Virginia at her word, as declared in the ordinance of secession passed yesterday. I am under no constitutional obligations to a foreign country, which Virginia now claims to be.'"[98]

Butler's position—describing human beings as "contraband"—did not sit well with some abolitionists like Frederick Douglass, who thought it dehumanizing.[99] Nevertheless, it seemed to have some rhetorical value and provided another argument for supporting the emancipation of slaves generally. An editorial published in the *Atlantic Monthly* offered the view that Butler's actions, although framed in "technical phrases," still had "great virtue" because they could play a role in "shaping public opinion." As that editorial argued, even the reader of "conservative" newspapers, who "prefers confiscation to emancipation" and is "reluctant to have slaves declared freemen," would have "no objection to their being declared contrabands." When a preacher announces that the enslaved persons should be freed because "it is a duty," the conservative mind rebels. But it "yields gracefully when Butler issues an order commanding it to be done because it is a military necessity."[100]

Months later, another Union general, John C. Frémont, leading Union troops in Missouri, issued a more sweeping order freeing the enslaved persons of any enslaver who was a resident of Missouri who took up arms in support of the rebellion.[101] President Lincoln would ultimately rescind that order as fears grew that such efforts might push the border states that still permitted slavery but had not seceded to rethink their position toward the Union.[102]

These sorts of arguments, however, would ultimately inspire Lincoln, another lawyer, of course, and help him devise a strategy to support broader emancipation.[103] To keep his fragile coalition of abolitionists and unionists together, he would argue that freeing the slaves could support the war effort and that it would provide a new group of potential recruits to shore up the Union army—freed, former enslaved persons and Northern Blacks in general, an argument Frederick Douglass had been making since the start of the war.[104] Not only would these individuals have the opportunity to enlist; they would also have a reason for doing so if they understood the war was being fought over the end of slavery, at least in the secessionist states.[105] This approach provided much of the arguments in favor of the Emancipation Proclamation, which freed formerly enslaved persons who found themselves behind Union lines and those in Confederate territories occupied by Union troops. Emancipation thus would satisfy the demands of the abolitionists while also addressing the interests of those who saw the fight to preserve the Union as the paramount objective of the war effort.[106]

In some ways at least, Lincoln's maneuvers endorsed Butler's seat-of-his-pants and lawyerly solution to the situation (what Lincoln would call "Butler's Fugitive Slave Law"[107]) that arose under Butler's command earlier in the war. But legal issues would arise throughout the conflict and immediately after: for example, whether the Union navy could blockade Confederate ports and seize the contents of merchant ships on the high seas;[108] whether President Lincoln could suspend the writ of habeas corpus;[109] or whether Jefferson Davis could face prosecution for treason before a military or civilian tribunal.[110] Lawyers would obviously play critical roles in all these debates.

The law and lawyers would also figure prominently in the immediate aftermath of the Civil War, as America's "second founding" as it is sometimes called[111] represented an effort to reform the Constitution through adoption of the Thirteenth, Fourteenth, and Fifteenth Amendments that, for their backers, were designed to recognize true equality under the law (at least between men).[112] The period of Reconstruction also sought to make good on this promise of equality, until law and lawyers stepped in, once again, to enshrine white supremacy in the legal system through Jim Crow and to protect the use of violence in an effort to terrorize the Black population.[113] The decades following the Civil War through to the end of the century marked a period where a war waged on the battlefield very much moved to the legislatures and the courtrooms, as law and lawyers advanced civil rights but also restrained them and their enforcement.[114] Nowhere was this more apparent than in the Southern states; as historian Eric Foner explains, by 1890, "the system of racial segregation [became] embedded in Southern law."[115] And, once again, lawyers would be heroes, like John Mercer Langston, who would serve in Congress and become the first dean of Howard Law School,[116] and villains, like Supreme Court Justice Henry Billings Brown, who authored the infamous decision in *Plessy v. Ferguson* at the tail end of this period.[117] The transformation of the American economy that would also occur in the latter part of the nineteenth century, the introduction of new technologies, and an increase in immigration would also set the stage for the emergence of a new legal profession itself. The notion that the United States might have once needed a "large, amorphous, open-ended profession"[118] would face significant resistance during this time, mostly from within the lawyer class itself. While many of the changes in the law in the post–Civil War era would transform all of society, it was within the profession that change was also coming. In the remainder of this chapter, I will begin to chart the evolution of the profession in the last decades of the nineteenth century. This examination will lay the groundwork for the more substantial changes the profession would institute—and institutionalize—in the first decades of the twentieth, which are the subject of chapter 4.

The Emerging Crises and the Initial Institutional Response

Just as in the revolutionary era, lawyers played a prominent role in shaping the key debates related to the war and its aftermath: around secession, slavery, emancipation, and Reconstruction. After the war, several forces emerged that would accelerate the influence and role of law and lawyers in the last decades of the nineteenth century. Rapid industrialization, growing immigration, the increasing role of finance in economic development, and the advance of the railroads led to the emergence of the business corporations and economic activity that entrenched economic elites. These elites often turned to lawyers to support their schemes or to try to thwart those of their rivals. Two of the most significant scandals of the postwar era—the effort to consolidate and gain control of the Erie Railroad, and gold speculation (which would touch even Ulysses S. Grant's administration)—had lawyers at their center. One of those lawyers was Field, who had risen to prominence as one of the most well-known and powerful lawyers in New York, if not the nation.

Field represented Daniel Drew, Jay Gould, and Jim Fisk in their struggle against the shipping magnate Cornelius Vanderbilt. The latter was represented by another prominent lawyer, Charles O'Conor. The conflict was over Vanderbilt's efforts to consolidate and control the separate Erie, Susquehanna, and New York Central railroad networks.[119] Dozens of lawyers would ultimately represent each side in the running dispute, taking advantage of Field's innovations in the civil code to secure dueling orders from different judges in different parts of New York State. According to one report, five separate judges issued seven different injunctions, "all enjoining or commanding things wholly inconsistent."[120] Many feared that the judges issuing these orders were corrupt—that they were either accepting bribes or had essentially purchased their seats from party bosses, who controlled the judicial nomination process itself and determined whether judges could stand for reelection.

The lawyers on both sides of the sprawling railroad dispute would file a total of twenty-one separate lawsuits. At one point, a violent melee involving over one thousand brawlers occurred outside the city of Binghamton, prompting the governor to call out the National Guard to operate the rails. The state's attorney general felt compelled to file his own action to try to resolve the titanic corporate battle. The physical violence (which resulted in the death of one process server), the armies of lawyers flinging legal pleadings around in an effort to gain the upper hand, and the apparent corruption of the judges left even reform-minded lawyers in a bind. There was a perception that the system was so corrupt that any lawyers who criticized a judge would find themselves ostracized. Clients, too, might bemoan the state of the legal system, but they also wanted to win their cases and might turn to the lawyers most able to operate within that corrupt, extractive system.[121]

In the midst of these tensions, a *New York Times* editorial called for a "Mutual Protective Association"—in effect, an association of lawyers who would act to reform the practices of the bar and the judiciary. The editorial lamented what it perceived as judicial corruption and argued that "there is virtually a judicial 'ring' in this City, and [there] always will be as long as judges are chosen by the present constituency." What was needed was a "permanent, strong and influential association of lawyers for mutual protection and benefit," as there was in London and Liverpool, England, at the time, where they "have been found necessary and effective." Such associations, the editorial noted, were made up of "the most prominent, able[,] and independent members of the profession." They "wield so powerful an influence that the Judges are compelled to pay that regard to their collective power which they would fain deny to that of the individual members." The editorial implored the "respectable members" of New York City's bar—who, individually, were "powerless"—to "consult their professional interests and expectations" so that they might form such an association "at an early date." The "only protection of the members of the Bar is in united action and organization," which would "be mutually beneficial in establishing the standing of the members of the association[] and in separating the black sheep in the legal flock from the white."[122]

Six months later, the *Times* once again argued, albeit in somewhat more strident tones, that lawyers had to address the corruption of the bench: "If it be the supineness, the guilty silence of the lawyers, as officers of the people's courts, which have brought us to our present pass, it is their reawakened public spirit and activity which must help us back to a better state of things; we must again proclaim that the bar must lead the way."[123] As one commentator explained: "The failure of the lawyers to act in so many areas which seemed peculiarly their own inevitably contributed to the idea, which was gaining ground with the public, that justice in New York, city and state, was becoming a farce."[124]

Stepping into this breach, several lawyers in December 1869 began to circulate an invitation among the more prominent members of the New York City bar. (At the time, that meant lawyers practicing on the island of Manhattan because the extended city had not yet been formed with the neighboring counties.) The invitation was to gather together to try to form a bar association that would not only "lead to the creation of more intimate relations between its members that now exist" but also "sustain the profession in its proper position in the community and thereby enable it, in many ways, to promote the interests of the public."[125] There had long been a lawyer's association in New York City: the New York Law Institute, founded by Chancellor James Kent, a prominent jurist in the state during the first half of the nineteenth century.[126] But that body had evolved into what was primarily a social club that also curated a law library for its members.[127] While some lawyers resisted the call for a new organization, the need for an association that might take on the issue of law reform was apparent.[128]

Some of the most well-known members New York City's practicing bar responded to this call, including Field and Samuel Tilden, who would become the Democratic Party nominee for U.S. president and lose to Rutherford B. Hayes in the contested election of 1876. The call was also answered by such other prominent lawyers as former U.S. Attorney General Edwards Pierrepont; Alexander Hamilton, Jr., son of the late Treasury secretary; and Elbridge T. Gerry, grandson of former Vice President Elbridge Gerry. Others joining included lawyers whose names adorned the letterheads of some of the nation's most prestigious law firms for over a century, like the three Coudert brothers who formed the firm of that name. And still others headed firms that continue to this day—including John L. Cadwalader, the founder of Cadwalader, Wickersham & Taft; and Thomas Shearman (an original partner of Field), whose firm would become Shearman & Sterling.

At the group's initial meeting, Tilden offered his view on the need for the association, noting that "there has been, in the last quarter century, a serious decline in the character, in the training, in the education, and in the morality of our Bar."[129] As a result, the "first work of the Association" had to be to "elevate the profession to a higher and better standard."

He expressed concern that, "[i]f the bar is to become merely a method of making money, making it in the most convenient way possible, but making it at all hazards, then the Bar is degraded." Moreover, speaking directly to the issue of lawyers colluding with judges to advance their clients' interests, he would state that, if the bar "is to be merely an institution that seeks to win causes and to win them by back-door access to the judiciary, then it is not only degraded, it is corrupt." At the same time, he appealed to his fellow lawyers' self-interest and the desire to promote the commercial activity in and the prominence of New York City, which he described as "the commercial and monetary capital of this continent," by stressing the need for lawyers to defend the rule of law. If the city was to maintain this role, "it must establish itself an elevated character for its Bar[] and a reputation throughout the whole country for its purity in the administration of justice." Indeed, he argued that "it is impossible for New York to remain the [center] of commerce and capital for this continent, unless it has an independent Bar and an honest judiciary."[130]

This newly formed organization called itself the Association of the Bar of the City of New York. It adopted a constitution, which provided that the purpose of the organization was to "maintain the honor and dignity of the profession of the law, to cultivate social intercourse among its members[,] and to increase its usefulness in promoting the due administration of justice." The organization created committees for amending the law, reforming the judiciary, and hearing attorney grievances.[131] Roughly five hundred of the four thousand lawyers practicing in Manhattan joined the association, but it was still an exclusive club. In today's dollars, the cost to join was roughly $1,500, with annual dues of $1,200.[132]

An editorial in the *Albany Law Journal* criticized the association for having accomplished little in the way of reform in its first year of operation, attributing it in part to the fact that only a small fraction of New York City's practicing lawyers were members. For the association to accomplish its goal of restoring the "ancient dignity and position of the legal profession," it could not operate as an exclusive club.[133] If all members of the practicing bar were to engage with the mission of the association, the editorial argued, "they would constitute a formidable element in our political system" and would be "invincible" if they were to act "in concert" to achieve reform with lawyers from throughout the country. The association was thus urged to make itself "accessible to every member of the profession who is not grossly immoral."[134] The editorial would go on to argue that an accessible, inclusive association "is precisely what the New York City Bar Association is not." As a result, "the influence of the organization is seen neither in court nor legislature, nor in the morals or manners of the bar."[135]

After receiving these criticisms for its somewhat underwhelming first year of existence, the association began to engage with some of the critical corruption scandals of the time, acting explicitly as an organization or through its prominent members who held central roles in some of the high-profile litigation and other efforts designed to root out that corruption. The association also set its sights in particular on malfeasance in the judiciary. It called for the impeachment of several judges involved in the Erie controversy, including George Barnard and Albert Cardozo (father of Benjamin Cardozo, who would later become a Supreme Court Justice).[136] In recommending these and other judicial impeachments, the association recognized the ties between the proper administration of justice, the rule of law, and the prospects of New York City's economy. It argued that charges of corruption against the city's judges "have been repeatedly made in the most explicit manner in many of the principal journals of the day[] and thus circulated throughout the United States and foreign countries."[137] As a result, "the administration of justice" in New York City "and the honor and fair fame not only of that city but also of the State have become widely involved in doubt and suspicion."[138] Because of these conditions, "capitalists have been alarmed, and important commercial and financial enterprises have been diverted from said city, and . . . its general prosperity is likely to be still further materially retarded."[139] The association would ultimately secure the impeachment or resignation of several prominent judges, including Cardozo.

Members also addressed corruption in New York City's government. A scandal emerged involving the outfitting and renovation of what has come to be known as the Tweed Courthouse in Lower Manhattan. Investigations revealed that the so-called Tweed ring spent over $54 million in taxpayer money (in today's dollars) on carpentry, roughly $87 million to plaster the facility, and nearly $150 million on carpeting.[140] When this news broke, several prominent members of the association led the effort to rouse public sentiment against the boss of the Tweed ring, the eponymous William Tweed, leader of the infamous Tammany Hall club. Calls for his prosecution reached Albany, where O'Conor— the former Vanderbilt attorney from the Erie conflict and a member of the association—was tapped as private attorney general to lead the case against Tweed. Field had previously offered his services for this role but was rebuffed.[141] He would soon enter the fray as counsel for the defense.[142]

Previously, Tweed had wriggled out of the first corruption case brought against him by virtue of a hung jury. In this second trial, in which prominent members of the association had appeared as prosecution and defense counsel, the outcome would not be as inconclusive. The defense team thought it could disqualify the judge, Noah Davis, who had recently served in Congress and as U.S. Attorney for the Southern District of New York. Tweed's lawyers claimed Judge Davis was biased against Tweed, echoing concerns of corruption the association had levied against other judges in prior impeachment campaigns. Judge Davis would not tolerate such charges. He reviewed their petition to disqualify him and essentially ignored it until after the verdict was rendered against Tweed.[143] Once the jury convicted Tweed—and after Davis imposed a much harsher sentence on Tweed than his counsel believed was possible—the judge then admonished defense counsel in open court. Davis proclaimed that no lawyer may "act for the sake of his client" in a way that "tends to degrade the tribunal before which he appears[] or lessen respect for that official authority on which so much depends for the preservation of our institutions."[144] He fined each of Tweed's more senior lawyers the equivalent of roughly $10,000 today and said they would be sequestered until they paid the fine (although he said he could not fine Field because Field was in Europe at the time). As for the younger lawyers—including Elihu Root, future U.S. secretary of state and of war, and Willard Bartlett, who would later serve on New York's highest court and who Davis said "displayed great ability during the trial"—the judge provided the following "few words of advice": "[R]emember that good faith to a client never can justify or require bad faith to your own consciences."[145] While it be beneficial to be "known as successful and great lawyers, it is even a better thing to be known as honest men."[146]

From Tweed's conviction in 1873, through to 1898, when New York County became a part of the consolidated New York City, and the city population itself grew considerably, the association did not increase its membership as a percentage of the overall population of the practicing bar. It also began to stagnate, as the founding members continued to dominate the discourse and the direction of the bar.[147] In the 1870s, the Association of the Bar of the City of New York had embarked upon nearly a decade of muckraking advocacy to root out corruption in the judiciary, and it served in the vanguard of efforts to reform the law to address the changing nature of society. By the early 1880s, however, new leadership would place the association in opposition to efforts—long sought by once-prominent members like David Dudley Field and others—to reform the common law and promote the codification of New York's entire body of civil law.

Legal historian Morton Horwitz has explained that a new leader of the bar, James Coolidge Carter, "employed the language of popular government for essentially conservative ends."[148] For Carter, despotic nations were those where law is codified, because the despot must pronounce the law in order to stay in power. By contrast, in common law countries like the United States and Great Britain, Carter argued that the law is developed by the people, with judges simply identifying the logic of their customs and habits. Common law emerges from that judicial analysis, but the source of the law is always the people themselves. The slow evolution of the common law as the people shape their traditions, customs, and habits is, according to Carter, more consistent with the protection of "property, business, and liberty."[149] In contrast, the despot declares the law "by a positive command," which, in turn, becomes legislation: that is, code.[150] Such a position would certainly be a surprise to legal scholars from the early republic, like St. George Tucker, whose important work on Blackstone's *Commentaries* in 1803 showed how American law and its constitution diverged considerably from the common law as passed down from England.[151]

Carter's sleight-of-hand—cloaking conservative concerns in the raiment of democratic values—was an approach the legal profession would take in response to many efforts to reform not just the law but also the legal profession itself. Carter's ultimate ascendancy to the presidency of the association represented not generational change but rather the march of time that took the leaders with it in lockstep. By the 1890s, the association's leaders would age (or die, as was the case with Field in 1894), and yet their generation continued to assume the leadership roles in the organization.[152] And that cohort of leaders soon found that the desire for reform continued to burn despite their best efforts to snuff it out.

During this period, the profession itself was starting to change, albeit slowly. No state appeared to admit any women to practice before the Civil War, and the Supreme Court held that there was no federal right to bar admission for women, leaving the issue to the states to decide the issue.[153] By the end of the century, most states permitted women to enter the profession.[154] Their ranks were limited, however, leading one commentator at the time to quip "the newspapers publish and republish little floating items about women lawyers along with those of the latest sea-serpent, the popular idea seeming to be that the one is about as real as the other."[155] Blacks, too, began to join the profession, but they would number less than 800 in the entire country by one estimate and make up less than .5 percent of the legal profession by the end of the nineteenth century.[156] For women, Blacks, immigrants, and members of religious minorities, entry to the law firms that were beginning to form was extremely rare;[157] for women, at least one prominent firm would not even let them serve as secretaries.[158]

Apart from New York City's prominent bar association, other professional associations were also emerging in other states and even in the nation as a whole. Both the American Bar Association and the American Association of Law Schools would emerge from meetings held in the resort town of Saratoga Springs, New York, in 1878 and 1901, respectively.[159] Because the Association of the Bar of the City of New York would not admit women, the Women Lawyers' Club in New York would form in 1899.[160] Also in New York, calls for a new bar association—one that would be more inclusive and represent a larger percentage of the practicing bar—led to the creation of the New York County Lawyers' Association. J. Noble Hayes, a director of the new association, pointed out that there was a need for a new and more inclusive organization because the old one had become conservative politically, dominated by the "Old Guard." The leadership of the association had thwarted reform efforts, stifled debate, and had no interest in welcoming new members (let alone African American lawyers, women, and individuals from religious minorities). According to Hayes, the new organization was gaining members because it attracted lawyers who felt that such an association would serve as an ally in the efforts of reform and "not [as] a rival in the common cause of maintaining high standards upon the bench and at the bar[] and promoting efficiency of the courts of justice."[161] The annual dues were 20 percent of those of the association, and there was no admission fee. Anyone admitted to the bar could join. It is not surprising that in a short time the county association would have twice the number of members as the older association.[162] Trying to distinguish the new association from the old, Hayes offered the following assessment:

> If there is an essential difference between the two [associations] it consists in this, that the policy of the Association of the Bar has been to distrust the profession as a whole and guard against action by it, while the policy of the [Lawyers' Association] is to trust it and encourage it to action, in the belief that the real leaders will lead and the just cause triumph, and that anything is better than supineness,—a difference, perhaps, after all, of method.[163]

The reformist tendencies of the Association of the Bar of the City of New York in the 1870s had lapsed into a more defensive posture, attempting to thwart the progressive elements within the profession that were beginning to emerge. But such tendencies would not hold back the seismic changes afoot in the United States. Moreover, the legal profession would find itself at the center of many of these changes, both helping to shape them and being shaped by them. The profession's response to these changes, as I will show, created the core institutions of the American legal profession that are with us to this day—a phenomenon I will explore in depth in chapter 4.

4

The Profession in Crisis and the Institutional Response

In 1893, the Chicago World's Fair highlighted the social and technological changes underway in late nineteenth-century America. Transformations in architecture, urban planning, and technology were all on display. The "City Beautiful" movement, which emphasized order, grand buildings, monuments, and boulevards, had its coming-out party.[1] Exhibits by Westinghouse and General Electric highlighted advances in electrical generation and electrification.[2] These developments reflected broader and dramatic trends in the country: population growth, internal migration, immigration, urbanization, and increased industrialization. These led many, both new immigrants and those who had been in the United States for generations, to feel a loss of any connection to community, of self-determination. They felt that things were spinning out of control and unfolding at a pace not seen before.[3] A devastating financial crisis in the early 1890s also gripped the nation and shook many people's belief in Social Darwinism and laissez-faire economics.[4]

These forces spurred efforts to achieve some degree of control over communities, the marketplace, the workplace, and government, leading to a growth in organizations and corporations and an expansion of the regulatory state.[5] Informal local bonds and loyalties gave way to more formal institutions: social and political organizations and networks; nation-spanning and integrated business trusts; professional associations; and a new web of laws and regulations to rein in such institutions.[6] While businesses expanded, government oversight of those businesses tried to catch up, including through the adoption of federal antitrust laws; food safety regulations; and worker health and safety provisions.[7] Many believed that through technology, rigorous planning, and professionalization in a range of disciplines the world could be tamed, ordered, controlled, enhanced, and enriched.[8] Much of this ordering would occur through law, with lawyers at the center of these developments, sometimes leading the way, sometimes opposing them. Indeed, lawyers developed new legal structures for advancing the corporate business form;[9] defended corporate practices and health and safety regimes;[10] and created and maintained the legal infrastructure of Jim Crow.[11] For these and other reasons, lawyers often found themselves at the center of many of the forces that not only represented change but also created discontent and disillusionment in turn-of-the-century America.

This charged environment prompted an assessment of existing institutions and the development of new institutions to address these broad societal changes. It would also lead to an appraisal of the proper role of lawyers in the community and the economy. Those who gazed upon the practices of the profession at the time did not like what they saw—from across the political and economic spectrum and from within and outside the profession. As with the broader changes, and the responses to those changes, the legal profession sought ways to develop new institutions and strengthen existing ones to enable the profession to keep pace with the changes all around it and to stay relevant in a rapidly growing and evolving nation.

In this chapter I will trace the development of the modern legal profession through the institutions the profession either formed or strengthened from the late 1870s through the 1920s. This institutional history is essential to understanding how the profession established these institutions in the first place. Because this institutional structure still provides a logic and coherence to the legal profession today, it is even more important to delve into this history. In order to conduct this assessment, I will begin with the forces the profession faced at the dawn of the twentieth century and then describe the profession's institutional responses to them that followed.

A Profession in Crisis

Wherever one identified social, economic, and political tensions at this time, one would find lawyers. They were also not immune to them, as demographic change, new modes of technology and communication, and even such innovations as the telephone and the typewriter had an impact on the practice of law itself.[12] Throughout the nineteenth century, for those who were white, male, and of Northern European stock, access to the profession was fairly easy. By century's end—as the U.S.

population grew and changed and the economy expanded, which led to major opportunities for lawyers to achieve economic gain through the practice of law—some of the more traditional members of the bar saw peril.

One bar committee report in the early 1900s described these forces and the state of the legal profession as follows:

> With the marvelous growth and development of our country and its resources, with the ranks of our profession ever extending, its fields of activities ever widening, the lawyer's opportunities for good and evil are correspondingly enlarged, and the limits have not been reached. We cannot be blind to the fact that, however high may be the motives of some, the trend of many is away from the ideals of the past and the tendency more and more to reduce our high calling to the level of a trade, to a mere means of livelihood or of personal aggrandizement. With the influx of increasing numbers, who seek admission to the profession mainly for its emoluments, have come new and changed conditions.[13]

David Brewer, then a Justice of the U.S. Supreme Court, complained in a commencement address at Albany Law School that, in the legal profession as elsewhere, there were "many weak characters who, while they might not deliberately do a dishonest thing or deliberately prove false to an oath or obligation, yet yield to pressure of corporate interests, deluding themselves with the idea that those interests are synonymous with the interests of the nation."[14]

Others would share similar sentiments. One prominent San Francisco lawyer, George Shelton, would complain that lawyers as a class were once seen as "one of the exclusively learned" professions; the lawyer found "his influence powerful, and his scholarship enhanced the esteem with which he was held."[15] At the turn of the nineteenth to the twentieth century, however, Shelton believed that lawyers' motives were "sordid" and "mercenary."[16] Such an approach was "suicidal" for the profession where the lawyer is "willing to measure his activity at the bar by the standards of the counting-house and the pawn-shop." As long as lawyers do this, they are "looked upon as a class of mercenary sharpers whose best is ever at the command of the long purse."[17] Another critic recounted a dialogue between a young lawyer and a seasoned judge that he claimed to have overheard at a bar committee meeting. He described the judge as explaining that "'[e]very year, a horde of young men are entering law, far more intent on making money than on living up to professional standards.'"[18] At this time, "ninety-nine out of a hundred lawyers" engage in the practice of law "'for all it is worth as a living.'"[19] These forces were unlikely to leave "'the law anything but a sordid trade, based still on the false pretense that it is a dignified professional calling.'"[20]

Leaders of the legal profession at the time harbored fears that the public did not view lawyers in high regard. For at least some of these leaders, however, their own concerns were different from the voices criticizing lawyers for too often choosing to promote the interests of wealthy clients over the needs of the community. Many prominent leaders of the bar recast the concern that the legal profession was becoming too profit-oriented as one of charlatans and scam artists subverting the high-minded values of the profession.[21] These unscrupulous lawyers were on the lower end of the lawyer-status spectrum: thinly credentialed and shameless practitioners who saw law as a means to personal financial wealth rather than as a vocation. For these leaders, the ranks of the profession were swelling—like the teeming streets, tenements, and factory floors—with immigrant strivers.[22]

Indeed, for many of these elite lawyers, the growth—and the new demographic heterogeneity—of the bar were to blame for this state of affairs. In 1903, a committee of the American Bar Association tasked with studying legal education and access to the bar lamented that some law students were "illiterate foreigner[s] who can hardly read or write English."[23] This type of individual, the committee asserted, wishes to become a lawyer "almost as soon as he becomes a citizen, with the lowest ambitions and ideals, who earns his living while studying law as a runner for a pettifogger."[24] Another ABA committee reported that, at one time, "possible ostracism by professional brethren was sufficient to keep from serious error the practitioner with no fixed ideals of ethical conduct," but, with new elements in the bar, "the shyster, the barratrously inclined, the ambulance chaser, the member of the Bar with a system of runners, pursue their nefarious methods with no check save the rope of sand of moral suasion so long as they stop short of actual fraud and violate no criminal law."[25] Such men "believe themselves immune, the good or bad esteem of their co-laborers is nothing to them provided their itching fingers are not thereby stayed in their eager quest for lucre."[26] These men "are enemies of the republic[,] not true ministers of her courts of justice robed in the priestly garments of truth, honor and integrity," and are "unworthy of a place upon the rolls of the great and noble profession of the law."[27]

Similarly, George Costigan, dean of the University of Nebraska Law School, expressed his concern that newer lawyers at the turn of the nineteenth to the twentieth century had a "growing tendency . . . to regard their calling either as a money-getting trade or as a stepping stone to politics rather than as in itself a noble and inspiring calling to which money getting is merely an incident."[28] Sharing some of the sentiments regarding the demographic background of some of these newer lawyers, he would declare this state of affairs was a product of the "democratization of the bar" and a result of the profession's members being drawn from "widely varied walks of life."[29]

The practicing bar's concerns were summed up by legal scholar Everett V. Abbot: "It is a frequent observation that the practice of law is taking on, especially in the large cities, a distinctly commercial character."[30] For Abbot, this was a product of three things: first, the change in the relationship between lawyer and client as one focused on profit maximization; second, "lowered standards"; and third, "*personnel.*"[31]

Crass commercialization within and extractive practices by the profession were nothing new. In colonial times, John Adams complained of "pettifogging meddlers" who, for a profit, attempted to take advantage of a client's trust or lack of superior knowledge of the legal system.[32] At the dawn of the twentieth century, however, something had changed. While the Jacksonian ethos had certainly led to a fairly open legal profession, it was still mostly white, male, and Protestant, its members mostly descended from Northern European immigrants.[33] Changing demographics in the nation meant that a relatively open legal profession would also be open to individuals from religious, racial, and ethnic groups not historically found among the ranks of the bar.

Lawrence Maxwell, in his 1905 report as chair of the ABA's Section on Legal Education,[34] recounted a conversation he had with a justice of a state's highest court who asked: "What sort of a learned profession is it a majority or any considerable part of whose members have not sufficient command of the English language, or comprehension of their subject, or logical faculty, to be able to present the questions in a case which has reached the court of last resort in a clear and orderly way?"[35]

Henry Drinker, a prominent Philadelphia lawyer, who would author a well-regarded treatise on legal ethics later in the century, expressed his dismay over the state of the profession, attributing much of that condition to the influx of new immigrant lawyers. He explained that he had served on a local attorney grievance committee and thus had a sense of "the type of lawyer that [the ABA] wants to keep from studying law."[36] He would argue that there were some lawyers who had come "up out of the gutter and were catapulted into the law."[37] For Drinker, these lawyers "did not associate with the American boys" in college and thus "were not apt to realize they were doing anything wrong."[38] These uneducated lawyers "were merely following the methods their fathers had been using in selling shoe strings and other merchandise, that is[,] the competitive methods they use in business down in the slums."[39] He estimated that "three-fourths of the offenders" before the grievance committee "came right up out of the gutter into the Bar."[40] And he described what he believed to be the family practices of these lawyers: they would "have four or five boys and two or three girls, [and] when they get big enough they pick out the one that is the smartest, and they all make a sacrifice to let that boy get an education . . . and lots of them become lawyers and doctors." Since that boy-turned-law-student "works in a sweat shop or somewhere in the daytime and he studies law at odd times mostly . . . he has not had a chance to absorb American ideals." This situation, Drinker argued, applies to "any number of foreign boys." However, Drinker was not satisfied with the use of code words like "shyster" that others might have used to describe these individuals. He made his comments quite specific, stating that "an extraordinarily large proportion" of those who came before the grievance committee "were Russian Jew boys, young fellows who had been at the Bar a few years."[41]

For Elihu Root, a former U.S. senator who had also served as a cabinet secretary to President Theodore Roosevelt, and who cut his teeth in the Boss Tweed trial described in chapter 3, the new class of lawyers entering the profession were "acute, subtle, adroit, [and] skillful" and merely "crammed" for the bar examination.[42] This meant that, although they could "trot around any simple-minded American boy," the new class of lawyers had at least two failings.[43] First, they had no moral compass to make them familiar with the ways of the American legal profession because they had not been trained in a law office.[44] Second, and more important, for Root, they were born of foreign stock, hailing mostly from "Continental Europe."[45] There was thus a "great influx in the bar of men with intellectual acumen and no moral qualities."[46] Root argued that "American institutions" grew from the "struggle and sacrifice" that emerged from "the long centuries of the Anglo-Saxon fight for freedom" that received a new birth in the United States.[47] Yet "today," Root continued, individuals were coming to the profession "by the hundreds" who had "no conception of the moral qualities that underlie our free American institutions."[48]

Despite the claims that uncouth, untrained, and un-American lawyers were besmirching the profession by peddling their wares to the masses, in reality most of these "masses" had no access to the legal profession to meet their legal needs. This state of affairs led to the sentiments offered by Roosevelt and Brandeis that opened this work: if the legal profession and the legal system were essentially inaccessible to the general population, and lawyers were seen as manipulating the legal system to serve their wealthier clients, the underserved population would take the law into its own hands. In particular, the influx of immigrants into the United States raised concerns that individuals from foreign countries with different democratic traditions (and, at times, even experiences with violent revolution) might resort to extralegal means of promoting their interests—if not seek to overthrow the system itself.[49] What is more, if the practice of law was perceived as a means of making money—if justice was seen as being for sale and the legal system as not dispensing equal justice, favoring moneyed interests—there was no lawful way for the poor and middle class to protect their rights and interests. As George Shelton would argue, inappropriate practices by lawyers undermined the rule of law and would lead people to take the law into their own hands because "popular sentiment is crystallized into the belief that unscrupulous attorneys can be found to provide loop-holes for the escape of transgressors if the fee is forthcoming."[50]

For these reasons, the legal profession was facing a series of crises. The first was a crisis of professionalism. Whether it was well-heeled lawyers serving their wealthy clients, or immigrant strivers serving the working class in unscrupulous ways, there was a general sense that the practice of law had devolved into a sordid trade. Within the profession, this was viewed as a function of there being few barriers to entry, which created a second crisis: the perceived need to limit access to the profession. Efforts to address the second crisis created yet a third: one of exclusion. The poor and working class needed to feel included in the American legal system and its institutions; otherwise there would be threats to the rule of law. As with other sectors of the economy and society as a whole—in which Progressive Era reforms sought to create new institutions, and strengthen existing ones, to address the needs of a changing nation— the legal profession embarked on an effort to build the institutions that would shape the profession with designs on responding to the crises before it. The institutional turn in the profession's crisis-response approach included the development or strengthening of six key institutions: bar associations, law firms, codes of ethics, law schools, barriers to entry to the profession, and a fledgling public interest bar. I will discuss the emergence of each of these throughout this chapter, with my primary focus on codes of ethics, law schools, and barriers to entry.

Organizing Lawyers, Organizing the Bar

The first institution the legal profession developed as a response to the changes in the economy and society was the law firm. Here we see the profession, by organizing itself into firms, attempting to adjust its practices to meet the needs of its clients, a changing economy, and the introduction of new technologies to the practice of law. In the late 1800s, most lawyers practiced as solo attorneys or associated with one or two others in order to share office space.[51] But the growing and newly industrialized nation needed lawyers to help craft the legal forms, create the financing arrangements, and negotiate the business deals that would help build a transcontinental railroad, increase interstate commerce, and form national corporations.[52] Just as businesses organized into "vertical" entities, the legal profession adopted what came to be known as the Cravath Model, named after the corporate law firm that now bears the name Cravath, Swaine, and Moore.[53] This firm had tiers of practitioners who gained promotion based on merit and accomplishments.[54] The purpose of this tiered organization was to make the delivery of legal services more efficient and more effective in a fast-paced, national economy.[55] It was also a response to technological advances like the telephone, typewriter, industrial typesetting, and the capacity for rapid reproduction of judicial opinions. The introduction of these innovations into the practice of law enabled lawyers to communicate with their clients in more efficient ways, track outcomes in cases, and generate more work.[56] Some more traditional lawyers lamented many of these newfangled contraptions, which, they argued, tended to diminish the trust between the lawyer and client because it displaced face-to-face communication.[57] But lawyers had to adapt to and adopt the new technologies and explore the creation of new partnerships that facilitated more efficient practices.[58]

The law firm was not the only organizational structure the profession embraced, however. Interfirm networks—in the form of bar associations—also left their mark on the profession, in particular because of the ways in which they strengthened other critical institutions: codes of ethics, law schools, and barriers to entry. In chapter 3, I closed with the formation of an impactful bar association in New York City in the post–Civil War era. Much of the legal profession's crisis-response approach followed and was catalyzed by the emergence and rise to prominence of another association, the first of its kind because it was national in scope. Founded by elite lawyers who summered in the resort town of Saratoga Springs, New York, the ABA ensured that the professional bar would have an organized voice to promote the interests of its members—all of whom were white and male, by design, and most of whom represented corporate clients.[59] Founded in 1878, one of this body's most important acts did not occur for another thirty years: the codification of rules of ethics for the profession that would serve as a guide for the states, which had the primary responsibility for overseeing the lawyers who practiced within them. In many ways, the development of this code was one of the primary institutional responses of the profession to the challenges before it, and I explain its origins in some depth next.

The ABA's 1908 Canons of Professional Ethics

By the end of the nineteenth century, new technologies, new means of communication and travel, and the growth of mass production all transformed how people worked, lived, moved, shopped, and entertained themselves. These changes also spurred increased legislation and regulation to provide some degree of oversight and accountability in a rapidly changing economy.[60] In one critical sector of the economy—the legal profession—this movement to enshrine guidance and accountability into legal mechanisms had not quite caught up to the trends shaping all aspects of life. Indeed, at this time there was no codified set of rules of ethics for lawyers to follow or for clients and the courts to hold lawyers accountable for misbehavior.

In the first half of the nineteenth century, a patrician lawyer from Baltimore, David C. Hoffman, who would teach a course in law at the University of Maryland, developed what he called the "Fifty Resolutions in Regard to Professional Development," which he updated over time.[61] Hoffman was disturbed by the Jacksonian ethos that dominated the time, and he was concerned by what he perceived to be a growing lawlessness and mob rule.[62] His resolutions, which read today as quaint at best, are more like rules of etiquette as opposed to a code that could guide lawyer behavior given the tumult of the late nineteenth century. For instance, in court a lawyer should resolve "ever to be courteous," and "no man's ignorance or folly shall induce me to take any advantage of him."[63] If a client owes a debt, and yet the statute of limitations on that debt has run, the lawyer should not assert that defense for fear that the client would make the lawyer "a partner in his knavery."[64] When it comes to the setting of fees, the lawyer should be careful so as not to charge less than what other lawyers in the community charge because "all underbidding of my professional brethren" is "eminently dishonorable."[65] Hoffman's final resolution is simply that the lawyer should "read the foregoing forty-nine resolutions twice every year during my professional life."[66] Hoffman's Resolutions gained little traction with the practicing bar, however.

The next lawyer to generate a body of rules for practicing lawyers was George Sharswood. A lawyer from Philadelphia, he served as a professor of law at the University of Pennsylvania and held several elected legislative offices and then several judicial positions, including a seat on the Pennsylvania Supreme Court, becoming its chief justice in 1879.[67] In 1854, he produced "An Essay on Professional Ethics," which would go through several editions, including a fifth, published posthumously in 1884.[68] In that fifth edition, Sharswood's Essay proclaimed that "[t]he dignity and importance of the Profession of the Law, in a public view, can hardly be over-estimated."[69] For Sharswood, this is due to the profession's influence over both the writing of the laws and the administration of justice.[70] The lawyer "is as frequently called upon to inquire what the law ought to be as what it is."[71] What is more, the legal profession has a prominent role to play in the functioning of American democracy due to its role in drafting and amending constitutions, defending "the weak and the oppressed," standing as a "bulwark of private rights against the assaults of power," preparing legislation, arguing cases in court, communicating the contours of the law to the public, and holding "the most important public posts."[72]

Sharswood then developed what he described as "accurate and intelligible rules by which to guide and govern the conduct of professional life"[73] because "no man can ever be a truly great lawyer, who is not in every sense of the word, a good man."[74] This was the case even though he asserted that "[t]here is no class of men among whom moral delinquency is more marked and disgraceful than among lawyers."[75] Sharswood, like Hoffman, made recommendations that sounded more like rules of civility than those that would govern the serious practice of law. For example, "[e]quanimity and self-possession are qualities of unspeakable value."[76] Conduct before a court requires "outward respect in words and actions."[77] The lawyer should "neither give nor provoke insult"[78] and should "shun most carefully the reputation of a sharp practitioner."[79] And "if it be necessary to say severe things of" an adversary or witness "let it be done in the language, and with the bearing, of a gentleman."[80] Sharswood also discussed what can only be described as good law practice management, cautioning the practicing lawyer that "dishonor and obscurity, if not ignominy, has often taken its rise from the fountain of a little habit of inattention and procrastination"[81] and that the "importance of good hand-writing cannot be overstated," which becomes a "passport to the favor of clients[] and to the good graces of judges."[82] He also cautioned members of the profession "not to settle down into a mere lawyer."[83] Instead, they should elevate themselves by cultivating "polite literature in hours of relaxation," making sure not to lose "acquaintance with the models of ancient taste and eloquence"[84] lest they succumb to the "great danger that law reading, pursued to the exclusion of everything else, will cramp and dwarf the mind, shackle it by the technicalities with which it has become so familiar, and disable it from taking enlarged and comprehensive views," even on topics "lying beyond" one's "legitimate domain."[85]

At the same time, Sharswood criticized direct and secret communications with judges as undermining the rule of law because such communications have a "tendency to impair confidence in the administration of justice, which should not only be pure but unsuspected."[86] He also proclaimed, in an oft-quoted phrase: "Entire devotion to the interest of the client, warm zeal in the maintenance and defence of his rights, and the exertion of his utmost learning and ability[;] these are the higher points, which can only satisfy the truly conscientious practitioner."[87] If the lawyer comes to believe that their client is pursuing an "unrighteous object," the lawyer "ought to throw up the cause, and retire from all connection with it, rather than thus be a participator in other men's sins."[88] Sharswood also asked whether, citing what he described as the history of the decline of the legal profession in other societies over time, this was a product of the descent from "an honorable office" into a "money-making trade."[89] Seemingly answering his own question, he would assert that a "horde of pettifogging, barratrous, custom-seeking, money-making lawyers[] is one of the greatest curses with which any state or community can be visited."[90]

Unlike Hoffman's resolutions, Sharswood's essay seemed to influence a small wave of state ethics codes, beginning with Alabama's, adopted in 1887 and culled from Sharswood's recommendations.[91] By 1906, ten more states had adopted similar codes, some almost a word-for-word match with Alabama's.[92] Louisiana also had its own brief code, which consisted of eight points, filled no more than a page, and included the directive that the lawyer is to "live uprightly; and in our persons, to justify before men the dignity, honor, and integrity of a great and noble profession."[93]

Due in part to the criticisms of the profession, and the fact that there was no national guidance for state bar associations looking to adopt their own codes of ethics, the ABA set out to establish just such a national model code. At its annual meeting in 1904, held in Narragansett, Rhode Island, it charged a five-member panel to study the issue and "to report at the next meeting of this Association upon the advisability and practicability of the adoption of a code of professional ethics by this Association."[94] One year later, this committee would present to the ABA a brief report, spelling out its position on the need for the promulgation of such a code, arguing as follows: "[H]ere in America, where justice reigns only by and through the people under forms of law, the lawyer is and must ever be the high-priest at the shrine of justice."[95] Echoing the concerns of lawlessness brought about by a failure of the profession to uphold the equitable administration of justice, the committee added that, without "continued confidence on the part of the public in the fairness, integrity[,] and impartiality of its administration, there can be no lasting permanence to our republican institutions."[96] The committee described the legal profession as "the keystone of the republican arch of government," but it also warned that if the profession were to "[w]eaken this keystone by allowing it to be increasingly subject to the corroding and demoralizing influence of those who are controlled by graft, greed[,] and gain, or other unworthy motive . . . sooner or later the arch must fall."[97] Since the "future of the republic depends upon our maintenance of the shrine of justice pure and unsullied," that future cannot be "maintained unless the conduct and motives of the members of our profession, of those who are the high priests of justice, are what they ought to be." It was thus the legal profession's "plain and simple duty, our patriotic duty," to help make the ABA "what it ought to be," and such a code of ethics, "adopted after due deliberation and promulgated by the American Bar Association, is one method in furtherance of this end."[98]

Over the coming year, a now-expanded bar committee would draw from a range of sources—including the codes of the few states that had adopted them, as well as Sharswood's Essay and Hoffman's Resolutions—and circulate them to every member of the association throughout the country. The committee asserted that, in preparing a model code, it "should have the active assistance of every member of the Association with thoughts upon the subject."[99] The committee would then gather the comments received and report out many in subsequent publications. To begin, the committee asked ABA members to comment on the Alabama Code, as if the ABA might consider adopting it.[100] It went on to issue several draft versions of its own Ethics Code, with several iterations, from March 1908 through August 1908, when the final code was adopted at a national meeting of ABA delegates. While many aspects of the Alabama Code proved unobjectionable to the vast majority of members, debate over several key issues reveals tensions inherent in the

ABA's challenge to address the profession's crises of professionalism, access, and inclusion.

The use of the Alabama Code is itself notable. It was certainly the first such state code adopted, but that use also provides some insight into the cultural setting in which the drafters of the ABA's code found themselves. Charles A. Boston, who would later serve as president of the ABA, would discuss the difference in the legal profession at the time the ABA was considering adopting a code of ethics, and the practice in Alabama at the time its code was adopted, as follows: then, Alabama "was a homogeneous community, where the law was an honorable profession, and not a trade, and where the practices of many races and of commercial craft had not destroyed notions of ethical standards, nor introduced practitioners actually ignorant that there might be such standards."[101] One of the main architects of Alabama's code, Thomas Goode Jones, was a prominent lawyer in Alabama at the time who served as governor and as a federal judge from the state. He was also a rank segregationist and helped to draft Alabama's new constitution in 1901 that enshrined Jim Crow into that state's laws.[102]

By 1908, the committee tasked with drafting the code had nearly tripled in size. Originally five members, it now had fourteen, and all were urban lawyers in the elite of the profession, with three from New York City, two from Chicago, and the rest from cities like Philadelphia; Washington, D.C.; Norfolk, Virginia; Montgomery, Alabama; and Boston.[103] None of these lawyers had offices in rural communities, nor did they represent the emerging public interest bar. Jerold Auerbach's historical and economic analysis of the members of the bar suggests that the elite members of the bar crafted the rules to serve elite ends.[104] According to Auerbach, the movement for a code of ethics "concealed class and ethnic hostility" because "Jewish and Catholic new-immigrant lawyers of lower-class origin were concentrated among the urban solo practitioners whose behavior was unethical because established Protestant lawyers said it was."[105] In the ensuing debates over the ABA's new code, elite interests would have a modicum of success in curbing at least some of the perceived disfavored and undignified practices of nonelite lawyers; but they were not as successful in this area as they might have hoped, which would lead them to pursue other avenues to do so, as I will explore shortly.

In the debates over a national code, there were certainly efforts to rein in contingency fee arrangements, which allow the lawyer to receive payment only if victorious on behalf of the client. This was the main mechanism by which lower-income clients could retain lawyers to bring personal injury, wage-theft, and other types of cases against wealthier adversaries. In the early twentieth century, criticism of contingent fees was common. A former president of the ABA and one of the cofounders of the National Association for the Advancement of Colored People (NAACP), Moorefield Storey, labeled contingent fees "legalized piracy" through which lawyers "plunder both clients and opponents."[106] Reginald Haber Smith, whose work on access to justice I will highlight shortly, also criticized contingency fees. While admitting that they were "better than nothing," and that a worker "whose leg or arm had been cut off would prefer to accept half of the amount awarded him by a jury than to receive nothing through the inability to get his day in court,"[107] nevertheless he called the contingency fee system "the greatest blot on the history of the American Bar."[108] He asserted that, as a public relations matter, many Americans in the "lower social stratas" have "been taught from infancy that lawyers are a class who prey on the weak, who profit out of their misery, and who are so strongly entrenched that the state cannot curb them." He associated these perceptions not just with the "commercialization of the profession" and "the lowering of standards" but also with the existence of the contingent fee.[109]

The first draft of the code provided as follows: "Contingent fees may be contracted for, but they may lead to many abuses and should be under the supervision of the court."[110] While this draws loosely from the language on contingency fees from Alabama's code, the various provisions in that code referring to fees make routine, even offhand, reference to contingency fees, never prohibiting or restraining them in any way, and even acknowledging that "the element of uncertainty of compensation where a contingent fee is agreed on[] justifies higher charges than where compensation is assured."[111] While stating that contingent fees "lead to many abuses," the Alabama Code said simply that "certain compensation is to be preferred"[112] and contains no reference to court supervision of this type of fee arrangement.

Advocates for the new code who recognized the value of contingent fees appeared to hold the more popular position and ultimately succeeded in having the new code recognize their legitimacy, albeit with limitations. Edward B. Whitney, a law firm partner in New York City who had served as assistant Attorney General of the United States and would later serve on the New York's highest court,[113] "noticed that the majority" of contingent fee opponents "have always been those whose clients are rich enough to pay whether they win or lose." But, he argued, "[v]ast injustice would go unaddressed if it were not for the contingent fee."[114]

The New York State Bar Association's comments on the draft code described in powerful terms not just the historical rise of the contingent fee but also its importance in ensuring access to justice, particularly for the poor. "The justification for the contingent fee is summed up in one phrase," the association argued: the contingent fee is "'The poor man's fee.'"[115] These comments sought to remind the committee that "the legalization of the contingent fee took place shortly after the beginning of that time which we now call the age of machinery."[116] The "advent of steam" and its application to the "service of mankind" brought with it "a multitude of casualties."[117] This then led to the poor litigant "pitted, not against another poor man, but against corporations entrenched in wealth and power."[118] Not only was litigation expensive, but the injured worker, dependent on a wage to live and to pay a lawyer, was also "deprived of his ability to earn that wage" by the very injury that would form the basis of a lawsuit.[119] It thus became "imperative" to allow the injured worker to pay the lawyer "out of the proceeds of his litigation." In fact, "there was no other way."[120]

The Bar Association of the City of Boston's comments included that contingency fees "tend to promote litigation and to degrade the practice of law from an honorable profession to a mere money getting trade."[121] Boston's committee suggested that the language of the code regarding contingent fees should read as follows: where "'a client may have a meritorious cause of action and yet be unable unless the litigation proves successful to pay the fees of counsel,'" in such case it "'is proper for a lawyer to agree that he will look to the amount which may be recovered for the payment of his fees.'"[122]

For the most part, though, the reported criticisms of such fees were often couched in terms that acknowledged their importance to ensuring access to justice and sought, instead, to tinker around the margins concerning when and how such fees should be monitored by a court.

One anonymous submission, reported as a private communication from a "distinguished member of our profession in judicial office" who had "made a close study of the subject" of contingency fees "for some years,"[123] complained that he had "'known a number of cases, particularly in the counties, where prominent members of the bar, of the highest character, have refused to accept appointments as counsel for railroads and other corporations, because it was more profitable to take cases against them.'"[124] This judge argued that leaving review of contingency fee arrangements to occur at the end of the case offered too much opportunity for mischief and that "the court's action" in overseeing contingency fee arrangements "should occur at the beginning of the case."[125]

At the conclusion of the drafting process, the ABA committee, responding to feedback from the association's members that the contingency fee was an important tool to ensure access to justice, removed the language that contingency fees caused "many abuses." Ultimately, the final version provided as follows: "Contingent fees, where sanctioned by law, should be under the supervision of the Court in order that clients may be protected from unjust charges."[126]

While they may not have succeeded in banning contingency fees altogether, elite members of the bar *were* successful in reining in other practices they also saw as threatening their own clients' interests—and their own business. The ABA's new code would include outright prohibitions on lawyer advertising, fee-splitting with nonlawyers, and the payment of referral fees to nonlawyers. Elite lawyers generally did not have to advertise because they were already well-established practitioners with wealthy clients.[127] Apart from the effort to rein in contingency fees, the ABA's leaders also sought to rein in advertising, what was considered stirring-up of litigation, and the payment of referral fees.

Once again, it is interesting to look at what the Alabama Code said on the issue of advertising to see where the ABA intentionally diverged from that source text. That code was quite generous on the question of advertising, providing that "advertisements, circulars, and business cards, tendering professional services to the general public, are proper." At the same time, "self-laudation" by indirect marketing to drum up newspaper stories and other attention for a lawyer's practice was "of evil tendency[] and wholly unprofessional."[128] The ABA committee referenced the report and recommendations of the grievance committee of the Bar Association of Erie County in Buffalo, New York, which had recommended to its own members that reining in advertising was necessary to "maintain the dignity of the profession," to "elevate it to its exalted and deserved position, and to free it entirely from the baser taints of commercialism."[129] Thus, that group recommended that its members "incorporate[] into the by-laws" of its association "'a rule making it unprofessional and undignified for any member of the bar to advertise in any way whatsoever.'"[130] With little fanfare, the ABA committee recommended, and would ultimately adopt, a canon that considered it "unprofessional" to solicit business "by circulars or advertisements" and by "personal communications or interviews, not warranted by personal relations,"[131] even where Alabama's code explicitly provided that advertisements "tendering professional services to the *general public*" were proper.[132]

The committee and those who submitted comments mostly addressed what they would consider lawyers stirring-up of litigation; deploying litigation as a means of harassment; and, most important, paying for referrals from nonlawyer agents. William Wirt Howe, a lawyer from New Orleans and a former president of the ABA, combined a range of concerns in one broadside, proclaiming:

> There is a ragged fringe to every learned profession, and the profession of law is not exempt. Men are admitted to the bar and are tempted and yield to temptation. They become, for example, what are called, for convenience, "shysters," "calaboose lawyers" and "ambulance chasers." They promote suits for personal injuries and promote them in such a way as to lead to scandal and perjury of the worst kind . . . It is well known that many of these shysters, who bring personal injury suits, employ "runners" who at once pursue the injured person, induce him to put the case in the hands of their employer and have it prosecuted upon a large contingent fee, whether the real facts will maintain a claim or not.[133]

The Boston committee argued for an express rule against what it called the "practice of entering into a partnership or arrangement with a physician, nurse, hospital attendant, apothecary, hackman, policeman, railway employee, or other person who is likely to be brought into contact with people who sustain personal injuries, to give him some fee or reward in consideration of his steering the injured person to the lawyer's office."[134] Since an individual like a doctor or nurse is shielding their relationship with the lawyer from the injured, the lawyer thus begins their representation with the client through an abuse of confidence. Given that, the Boston committee noted that it could "hardly be expected" that the lawyer will "maintain through the litigation that fidelity to the interests of his client which ought to characterize all a lawyer's dealings."[135]

In the end, the ABA's new code, the Canons of Professional Ethics as they were called, included provisions that deemed it unprofessional to "procure business by indirection through touters of any kind, whether allied real estate firms or trust companies advertising to secure the drawing of deeds or wills or offering retainers in exchange for executorships or trusteeships to be influenced by the lawyer."[136] The code considered it not just "unprofessional" to volunteer advice to bring a lawsuit, "except in rare cases where ties of blood, relationship or trust make it his duty to do so"; it was also "indictable at common law."[137] The ABA also found that it was "disreputable to hunt up defects in titles or other causes of action and inform thereof in order to be employed to bring suit, or to breed litigation," by seeking out those in need of representation or "to employ agents or runners to do so."[138] It also prohibited lawyers from paying "policemen, court or prison officials, physicians, hospital *attachés*[,] or others who may succeed, under the guise of giving disinterested friendly advice," to seek out the lawyer's services.[139]

Another aspect of the code that reflects the fact that a quaint, nineteenth-century sense of collegiality among members of the bar still hung over it in many ways was the fact that the ABA had no enforcement powers and could not create any through the ABA Canons of Professional Ethics. The drafters knew that, in order for any code of ethics to be enforceable, state and local bodies that might adopt some version of the Canons would have to create their own within their respective jurisdictions.[140] Fifty years later, as the ABA was considering adopting new rules of ethics, the future Supreme Court Justice Lewis Powell would argue that the Canons themselves were simply unenforceable, and he advocated for an adoption of rules that had more bite.[141] While he would complain that there was "a disquieting reluctance on the part of courts and bar committees to discipline fellow lawyers," the "more fundamental problem" was "that the Canons, in their present amorphous form," were "simply not capable of enforcement."[142] Still, regardless of later critiques that had the benefit of decades of experience with the Canons, the ABA's adoption of those rules in 1908 was an attempt to rein in conduct that the elites of the profession believed unbecoming of professionals.[143]

Yet Auerbach's verdict—that the ABA's code of ethics was made for and by the elite lawyers and only served their interests—is one that some scholars do not fully embrace,[144] and it is hard to square with the fact that some of the more aggressive efforts to curtail the practices of nonelites lawyers did not always succeed. As we can see, at key points the ABA committee—and those who submitted comments to it on the proposed code—held divergent opinions on key issues like contingency fees and advertising. These views of even elite members of the profession were by no means uniform, and the code that ultimately passed was somewhat ambiguous in terms of serving exclusively to rein in nonelite lawyers, although it certainly did strive to accomplish that to a certain extent. At the same time, a parallel debate was happening as the code was first being considered, and it would continue for roughly the next two decades (and continues, in many ways, to this day). That debate— over the state of legal education and admission to the bar at the turn of and the first decades of the twentieth century—perhaps affords us greater insights into the views of the leaders of the bar during this period. When we read those discussions as a data source on what elites of the bar were trying to accomplish through the institutionalization of reform, a clearer picture of some of the sentiments that informed those elites comes into view, and it is not a pretty picture. It is to that debate that I now turn.

The Institutionalization of Exclusion: Law Schools and Higher Admission Standards

While the concerns that "shysters" were stirring up litigation among recent immigrant communities against the established bar's corporate clients might have been code for underrepresented groups within the profession,[145] it is in the debates around admission to the bar itself, whether it is discussing minimum standards for admission to law school, for taking the bar, or respecting the operations of law schools themselves, where some of the biases of that established bar, and the desire for exclusivity, are more apparent. What is more, it would be hard to make admission to the bar harder for those traditionally excluded from the ranks of the profession, and the efforts at the turn of the nineteenth to the twentieth century would not exactly address those exclusions. Nevertheless, just as the debate over the adoption of a code of ethics was an effort to rein in the abuses of the striving, arriviste lawyers, one way to limit them from ever joining the legal profession in the first place would be to make access to the profession more difficult—which is exactly what the ABA set out to do. While code words were more common to refer to the less-favored class of lawyers in earlier discussions over legal ethics,[146] more explicit language entered the discourse as the debate over barriers to entry ensued through the 1920s. Much of that debate focused on urban lawyers, immigrants, the foreign born, and even the children of foreign-born parents. In other words, there were concerns among the established members of the bar that the floodgates had been open to those elites considered *un-American.*

As Richard Abel has explained, "[t]he profession reinforced the exclusion of immigrants and their sons with every new barrier it erected," from prelaw educational requirements ("when," Abel explains "many universities discriminated against religious and ethnic minorities") to more stringent requirements for accreditation of law schools, among others.[147] Throughout much of the nineteenth century, the predominant mode of gaining access to the legal profession was to serve as an apprentice at a law office and seek admission from the court in which the individual wanted to practice. Each state's rules varied in terms of the number of years one needed to apprentice before one could apply for admission, if a state required any at all.[148] Some universities might have a faculty member who taught courses in the law,[149] like George Wyeth of the College of William & Mary in Virginia, who would guide the legal training of Thomas Jefferson, John Marshall, and Patrick Henry, among others, and was appointed as the first American law professor in 1779.[150] Some lawyers, like Lemuel Shaw in Boston, seemed to have a pedantic streak and enjoyed having interns on hand he would instruct in a systematic way.[151] Tapping Reeve was another lawyer with a penchant for educating young lawyers. Around 1784, he started what is generally recognized as the nation's first law school, in Litchfield, Connecticut.[152] Students came from across the nation for Reeve's lectures in the common law. Then they often returned to their hometowns to seek admission. Having trained under Reeve for a few months (which was the duration of one's studies in Litchfield) would often serve as a passport to the profession. By midcentury, independent law schools had emerged. Some of the nation's leading universities also created law departments and law schools, some of which were closely tied to the university; others seemed connected in name only, serving as a professional adjunct to the important, scholarly work of the greater university.[153]

By the beginning of the twentieth century, the ABA was ready to connect educational and other requirements to admission to the bar. As Lawrence Maxwell argued at the time, "ignorance and mismanagement" by incompetent lawyers was causing cases to be reversed because of procedural errors, being filed "without merit," or "defended without justification."[154] This was the "natural result of a long course of indifference in this country to the proper requirements for admission to the Bar."[155] The unqualified lawyers' "bungling and wasteful ways" cost the legal system and the unsuspecting clients dearly.[156] While recognizing that efforts by the ABA could not "make Daniel Websters or Rufus Choates out of every young man who aspires to be a lawyer," it could "stop general incompetence at the Bar and raise its moral tone."[157] Maxwell's prescription for how to accomplish this task was "first, education, second, education, and third, education." This would include "education of the mind to the point of power and maturity necessary to enable it to grapple with the complicated questions of the law," as well as "education in the doctrines of the law itself which cannot be dreamed or imagined, but must be learned," and lastly "education of the soul to an appreciation of the divine principles of justice which underlie all law."[158] He added that "[t]he law is not food for infants or work for children. It is for those only who have the mental and moral stature of a man."[159]

In 1905, Maxwell recounted that, since the ABA's formation, "only seven of the forty-three schools then in existence had a three years' course and a still less number enforced any substantial requirement for admission."[160] He added that "[i]t was not until 1875 that any of the law schools subjected applicants for admission to examination[] or prescribed any definite or substantial condition of preliminary education."[161] While there was cause to celebrate some of these changes, for Maxwell "much remain[ed] to be done."[162] He lamented that in many states there was "no standard for admission to the Bar" and that, in others, any standards that might exist "on paper" were "not enforced."[163] Half of the law schools in the country did not require applicants to have completed high school, and, according to Maxwell, 25 percent required no educational training at all.[164] For Maxwell, "the supremely urgent and important duty of the Association" was to "secure the enforcement of proper standards for admission to the Bar, the enlargement of the course of professional study in all schools to three years, adequate preliminary education on the part of those who undertake to study law[,] and the suppression of fake schools."[165] The Maxwellian maxim—"education, education, education"—could very well have been "tighten, tighten, tighten": reduce the number of law schools, make it harder to get into those that did exist, and make it more difficult to gain admission to the bar once a candidate concluded their studies. The ABA would pursue all three of these strategies.

It seemed that one of the most pressing issues, for the bar and the more established law schools alike, was the problem of so-called fake law schools. At the meeting of the ABA's Section on Legal Education, George L. Reinhard, dean of the law school of Indiana University, lamented that in Indiana "anybody can start a law school who wants to . . . just as anybody can start anything else as a business enterprise."[166] He added that the existence of these types of schools was a product of the fact that, in many parts of the country, there were no "considerable requirements for admission to the Bar" and that both the legal profession and the public were indifferent to raising those requirements.[167] For Maxwell, these fake schools were "for the express purpose of providing shady avenues to the Bar for those who wish to evade proper and reasonable requirements and whose only aim is to get a license to practice as quickly and cheaply as possible."[168] These schools operate by charging fees, "small in amount, but considerable in the aggregate," to "clerks, officeholders, real estate brokers[,] and detectives to whom they hold out, in true quack style, the prospect of attaining positions of eminence at the Bar or in politics if they devote a few hours in the evening to the so-called study of law."[169] For Maxwell, such schools were not just "bogus"; they were a "public evil."[170]

Henry H. Ingersoll, another law school dean, heading the law department of the University of Tennessee, would describe one of these schools, which he claimed existed in his state, as being "organized by a single person under a charter obtained from the state in pursuance of a general law, in which the president was the mother-in-law of the incorporator-in-chief and where half a dozen men unknown to the members of the Bar and to the community generally composed the faculty."[171] A degree was issued by the school to its students "without a single hour's attendance."[172] Those students "simply wrote requests from a distance for a degree, and . . . the institution, upon receipt of the requisite fees as fixed by the incorporator, gave the degree."[173] At the time, Tennessee had a "diploma privilege": any student holding a degree from a law school in the state could gain admission to practice in that state. Because this law school existed in the state and offered the requisite degree, its students could gain admission as a result of obtaining a degree from the school. For Ingersoll, "that is a fake law school according to our understanding."[174]

Addressing the problem of such fake schools was but one issue with which the ABA attempted to grapple. A second was admission standards, both for law schools and the bar itself. In order to make admission to the bar more difficult generally, one could make it harder to get into law school; make law school itself harder, longer, and more of a commitment of time, expense, and effort; require that admission to a law school that met certain educational standards would serve as a prerequisite to admission; or make ultimate admission to the profession itself harder by requiring more education prior to taking a bar examination and imposing a more difficult examination as an ultimate barrier to bar admission. Pushing forward on any of these strategies would necessarily make the process to secure admission to the bar more onerous, expensive, and time-consuming. It would also make the profession itself more exclusive. Nevertheless, the ABA, often in collaboration with the more established law schools, pressed forward on all of these fronts and, over the course of the next three decades or so, realized dramatic changes in all of these areas, raising the standards for law schools, for admission to law schools, and for admission to the bar itself.[175]

Such changes were bound to make the practice of law more exclusive. At the turn of the century, this did not seem to be much of a concern for the ABA. Recognizing that increasing admissions requirements for law schools—for example, requiring that some formal education, including a college degree, was a prerequisite to attending law school—could make it harder for someone of lower income to attend, the general sentiment seemed to be that those of merit and drive would not let such barriers stand in their way. As James B. Brooks, dean of the college of law at Syracuse University, would argue: "[T]he legal degree should be made difficult, so that when a man gets one it shall mean something and be worth something."[176] Henry Wade Rogers of Connecticut, a professor of law at Yale at the time who had taught at several law schools and would later become a federal appellate judge, acknowledged that such requirements might have kept Abraham Lincoln from joining the bar. But, he would retort: "We know that poor boys work their way through colleges and through law schools, and through both, and Abraham Lincoln could have done the same."[177] Lawrence Maxwell's address to the ABA's legal education committee that he chaired also argued as follows: "If he has the right stuff in him, he finds ways and means to secure the proper education." In response to the argument that higher standards will make the profession harder to access for all but the wealthy, he also stated that "[t]he law is the last vocation in the world to attract a rich man. It is too laborious and wearing. If I were rich, I think I should look for an easier job."[178]

To this point, I have mostly talked about systemic changes sought by elites in the profession to make it harder for *white men* to become lawyers. It is important to recognize that it was not really necessary to tighten restrictions on the admission of women, African Americans, and others who were not white and male and from the right religious and class upbringing because the system worked exquisitely well already in keeping such individuals out of the practice of law to begin with or to exclude them from important or lucrative areas of practice and opportunities for advancement within it. When lawyers could refuse to offer an apprenticeship to an aspiring lawyer, law schools could exclude anyone from enrolling at their discretion, firms could choose not to hire someone, and judges could simply reject any applicant seeking admission, the legal profession was able simply to reproduce itself however it wanted.[179]

As touched upon in chapter 3, before the 1870s, no women practiced law anywhere in the United States.[180] After that, women had several hurdles to overcome: they had to find a law school that would admit them, have an opportunity to sit for the bar, and then petition a state's highest court for admission to the bar.[181] Myra Bradwell took her case to join the ranks of the Illinois bar to the U.S. Supreme Court, where she lost, with the Court finding it was up to the states to determine who to admit as attorneys to practice in their respective jurisdictions. While state courts might have been resistant, lobbying at state legislatures in Illinois, Massachusetts, and California secured legislation recognizing that women could become lawyers.[182] In New York, Kate Stoneman secured an opportunity to apprentice at a law office in Albany, New York, as well as to take the bar exam, which she would pass, becoming the first woman in New York to do so.[183] She was nevertheless prevented from becoming a lawyer because New York's laws prohibited women from the bar and the state's highest court denied her petition for admission. After successfully lobbying the state legislature to amend the law, she gained admission in 1886.[184]

Still, by the end of the nineteenth century, women did not exactly fill out the profession. In Massachusetts, for example, there were just fifty women practicing in the state, roughly one-third of them in Boston. These fifty made up less than 2 percent of the more than 3,400 lawyers in the state as a whole.[185] African Americans fared even worse. While several law schools for African Americans opened in the years following Reconstruction, most would close soon thereafter.[186] By 1900, there were 730 Black lawyers in the country, representing just .5 percent of the profession, while 11.6 percent of the population as a whole was Black.[187] By 1935, no law schools south of the District of Columbia even admitted Black Americans; many in the North, though nominally accepting African Americans, still did not enroll many, which had the effect that, by the mid-twentieth century, Black Americans made up only 1.1 percent of the legal profession.[188]

While not addressing the lack of diversity in the profession, the sheer number of law schools would increase dramatically in the early years of the twentieth century, with most of the increase coming from the creation of night schools and others that catered to those who were mostly excluded from elite practice, like the Portia School of Law in Boston, a part-time, for-profit school set up to enroll and graduate women, who would go on to pass the bar at a higher rate than many other part-time law schools.[189] From 1900 to 1940, the number of law schools nearly doubled, from 100 to 190, with most of the growth occurring in schools providing part-time and evening programs.[190] Less than half of the law schools in operation in 1936 were approved by the ABA. But law school enrollment numbers reflected an even greater imbalance. In 1928, only one-third of the students enrolled in law schools in the country were matriculated in ABA-approved schools.[191] What is more, the balance of full-time law schools that had their students enroll during the day, as opposed to part-time and evening schools, was even further skewed: In 1936, of the ninety-four ABA-approved law schools, seventy-five offered full-time programming; eighteen had mixed part- and full-time students, and only one was a part-time school; in contrast, of the unapproved schools, eight were full-time, seventeen mixed, and seventy-one enrolled students on a part-time basis.[192]

As the ranks of the legal profession swelled through the 1920s, concern grew that the market for legal services would become saturated. Some at established law schools were also worried that the market for their product would weaken as these newer schools continued to flourish. The legal profession looked to what had unfolded in the medical profession as a possible example of what could be accomplished with the law.[193] The American Medical Association had lobbied for changes in the education of doctors with the goal of raising standards to practice and lowering the number of individuals entering the practice. These efforts were designed with an eye toward not just improving the quality of the profession but also improving the market for doctors. They would do this by raising entry standards, training and accreditation requirements; and requiring board certification.[194] These changes proved wildly successful in transforming the market for doctors: from the start of the twentieth century through 1915, the number of medical schools decreased from 131 to eighty-one, and the number of graduates of these schools dropped by more than 50 percent: from 5,440 to 2,529.[195]

Inspired by this effort, the ABA teamed up with the still-fledgling American Association of Law Schools, which represented the more-established schools, to work for more, and more difficult to overcome, barriers to entry.[196] And these barriers certainly had the effect of making it difficult to chart a path toward the profession if an aspiring lawyer was not in a position, economically, to satisfy them.

Participants in a 1920 meeting of the ABA's committee on legal education and admission to the bar discussed whether there should be an educational requirement, either to enter law school or to sit for the bar.[197] The ABA would also seek to require that most schools have a significant number of their faculty teaching full time; that schools have robust curricula; that students finish their studies in three or at most four years; and that schools have substantial law libraries.[198] A former U.S. president and then–Chief Justice of the U.S. Supreme Court, William H. Taft, was present at the meeting. Taft would note that some current members of the bar had not gone to college. Referencing the sixteenth president of the United States, like so many others, he would assert that because Abraham Lincoln "did not have the benefit of such an education," perhaps such educational requirements were not necessary.[199] Nevertheless, Taft believed the changes the ABA was considering that would make it more difficult to become a lawyer would have the effect of "saving society from the incompetent, the uneducated[,] and the careless, ignorant member of the Bar."[200] Still others believed the efforts to impose these requirements, which would necessarily impact the less prestigious law schools, were designed with the "deliberate purpose on the part of the great law schools of the country . . . to thrust out from the teaching of law all other law schools" that were not a part of the AALS.[201]

Still, there were some who argued against imposing some of these requirements. Their critics raised the concern that these new barriers to entry would tend to make it more difficult to seek a law degree for individuals who were unable to devote the majority of their time to their schoolwork or who could not afford to forego paid employment while they attended school. One critic argued that these requirements would "close the profession of law to all save the leisure class of youth . . . and would bar hundreds of naturally well-endowed, zealous[,] and industrious youths from attaining an honorable ambition."[202] The requirements would also "discourage legal education throughout the country, decrease legal knowledge everywhere, and deprive masses of people in our large cities, many of them of foreign extraction, from access to our courts and legal aid for want of lawyers familiar with their language and distinct customs."[203] When emerging from such communities, the individual becomes not just a "mere lawyer" but also an "interpreter of the spirit of our laws and of our institutions in his social and political contact with his kindred."[204] What is more, by bringing such lawyers into the fold, they will "have a safe and conservative influence in our midst."[205]

Despite these protests, the committee made the recommendations to the ABA as described, claiming that it was necessary to "purify the stream" of lawyers "at its source by causing a proper system of training to be established and to be required."[206] The committee thus recommended increasing admissions requirements for law schools; imposing higher standards around faculty, curriculum, and law libraries; and expecting students to finish their studies in, at most, four years.[207]

Not content to conclude with making law schools alone more exclusive, a special conference was convened the next year with representatives of bar associations from across the country, where one of the purposes was to gather support for tightening requirements for bar admission itself. This meeting focused, at least in part, on having such requirements dovetail with those related to law schools: that is, having states only permit candidates for the bar who had graduated from law schools that conformed to ABA guidelines, which included requiring at least two years of college prior to admission to law school, at least three years of legal study, full-time faculty members, and an adequate law library.[208] Elihu Root, chair of the ABA committee that convened the gathering, argued for these requirements, particularly the one regarding prelaw educational qualifications, because of what he perceived to be the shortcomings of the new breed of lawyers.

For Root, two years of college were required of these individuals with "Continental" upbringing so they could "mingle with the young American boys and girls" to begin to understand the "community spirit of our land."[209] Root's arguments echoed those of Henry Drinker, who said that it was in college where these individuals would learn "the American spirit of fair play." In college, Drinker argued, one learns the "way the Americans live," which is "if you don't play the game fair, somebody is going to bust you one."[210]

Once again, defending against the argument that an educational prerequisite to law school, and thus the bar, would exclude individuals of lower income, and deflecting the argument that this would prevent someone like Abraham Lincoln from becoming a lawyer, Root protested rhetorically: "Do you suppose such a thing" as a college prerequisite "would have kept Lincoln out?"[211] Similarly, I. Maurice Wormser, who taught at Fordham University's newly formed law school at the time, and also speaking in favor of the college prerequisite, said that his "cross in life" was that he had to read the records of legal proceedings in the New York courts. He claimed that "almost with uniformity" these records showed that it is the "uneducated, the illiterate, and, more particularly, the immigrant lawyer, the lawyer from a foreign country, or son of parents from a foreign country with whom we have difficulty."[212] Invoking Lincoln yet again, and anticipating the criticism of the college prerequisite position, Wormser declared: "If Lincoln were living today, he would have a college education."[213]

By the end of the 1920s, the ABA Section on Legal Education would attempt to pass a resolution designed to rein in some of the practices of the night law schools. Here we see the use of some of the most explicitly exclusionary language to refer to the new lawyers who were entering the market to provide legal services. Indeed, the demographic change in the profession from the late 1800s to the 1920s had been dramatic, although it was still not keeping pace with the larger demographic changes in the United States as a whole. In 1910, 74 percent of lawyers in the country were native-born white children of native-born parents.[214] But change was underway, particularly in the nation's largest urban centers. Just ten years later, in New York City and Chicago, the number of practicing lawyers who were themselves native born and of native-born parents was now just 45 percent of the profession in those cities.[215]

While the efforts to raise ethical standards earlier in the century did not seem to have the effect of reducing the number of lawyers, the systematic campaign to raise barriers to entry did. The elites of the bar left no stone unturned, establishing minimum educational requirements for attending law school; raising the standards for accreditation by the ABA, with most states to make attendance at an accredited law school a prerequisite for application to the bar; and imposing a bar examination in most states.[216] The cumulative impact of these efforts certainly made it more difficult to practice law for those who were not white and male, but they also had another effect: they prompted the emergence of a new type of lawyer and law practice.

The Rise of the Public Interest Bar

The combined efforts of the established bar certainly made it more difficult for individuals who were African American, women, and not of a

Protestant faith to earn a law degree from a top school and practice law in the more prestigious law firms. Still, those less-prestigious schools that survived the ABA's efforts to reduce the number of law schools continued to educate students, and lawyers from religious and racial minorities and women continued to claw their way into the practicing bar.[217] With the more lucrative avenues of practice mostly closed to them, they would soon find opportunities in a new kind of practice: the public interest law office. While nominal "law reform" may have been one of the goals of elite organizations like the Association of the Bar of the City of New York, legal organizations began to emerge in the late 1800s that were organized to provide affordable legal services to families of low income. The first of these was originally organized as Der Deutsche-Rechtsschutz-Verein, or the German Legal Aid Society, to serve German immigrants settling in New York City in the late 1870s. That organization would soon open its doors to individuals of different ethnic backgrounds and national origins and rename itself The Legal Aid Society of New York.[218] It would handle routine matters and wage-theft cases, often by offering advice only, and the organization urged its lawyers to settle cases whenever possible—even, on occasion, over the objections of their clients.[219] At the same time, other lawyers also emerged to promote progressive interests, even if they did not necessarily have much success. Indeed, the effort to challenge Jim Crow segregation, which culminated in the Supreme Court's tragic decision in *Plessy v. Ferguson*, was actually part of an orchestrated campaign to fight discriminatory practices in the South,[220] just as lawyers worked with clients to address racist immigration laws[221] and undermine efforts to suppress labor organizing.[222]

Thus, in addition to the other institutions created by the legal profession in the last decades of the nineteenth century and into the twentieth, the nation saw the emergence of a new type of lawyer, the legal aid lawyer, often taken from the ranks of the profession excluded from its most elite ranks: women, African Americans, and religious minorities.[223] What is more, such legal aid organizations were often created with the goal of assimilating immigrant communities to the democratic values and practices of American society and offering them an outlet within existing institutions to resolve their disputes peacefully and in a manner consistent with the rule of law. Just as leaders of the bar thought lawyers from immigrant communities were not sufficiently steeped in "American values," so, too, were many concerned that these communities, unfamiliar with concepts like the rule of law, would resort to violence and mob rule if left without legitimate legal recourse. The lawyers, once again, were seen as a way to curb the excesses of the masses.[224] As Reginald Haber Smith—a Brahmin lawyer from Boston who assisted the local legal aid organization there and would write an important work on access to justice for the poor in 1919—explained: "[F]reedom and equality of justice are essential to a democracy and . . . denial of justice is the short cut to anarchy."[225] In a foreword to Smith's work, Elihu Root echoed this sentiment, praising the report and stating that it would be of use to those "who are interested in the Americanization of the millions of foreigners who have immigrated to this country[] and who fail to understand or who misunderstand American institutions."[226] While asserting that the United States has had "in the main just laws and honest courts" that offered "poor as well as rich" an avenue through which to "obtain justice," at the same time, the "rapid growth of cities, the enormous masses of immigrants (many of them ignorant of our language), and the greatly increased complications of life" meant that the "provisions for obtaining justice . . . are sufficient no longer."[227]

Smith's study connected the lack of access to justice—not just in immigrant enclaves but in all low-income communities—as a threat to the rule of law. He argued that the "effects" of "denial of justice are far reaching" and added that "[n]othing rankles more in the human heart than the feeling of injustice."[228] This feeling breeds "contempt for law and disloyalty to the government[] and plants the seeds of anarchy."[229] What is more, people of low income come to believe that "there is one law for the rich and another for the poor." Lyman Abbott, a former lawyer and progressive advocate and editor, speaking before the annual benefit dinner for the Legal Aid Society in 1901, proclaimed that, when justice was solely for the rich and only a "golden key" will unlock the courthouse door, "the seeds of revolution will be sown[;] the firebrand of revolution will be lighted, and put into the hands of men, and they will almost be justified in the revolution which will follow."[230] Smith echoed these concerns: "[W]hen the law recognizes and enforces a distinction between classes, revolution ensues or democracy is at an end."[231]

The response to these concerns was to strive to provide some measures of access to justice, regardless of the ability to pay, with the goal of bringing outsider communities into the American legal system. "By their protection of the immigrant and their securing to the native born their legal rights," Smith wrote, "the legal aid organizations are each year proving to their hundred thousand clients the integrity and fairness of our institutions."[232] Such legal aid entities tended to be seen as charity, however, and not always as a means to promote racial or economic justice,[233] a necessary evil to permit the profession to continue to operate in a business-as-usual fashion.[234] Beholden to the charities and law firms that funded them, the lawyers who practiced within these groups were often restricted by the types of cases they could bring, the claims they could file, and how they could pursue their client's claims. The poor and marginalized got some justice, but not too much, and certainly not enough.[235]

A New Profession

In response to crises real and perceived, the legal profession created or strengthened a series of institutions in an effort to recalibrate a profession essentially created in the nineteenth century that reflected the values, structure, and organization of that century. The twentieth century posed new challenges. The profession attempted to develop an institutional response to those challenges and to shape the profession for a new century. The relative success of the profession in doing so; whether those institutions truly served the profession, and the nation, well over the next hundred years; and whether those institutions are adequate to address the challenges of the twenty-first century are the questions I turn to next and serve as the focus of the remainder of this work.

5

The Legal Profession as an Institution

In the first decades of the twentieth century, the American legal profession set a course for the future by creating institutions that form the bedrock of the profession to this day. Lawyers organized themselves into law firms and bar associations at the local, state, and national levels. They made access to the profession more difficult by requiring that would-be attorneys attend law school and take more challenging bar examinations prior to admission. The elite of the bar developed a code of ethics. On the fringes of the legal profession, a fledgling public interest bar emerged. These different components supplied the contours of a reformed American legal profession; in fact, these aspects of the profession are, in many ways, still with us, and they continue to provide shape and character to the profession of today.

Over the past three hundred years, lawyers have served as the guardians of what some might call the "institutions of democracy." They helped establish these institutions, playing central roles in crafting the arguments for independence, drafting the U.S. Constitution, and introducing new immigrants to democratic values and our system of justice. And they have defended these institutions: the integrity of elections and the expansion of the right to vote, our systems of checks and balances, the promotion of individual rights, and the preservation of the rule of law. In addition, since even before the birth of the republic, the American legal profession has itself been a critical institution, creating and maintaining other institutions that form American community life. Indeed, it is, perhaps, one of the most *American* of institutions, one from which other institutions—like the American legal and constitutional structure, our judicial system, the distinctly American dialogue around rights—have drawn to craft the uniquely American experience. These claims are not intended as a form of American exceptionalism but merely to assert that the American legal profession has had a significant role in shaping American institutions. That is not to say that the legal profession's impact on society has always been positive. The profession has been, on the one hand, a force for justice and opportunity and at the forefront of furthering and strengthening democratic values. On the other, it has undermined such values and placed them at great risk.

In this chapter I explore the legal profession and its elements through what I will call an "institutional lens." I ask whether or not the legal profession is an institution, has institutional elements, and has wider impacts on the institutions in society that surround it. I identify the profession's *internal* components—the rules, practices, and entities that govern and shape the profession—while also assessing the profession's *extra-institutional* effects: the ways in which the profession shapes the broader institutions of society. This analysis will not just serve a descriptive function; it will also provide a normative vision for how the institution of the legal profession *should* function so that it might serve positive ends within American community and cultural life. I will examine the values the profession should embrace with an eye toward the proper role the legal profession should and could play within the United States to preserve it as a multiracial, participatory, inclusive community that embraces the rule of law. This discussion will then set the stage for the remainder of the book, which applies these values to confront the forces currently impacting the future of the practice of law and society more broadly.

The American Legal Profession Through an Institutional Lens

A common approach to analyzing the legal profession is to view it as a profession per se, using theorists such as Max Weber, Émile Durkheim, and Karl Marx to assess its practices, beliefs, rituals, role in society, and impact.[1] Media theorist Clay Shirky has described a professional as an individual who "learns things in a way that differentiates her from most of the populace" and who "pays as much or more attention to the judgment of her peers as to the judgment of her customers when figuring out how to do her job."[2] Roscoe Pound classified lawyers as members of a profession by defining the term "profession" as a "group pursuing a learned art as a common calling in the spirit of public service."[3] In the 1980s, the ABA formed a commission out of fear that the profession was "moving away from the principles of the profession" with a stated goal to "rekindle" professionalism.[4] That report adopted Pound's definition of a profession, particularly the public service aspect of the concept, but also expanded on it. The report borrowed from sociologist Eliot Freidson's work when it outlined four core concepts that, it argued, make the legal profession a profession. First, its members have "special privileges" that are justified by the complex judgments lawyers must make based on the special training they receive. Second, clients must trust the actions of their lawyers because clients cannot properly evaluate lawyers' work. Third, trust is properly placed with the lawyer because the lawyers' self-interest is outweighed by their "devotion to serving both the client's interest and the public good." Fourth, the profession is self-regulating, policing the extent to which its members uphold their fiduciary obligations to place clients' interests ahead of their own.[5] While we might not agree that, today, practicing lawyers always, and in every context, exhibit these four characteristics, this book does not attempt to debate this question and accepts that the legal profession is indeed a profession.

What I will do, instead, is analyze the legal profession as an institution, one that has both internal components and generates external effects. Such an approach requires some agreement around terminology, however. One dictionary defines an institution as "an established organization or corporation (such as a bank or university) especially of a public character."[6] But in political science, economics, and sociology, an institution is considered so much more than just an organization. Economist Douglass North—at the forefront of what has come to be the New Institutional Economics school—considered institutions to be laws, norms, and customs: what he would call "the rules of the game."[7] Others within this school, like Geoffrey Hodgson, have gone beyond a rules-centric definition to include organizations. For Hodgson, organizations are "a special kind of institution, with additional features," including a means of distinguishing members from nonmembers; systems for determining "who is in charge"; and a division of responsibilities within the entity along a "chain of command."[8] Sociologists Roger Friedland and Robert Alford have argued that institutions have both observable and unobservable elements, including that they manifest in social relations that "concretize" those institutions and assist individuals and the entities they form to both "achieve their ends" and "make life meaningful."[9] North seemed to accept the interplay between rules and organizations when he said that "[o]rganizations are created to take advantage of opportunities" that arise from rules, "and, as organizations evolve, they alter" those rules.[10] Organizations are "purposive entities" that have the goal of maximizing "wealth, income, or other objectives defined by the opportunities afforded by the institutional structure of society."[11] Those institutions are clearly shaped by the "rules of the game," but they also shape them, and are thus related, in a deeply symbiotic fashion, to those rules.[12]

Sociologist Eliot Freidson, upon whom the ABA relied when classifying the legal profession in the 1980s, explicitly looked at professions through an institutional lens, seeing both the material and immaterial manifestations of institutions within them. He believed that professional norms and values become *institutionalized* when they are embedded in organizations that create the "institutional circumstances in which members of occupations rather than consumers or managers control [the] work" of the professions.[13] Like other scholars of institutions, Freidson considered the term "institutions" to take both tangible and intangible forms. Professional institutions are the organizations in which professionals work. Those organizations advance the interests of a particular profession, shape the conduct of those within it, and further the norms to which those members are supposed to adhere. And it is this normative institutionalization—the extent to which habits and practices are embedded and realized in particular *organizational* settings—that sets particular professions and their organizations apart from nonprofessionals.[14] Freidson believes that professions operate as a "third logic," existing partially outside the free market (as one logic) and a second logic, what he would call "bureaucracy": command-and-control economies and political systems where "executives of organizations decide what product will be made or a service offered, who shall make it, by what methods, and how it shall be offered to consumers."[15] According to Freidson, the "*central principle*" of professionalism is that "*the members of a specialized occupation control their own work.*"[16] Members gain this privilege by, among other things, stressing "the importance of the body of knowledge and skill for the well-being of some significant segment of society" and the "grave danger to the public if there were no control over those who offer their services."[17] For Freidson, "the claims, values, and ideas that provide the rationale for" the professions are embedded in at least some of the institutions of the profession.[18] In other words, it is the institutionally embedded values that breathe life into and help to define and sustain the profession itself. Thus, "professionalism is more than the economic and political institutions which protect and empower the practice of a technical specialty."[19] It is also "a set of values rooted in the profession itself that directs the economic and political institutions of practice independently of the state."[20]

Here, I proceed on the assumption that institutions reflect a sort of duality: they are both material and immaterial. The nonmaterial institutions of the legal profession are the habits and norms that members practice, as well as the ethical rules that attempt to both reflect and channel members' behavior. In turn, those habits, practices, rules, and norms are embedded in, advanced by, and defended through material entities: organizations and systems in which members of the profession act and conduct their business as professionals—including law firms, nonprofit organizations, in-house counsel offices, government law departments, bar associations, and the legal system itself. In this way, the immaterial habits and practices become institutionalized in material organizations and the systems in which they are found.

One more aspect of the institutional analysis I will utilize is the typology advanced by economists Daron Acemoglu and James Robinson and mentioned briefly in the introductory chapter. Acemoglu and Robinson have identified what they call "inclusive" and "extractive" institutions.[21] Inclusive institutions "are those that allow and encourage participation by the great mass of people in economic activities that make best use of their talents and skills and that enable individuals to make the choices they wish."[22] To be considered an inclusive economic system, the institutions that constitute it include "secure private property, an unbiased system of law, and a provision of public services that provides a level playing field in which people can exchange and contract"; they must also "permit the entry of new businesses and allow people to choose their careers."[23] Such inclusive economic institutions "foster economic activity, productivity growth, and economic prosperity."[24] In contrast, exclusive economic institutions "have opposite properties" to inclusive ones and are "designed to extract incomes and wealth from one subset of society to benefit a different subset."[25]

Institutional scholars such as North, Acemoglu, and Robinson have all stressed the importance of inclusive economic systems for the long-term success of nations. Countries that protect property rights and pre-serve the rule of law are also those that have shown they can sustain themselves over time.[26] What is more, these theorists see institutions as being, at least in part, legal concepts like the rule of law, secure property rights, and the recognition of contracts. Such institutions are also central to the functioning of inclusive systems.[27] And such inclusive legal insti-tutions are unlikely to exist in closed, antidemocratic societies; indeed, inclusive economic systems both emerge from and help sustain inclusive *political* systems: effectively functioning democracies that protect politi-cal rights.[28]

Analyzing the American legal profession according to this typology, and viewing the first three hundred years of its existence, one can see that it has exhibited characteristics of both an extractive and inclusive institution. Lawyers have used their superior knowledge of substance, procedure, lawmaking, and regulatory processes to advantage their cli-ents to the detriment of adversaries—but also at times to harm the larger community. Lawyers have endorsed risky business ventures and harmful environmental practices and have attempted to shield notorious actors from accountability. Their efforts make significant economic develop-ment projects and important business transactions possible, promoting economic growth and financial stability for beneficiaries of their work. They have also been paid handsomely for their efforts. But lawyers do not just assist the well-off or the well-heeled. Virtually every American with even a toehold into the nation's economy has at some point been a member of a consumer class action, which might generate a few dollars in damages to each consumer while netting the lawyers millions of dol-lars in fees.[29] At the same time, lawyers have also been at the center of efforts to desegregate our public and private institutions, to advance civil rights, and to ensure access to the ballot box.[30] Thus, lawyers can serve and have filled both extractive and inclusive functions in virtually every aspect of American civil, political, economic, and social life.

While it is apparent that lawyers have engaged in both inclusive and extractive behavior over the course of the legal profession's history, what institutional role do we want the legal profession to play in American community and culture moving forward? Answering this question re-quires us to widen the aperture of our view and look at the legal profes-sion within the broader institutional field. Here questions of institutional fit, first introduced in chapter 1, arise. The concept of institutional fit is typically used in the environmental context to assess whether institutions in a particular ecosystem "are compatible with the biogeophysical systems with which they interact."[31] This fit occurs when a set of norms, practices, rules, laws, and organizations is appropriate to achieve a desired set of policy outcomes. A mismatch between institutions, and the needs of the ecosystem in which they operate, can lead to catastrophic results over time.[32]

In this context, I will utilize this idea of institutional fit to connect the elements of the legal profession to the legal infrastructure of the community to assess the relative match between the desired practices and institutions in society with the norms, functions, and organizations of the legal profession. Furthermore, using the Acemoglu and Robinson typology of institutions together with the concept of institutional fit, I will argue that an inclusive legal profession will serve an inclusive legal and political system.

The American Legal Profession and Its Institutional Role

The United States secured a political foothold on the Eastern Seaboard of North America with a small class of individuals holding a preeminent role in crafting and maintaining a legal structure that might sustain and expand the nation. These were exclusively white men, particularly those who owned property. Some of them owned slaves, and many of them were lawyers.[33] Over the next 245 years, the nation expanded westward; industrialized; built its cities and transportation, communication, and financial systems; and fought a Civil War and two world wars to defend democracy and overcome racial hierarchies, injustice, and political inequality. Throughout this dramatic political, social, economic, and cultural transformation, the United States has also experienced demographic change such that it is now, at its core, a multiracial democracy built on a regulated capitalist market. While law might not be "king," as Thomas Paine once wrote, it certainly serves as the institutional architecture that strives to preserve these core qualities, values, and characteristics of the American system. In fact, it is precisely because the United States has become a diverse, multiracial democracy that a mere reliance on norms rather than law may not be sufficient to protect potentially conflicting interests adequately.[34] Because of this reliance on law and the rule of law to manage these conflicting interests, the American legal profession is itself an institution that makes other institutions—American institutions—function.[35]

Early in the twentieth century, the profession's elites attempted to institutionalize certain values into the profession's norms and practices. I will argue that a similar values-based approach, when calibrated to the needs of the contemporary legal profession and mid-twenty-first-century America, can help chart a course forward for the profession that provides greater institutional fit for the needs of the contemporary manifestation of American democracy. I will also show that an embrace of these values can establish the profession as an inclusive rather than extractive institution in the broader institutional field in which the profession is embedded.

Toward a Professional Ideal for the American Legal Profession

As we saw in chapter 4, the institutions of the contemporary legal profession—broadly defined as both norms and organizations—were forged in the first decades of the twentieth century. A lawyer in 1945 surveying the legal profession of today would recognize it more than they would the American legal profession that existed in the first years of the twentieth century, at least in terms of its structure and its institutions, even as the demographics of the profession have changed and continue to change. While some of the more effective mechanisms put in place to limit entry to the profession did not take full effect until after the Great Depression and World War II,[36] what that lawyer of 1945 who could peer into the future would see is a profession that closely resembles the image the profession's leaders envisioned for the it in the 1920s.

While the demographic makeup of the bar has changed considerably, with far more women and members of ethnic, racial, and other minoritized populations playing much larger roles in the profession than in 1920, today, like in 1920, prospective lawyers are educated in law schools; are trained in and follow a code of conduct first initiated in 1908; and practice in law firms and law offices that do not resemble the loose relationships prevalent among individual lawyers at the turn of the nineteenth to the twentieth century. More-difficult bar exams introduced in the 1930s reduced passage rates, which helped control the number of practicing lawyers.[37] The burdens placed on law schools to earn accreditation by the ABA and the pressure of states to recognize only ABA-approved law schools meant that, between 1930 and 1950, seventy law schools would close, with sixty-nine of those being non–ABA approved schools.[38] Some lawyers practice in public interest organizations, and many are members of and advocate through bar associations at the county, state, and national levels. By creating these institutions, the bar's leaders sought to improve standards of practice of the bar, limit access to the profession as a means of achieving greater professionalism, and yet professed a commitment to access to justice as a way to bring and include otherwise marginalized communities within the legal system. The profession thus institutionalized its own understanding of the values of professionalism, access, and inclusion. Are these values worth keeping, and are they the ones the profession must advance to address the challenges it faces today and the needs of American democracy? To answer this question, it requires an understanding of those needs and the characteristics of the American system. It also warrants the application of the concept of *institutional fit*.

The Characteristics of the American System

To ensure appropriate institutional fit between the needs of the American system and the legal profession that should serve it requires that we define the features of that system—both what it is and what it aspires to be. Once this is done, we can then explore the proper role for the legal profession within that system.

The first of these features is that the American system purports to abide by the concept of the rule of law, broadly defined: that is, we are a nation of laws and not people. This concept dates back to at least Aristotle, who argued that it is better to be ruled by law than by any individual.[39] Over the years, the concept of the rule of law has taken different shapes and meanings. Loyalist lawyers in the colonial era thought that rule of law meant fealty to the king, whereas the revolutionaries believed despotism was a rule of men and not law. A multinational corporation today might take the position that the rule of law means that a collectivist state cannot expropriate that company's holdings within that country;

the employees of that company might also protest that the rule of law requires the company to adhere to basic concepts of human rights and that the legal system of that country must provide a viable channel through which to hold the company accountable to the law.

Despite potential disagreements like these, a general consensus exists around some core aspects of the rule of law. Legal scholar Ronald Cass has argued there are four "constitutive" elements of the rule of law: "(1) fidelity to rules (2) of principled predictability (3) embodied in valid authority (4) that is external to individual government decisionmakers."[40] This definition begs many questions, including the definition of terms such as "valid" and "principled." Another legal scholar, Paul Gowder, argues that the rule of law exists where there is regularity, publicity, and generality. There is *regularity* in the application of the laws when "the state's coercive power" is used only when "authorized by good faith and reasonable interpretation of preexisting, reasonably specific, legal rules." Law is subject to *publicity* when the "rules on which officials rely to authorize coercion are available for" the subjects of those laws; the law's subjects have the opportunity to "make arguments about the application of legal rules to their circumstances"; and the "public at large may observe these reasons and the arguments about them." Law achieves *generality* when the application of rules does not include making "irrelevant distinctions between subjects" of the law.[41]

The United Nations (UN) defines the rule of law as a "principle of governance in which all persons, institutions and entities, public and private, including the State itself, are accountable to laws that are publicly promulgated, equally enforced and independently adjudicated, and which are consistent with international human rights norms and standards." The UN definition further requires "measures to ensure adherence to the principles of supremacy of law, equality before the law, accountability to the law, fairness in the application of the law, separation of powers, participation in decision-making, legal certainty, avoidance of arbitrariness and procedural and legal transparency."[42]

Accepting that there are different shadings to the concept of the rule of law, what legal scholar Brian Tamanaha calls a "thick" version of the rule of law includes such additional ideals as respect for individual rights and equality before the law, which are, themselves, both central to the liberal democratic tradition and have deep roots in American democracy; this thick version is contrasted with a "thin" version, which looks to formal, procedural justice alone.[43] Equal dignity for the individual in the thick version of the rule of law means the individual has the same meaningful and equal role as other community members in both selecting representatives and participating in the deliberations that lead to the laws that govern society.[44] Political scientist Daniel Philpott describes this as consistent with French philosopher Jean-Jacques Rousseau's idea of personal autonomy, "the kind that is realized through governing oneself, shaping one's own political context and fate—directly, through participation, and indirectly, through representation."[45]

This connection between individual rights, freedom, and political participation is deeply rooted in the ideals of the republican form of government. As philosopher Michael Sandel explains, in such a system "liberty is understood as a consequence of self-government" and an individual is free to the extent they are "a member of a political community that controls its own fate[] and a participant in the decisions that govern its affairs."[46] Equal and fair participation in those processes leads to trust in and adherence to the systems and rules that emerge from such processes, regardless of their outcome.[47] As Robert Dahl posited: "Even when you are among the outvoted members whose preferred option is rejected by the majority of your fellow citizens, you may nonetheless decide that the process is fairer than any other that you can reasonably hope to achieve."[48] What is more, for a legal and political system to be perceived as just by those affected by it, those individuals must have a meaningful role in the creation and ongoing operation of the system, even as they might disagree among themselves about the substantive outcomes the system generates.[49] Jane Mansbridge calls this "adversary democracy," which strives to "aggregate conflicting interests fairly" but also has "its own intrinsic claims on legitimacy, based on each member of the polity having, in theory, equal power over the outcome."[50]

This notion of adversarial democracy introduces another critical component of the American legal system: it is fundamentally *adversarial* in nature, and, as such, the lawyer's role is paramount.[51] It is through adversarial, bottom-up processes—rather than top-down, command-and-control systems—that we realize individual rights, the rule of law, and participatory democracy.[52] While it may seem, at times, that we have relegated a great deal of legal authority to nine (or five) unelected Supreme Court justices, in theory, an adversarial, pluralistic system has several core features, and this system is not constituted simply as the legal system of courts and adjudicatory fora. No, whether it is the operation of processes that lead to legislative and regulatory outcomes that are a product of competition in the public square; business negotiations where the parties, represented by their lawyers, advocate for their respective interests; or formal adversarial proceedings in judicially managed settings, the practical and theoretical underpinnings of these processes all reflect a belief that it is through such processes that individuals and entities will advocate for their interests. But an adversarial system such as this depends not just on adversarialism but also on a rough equality of access to technical skills and resources to sustain individuals and entities through these processes.[53] I will return to this idea shortly.

On a broader level, the underlying logic of this system, as a whole, is that it should be the one best designed to sustain the community in the long run. Using the Acemoglu and Robinson typology, the characteristics of this system should be inclusive rather than extractive. When actors within the system behave in ways that threaten the community's well-being, there must be mechanisms in place to rein in such behavior. Neglect of the law, disregard for individual rights, and a lack of equality before the law will result in cynicism about the law by predator and victim alike. In turn, it will lead to disaffection and a dissatisfaction with the legal system, leaving actors within the system to resort to extralegal processes to defend themselves—or to simply disregard the law itself. The descent into lawlessness follows, leading to the collapse of the system.[54] An inclusive, participatory, and engaging system will help to prevent this descent.

Finally, another characteristic of the American system is its potential for change.[55] As the demographics of America have changed, the law has evolved—more slowly than some would like and more than others would prefer.[56] This evolution is a product of and has reflected not just changing demographics but also a changing and changed society. Thus, the American political system aspires to be participatory; multiracial; adversarial; democratic; and, finally, evolutionary, meaning these characteristics must adapt to changing sentiments and demographics.

A Values-Based Approach Informed by Institutional Fit and Institutional Needs

If we superimpose these characteristics of the broader American system onto the nation's *legal* system itself and the role the legal profession should play within it, a number of themes emerge. First, an adversarial system is believed to advance individual rights.[57] Second, the adversarial system operates under a set of principles and rules; those principles and rules must ensure relative equality before the law and must themselves be fair.[58] They must preserve the dignity and rights of individual actors within the system, even if it is simply to enable them to present their best case within the rules or to advocate for a change in the rules themselves.[59] Third, actors within the system must also adhere to those rules, even when seeking to change them or when interpreting their legal obligation to adhere to the law.[60] Fourth, those rules and the fact that they govern adversarial processes are both a reflection of participatory democracy and a means of realizing it.[61] The ideal, then, for the United States is that it should operate as a multiracial democracy with an adversarial legal system. That legal system strives for procedural fairness and broad participation in lawmaking and the functioning of the system itself. It also seeks to ensure the protection and furtherance of individual rights.[62] These components are seen, collectively, as advancing the betterment of the community as a whole. These principles become not just ends in themselves but also means to an end.[63]

How do these characteristics and features translate into institutional values for the American legal profession? At the start of the twentieth century, the bar's elites attempted to instill a set of values that they believed were needed to respond to the crisis in the profession at that time. They instituted their own take on concepts such as professionalism, access, and inclusion in that process. To what extent did they embed their conception of these values in the institutions they created at that time? And are those values and institutions adequate to respond to the institutional needs of the profession, and the broader community, today?

A current tenet of the first of these values—professionalism—is that the lawyer should always engage in "zealous advocacy" for their client but do so within "the bounds of the law."[64] The adversarial system requires this type of zealous advocacy, but, in a democracy, such zeal must be tempered by law, which is a reflection of the community's collective will and deserves respect as such.[65] As Elihu Root is reported to have said: "About half the practice of a decent lawyer consists in telling would-be clients that they are damned fools and should stop."[66] But in an adversarial system where we accept that the law is subject to change through the levers available to lawyer and client alike to foster that change, the lawyer should advocate for the client's goals in a manner consistent with the tactics the law accepts for the achievement of such goals.

There are, of course, tensions in this role. There may be instances where a client, in the pursuit of their individual rights and dignity, identifies a desired goal—a change in the law or the client's status—that is inconsistent with what the lawyer believes is in the best interests of the community as a whole. Since lawyers both shape and reflect community values, we may question whether the lawyer is capable of objectively evaluating whether the client's interests undermine important community interests that should be preserved—or whether those interests should be undermined. Indeed, even the lawyer's "objective" view is likely colored by the fact that the lawyer is a product of that community itself and as such may accept the community's values as appropriate. Furthermore, the lawyer may not wish to threaten their standing in the community by challenging the community's values.[67] At the same time, lawyers can also fall into a sort of "role morality," where the client's interest is always a good in itself and whatever the lawyer does in the pursuit of that interest is worthwhile.[68] Nevertheless, because the conscious or unconscious adoption of community values might color the lawyer's decision not to pursue a particular client's interests, thereby undermining the inherent dignity of the client, the lawyer should always take great care before deciding to reject the client's desired course of action—unless, of course, advancing the client's position would require the lawyer to break the law. F. Scott Fitzgerald once said that "the test of a first-rate intelligence is the ability to hold two opposed ideas in mind at the same time and still retain the ability to function."[69] At times, the lawyer must do just that: balance the rights of a particular client against the interests of the community as a whole.

Thus, critical to lawyer professionalism is that the lawyer's craft involves the ability to simultaneously acknowledge and balance: (1) the interests of the client; (2) the knowledge that the lawyer may have to correct for their own biases; (3) a sense of the bounds of the law; and (4) an ability to assess the long-term interests of the client and the community. Successfully managing these interests, which at times conflict, allows the lawyer to advance individual rights, ensure equality before the law, and promote community well-being by ensuring adherence to the rule of law—while also recognizing the law's capacity for change.

This version of professionalism requires the invocation of what the early republicans considered "disinterestedness." Today, one might think of disinterestedness as being aloof or uninterested. Through the prism of civic republicanism, however, it meant considering the good of the whole community when taking action and refraining from putting one's own self-interest ahead of that of the broader community.[70] For the civic republicans of the late eighteenth century, this form of disinterestedness was "the essential element of public life."[71] It was also difficult to maintain.[72] That is why this professional value is just that: a professional value. While we might hope nonprofessionals embrace it as well, the value is institutionalized, to an extent, in the rules of the profession. It also serves as an indicator of professional exceptionalism. And all professions, by definition, have a degree of exceptionalism to them. Indeed, that is why they are professions in the first place.

A robust professionalism, attuned to the needs and broader values of the American system, empowers the legal profession to fulfill its appropriate role within that system—that is, fostering the very institutions that advance equality, the rule of law, and respect for individual rights. This robust professionalism will inform the discussion in subsequent chapters around how to address the six forces currently confronting the profession.

But professionalism is not enough. To calibrate its role to American societal needs, the legal profession should also promote *access*: the belief that every American, regardless of their ability to pay, should be able to use the legal system and legal assistance to navigate their legal problems. At present, 80 percent of low-income and 50 percent of middle-income Americans face their legal problems without the benefit of legal representation.[73] If we value a participatory, multiracial democracy where legal disputes are resolved within the legal system under principles consistent with the rule of law, there must be some degree of parity between adversaries in terms of technical legal knowledge and resources available to advance interests. That need for parity, especially when it comes to resources, reveals the tension inherent in not just a market economy but also one, like the American political system today, where lawmaking itself is too often dominated by wealthy elites and is awash in funds supporting elected officials who will protect and advance elite interests.[74] The legal system must serve as a check on this inequality and preserve some semblance of parity of resources within it.

Returning to the inclusive/extractive typology: extractive legal systems are those in which the "haves" are able—at the expense of the "have-nots"—to advance their interests, capture those systems, and extract value from them. Put differently, an adversarial system where some adversaries lack meaningful capacity to defend their interests is not an inclusive one. Accordingly, as will be explored in chapter 8, access to justice is a critical value the legal profession must embrace to ensure it operates like an inclusive rather than an extractive institution.

This new version of access turns the profession's early-twentieth-century view of the concept on its head. The cartelization of the profession, solidified through denial of access, has ensured that access to the profession—and, in turn, access to justice—is limited to those aspiring lawyers who have the financial wherewithal and the ability to overcome the barriers to entry and to those clients who can afford the costs associated with retaining legal representation. This cartelization has access-to-justice implications because it means there are fewer lawyers available to serve the community. It also exhibits extractive features because the very means by which the lawyer monopoly is advanced and maintained permits those within the profession to catalyze their economic advantage to drive the price of representation even higher.[75]

Connected to professionalism and access is a third critical value: *inclusion*. To ensure the profession is acting in an inclusive and not extractive fashion, it must expand access not just to justice but also to the profession itself, particularly for those traditionally and historically excluded from its ranks. There are many reasons for the legal profession to embrace inclusivity as a means to achieve some of the rule-of-law and access-to-justice ends described above. As I will explore in greater detail in chapter 6, a legal profession that looks like the communities it serves and brings in perspectives different from those espoused by those already in power and authority helps shape the law to advance the interests of the entire community. It encourages those outside the mainstream to feel like they can turn to the legal system and to lawyers when they have a legal problem because there are lawyers with whom they share common life experiences and backgrounds. It is also likely that, when we draw individuals from communities traditionally underrepresented in the profession and underserved by it, there is a greater chance that those individuals will provide empathetic, conscientious, and effective legal services to such communities. Writing in 1935, Charles H. Houston would assert that there was an overwhelming need for African American lawyers who could serve as "interpreter and proponent" of the Black community's "rights and aspirations."[76] An increased emphasis on bringing in more prospective lawyers from diverse backgrounds will also engender some degree of trust in the legal system when typically minoritized and marginalized communities see and feel that they have representation in the halls of justice and corridors of power: this means both capital R Representation and lowercase r representation, a topic I will return to in chapter 6.

When the legal profession is embracing a robust professionalism and supporting full access to justice, the profession, as an institution, can be seen as also advancing inclusion. This stands in contrast to the parasitic role in which the lawyer is often cast. In pop-culture portrayals and in real life, lawyers are too often seen as benefiting from the harm suffered by their clients or as sucking resources out of transactions for their own gain. Putting those concerns to the side for the moment, many of which are legitimate, I want to return, once again, to the ideal. There are certainly beneficial roles for lawyers to play in economic transactions, in litigation over personal injuries, in crafting regulations, in defending against the encroachment on property rights, in the criminal justice system, in in-house counsel offices in corporations, and in defending and advancing individual liberty and civil rights. Lawyers can serve in a capacity that advances inclusivity, or they can extract value and benefit from the misery of others to reward themselves. If we consider the value of the professional ideal, however, one that advances disinterestedness and zealous advocacy at its core, we see the possibility that the legal profession can serve as an inclusive rather than an extractive institution.

In addition to playing a critical rule-of-law function and by engaging the community in the functioning of democratic institutions, an inclusive profession is also a good in itself. The profession should promote equal opportunity, nondiscrimination, and equality before the law as core aspects of the rule of law, for sure, but the profession itself also cannot discriminate in who it accepts, sustains, and promotes within its ranks. In its institutions—law firms, legal services organizations, governmental units, law schools, et cetera—greater attention must be paid to creating pathways and processes for individuals from all backgrounds to gain access to the profession. An inclusive professional institution is one that takes actions with positive, inclusive institutional effects. It is also one that is itself inclusive in who has access to it and how it supports its members to succeed.

A legal profession that fulfills its institutional role—that is, one that "fits"—within the fabric of American community life will promote a robust version of professionalism that embraces a thick version of the rule of law attuned to the needs of American democracy. It will promote access to justice and access to the profession. And it will embrace the value of inclusion.

Having set what I hope will serve as the scope of the discussion, I turn now to the forces that the profession faces at present and the ways in which these institutional values may help serve to address them.

The Profession and Its Crises

Since the colonial era, the American legal profession has faced crisis after crisis. Many of those crises involved members of the profession acting in a way that seemed to threaten the legitimacy of the institution of the profession itself. At the turn of the nineteenth to the twentieth century, the profession faced one of these crisis moments. The profession that existed at the time did not seem to fit the community it was supposed to serve. The profession responded by creating a series of institutions that attempted to address a threat to the profession's reputation and to align its functions with its perceived role. It did so by promoting one vision of lawyer professionalism, and that vision, though it claimed to have also embraced inclusion, attempted to do so by limiting access to the profession. Indeed, in the profession's efforts to address the crisis before it, it ended up undermining critical values that the profession should have embraced to calibrate its practices to the needs of a changing society.

This lack of institutional fit still lingers, and it is no wonder that there still exists a lack of access to justice and that the profession continues to have a woeful record on inclusion. Could a more robust, comprehensive approach to reform of the profession, one that sought to address professionalism and issues of institutional fit while maintaining a deep concern for the ways that the profession must also advance the values of access and inclusion, have helped the profession overcome the failure to advance those values? More importantly, are we at another key inflection point in the history of the profession? Might a more deep-rooted approach to resolve these issues assist the profession in confronting the forces that the profession currently faces? In the remainder of this book I will attempt to answer these questions.

6

A Public Health Crisis and the Institutions of Exclusion

In early 2020, supervising lawyers in law offices across the United States had not exactly embraced the concept of remote work by the lawyers who worked under their management in any significant way.[1] Some might have offered some flexibility for unique situations, and some would be more tolerant of the stuff of life: the child's recital parents had to attend, the doctor appointment to which they had to escort an elderly parent, the medical condition that made it temporarily difficult to travel. Some organizations may have had generous parental leave policies. Few would tolerate any supervisee spending a significant amount of time functioning in a remote setting. Many might harbor concerns that an employee working remotely might shirk their responsibilities, that the supervisor could not monitor the quality of their work, and that sharing confidential information or permitting the lawyer remote access to their files might open the organization to a security breach. Just three months later, all that would change. Forced by a global pandemic to adapt to practicing law through remote means, many attorneys with supervisory responsibilities found that the functions of the office did not cease once the members were operating in a virtual mode.[2] And the lawyers working under the previously watchful eye of their supervisors got a taste of what remote work could look like, and, for many, it was a revelation, showing what their professional life could be.[3] Months later, when the murder of George Floyd sparked a civil rights reckoning, coupled with the changes wrought by the pandemic, law offices had to address not just how their teams conducted business but also those they hired, promoted, supported, and represented.[4] The pandemic, the rise of the Black Lives Matter movement, the #MeToo movement that emerged years previously, and the 2022 decision in *Dobbs v. Jackson Women's Health Organization*[5] by the U.S. Supreme Court restricting abortion rights all called into question the way the profession practices and how the law and the rule of law function in this democracy; these events also led many in the legal profession to question the role and function of the profession itself and even American legal institutions.[6] Indeed, through the institutional lens I have embraced for my approach to the profession, such a review forces us to take a hard look at institutions the profession put in place roughly a century ago to ask whether they are adequate to address these and other challenges the profession faces at this time. It also invites us to assess those institutions—and the institution of the profession itself—to determine if there is effective "institutional fit" between how the profession operates and the needs of a multiracial, diverse, inclusive, participatory democracy that is supposed to honor individual autonomy, human dignity, the rule of law, and civil rights.

In this chapter, I will explore the impact of the pandemic on law practice as well as the racial- and gender-justice reckoning that the profession faces. I will also ask how the three institutional values—*professionalism*, *access*, and *inclusion*—might help address these forces in a robust way to adapt to and foster meaningful and lasting institutional change. First, I will address the impact of the pandemic on law practice and discuss the ways in which necessity became the engine of innovation. Contrary to the fears that gripped the profession prior to the pandemic—that remote legal work was not possible—the ways in which lawyers practice law changed dramatically in light of pandemic protocols, and the sky did not fall. Given this phenomenon, concerns that the practice of law was not ready for a radical shift in how lawyers operate turned out to be quite overblown. I will then turn to the issue of a century of institutional bias within the profession and argue that, just as with the dramatic changes to practice that the pandemic ushered in, perhaps a similar change to the way the profession operates in terms of addressing the continued exclusionary forces still rampant in the profession might help shift the profession from an exclusive and extractive institution to an inclusive and accessible one.

The Legal Profession and the Pandemic

Prior to the onset of COVID-19, few law offices embraced any meaningful flexibility as to where and when lawyers worked.[7] Pre-pandemic law offices had not changed much in the previous fifty years in terms of how the lawyers operated within them. Lawyers with supervisory and team-leading responsibilities wanted those who worked for them to be close by, physically. Those supervisory lawyers wanted ready and immediate access to their team members, not just to keep a close eye on them but also so that they could turn to them with assignments. Senior lawyers also felt that they could better mentor their supervisees if such junior attorneys were available for formal and informal sessions where those less-experienced lawyers could sit in on strategy meetings, listen in on communications with clients and adversaries, and engage in face-to-face brainstorming sessions. For many, these in-person interactions were essential to lawyer development.[8]

What is more, there was an ethical cast to the insistence on such oversight: supervisory and nonsupervisory lawyers alike have a responsibility to provide competent service to their clients. The belief was (and still is among many) that lawyers with less experience needed a degree of hand-holding to ensure that the office was meeting this ethical standard. And there is certainly something to this concern. As the practice of law has become more specialized, the fairly general education that most law students receive is not quite enough for them to enter the profession and immediately begin to handle matters on their own, with no oversight or ongoing mentoring as they develop expertise in their domain. Not only are they likely to face adversaries with much more experience; it is quite likely that they will not know the nuances of practice in a particular area. Because of this, they will not be able to meet that fundamental ethical obligation of providing competent legal services.[9]

In addition to the professional obligation that a lawyer provide competent service to the client, supervisory lawyers also have their own obligations to ensure that those lawyers operating under their supervision do just that: provide such competent service.[10] It is not an excuse that a new lawyer was left to "swim with the sharks" without guidance appropriate to the situation, guidance that would ensure that the lawyer satisfies the professional standard of care. Prior to the pandemic, the fear that newer, less-experienced lawyers would not satisfy their duty of care if they did not operate under the close eye of a supervisor prompted many law offices to eschew remote work options for the lawyers practicing within them. While there are many aspects of the rules that represent an effort on the part of elite interests to stifle innovation and frustrate change, the duty of competence is one of the lawyer's most important and worthwhile obligations to clients. There is certainly some credence to the notion that a supervisory lawyer must provide adequate supervision to their supervisees to ensure they meet this standard of care. And this requirement—that the supervisory lawyer has an obligation to ensure the lawyers they supervise are satisfying their own ethical duties—is, in fact, a separate obligation imposed on that supervisory lawyer, with good reason: the seasoned, experienced professional has a better grasp on their professional obligations than the newer attorney.[11]

Thus, the rules governing the profession create an independent duty on the supervising lawyer to oversee the work of those less experienced lawyers. At the same time, though, the pandemic put the following question to the test: Is in-person work a prerequisite to satisfying these twin duties, that of competence and to provide supervision that ensures that competence? From what we know so far, it appears that lawyers and their supervisors are more than capable of satisfying their obligations to their clients even when those lawyers are not physically working under the same roof.

Up against pandemic protocols, virtually every aspect of law practice was transformed practically overnight.[12] Law offices went virtual, with practicing lawyers scattered to the four corners of the country, with some even working overseas.[13] Perkins Coie is an international law firm founded in Seattle in 1912; it now has over 1,200 lawyers and over twenty-one offices, including domestic locations from Anchorage to Washington, D.C. and foreign offices in Shanghai and Beijing and a small office in Taipei. In the summer of 2019, the firm appointed a new managing partner, William Malley, who had previously directed the firm's Washington, D.C., office. A lawyer with experience in energy law and environmental compliance, Malley found himself spending much of the second half of 2019 traveling throughout the world to meet with members of the firm in all of its far-flung offices in an effort to develop deeper relationships with his colleagues.[14] In early 2020, as news of the rise of COVID-19 emerged, and because of their offices in Asia, Malley began to have to consider what types of actions the firm would take in response to the growing threat of a pandemic. Malley had a long-planned trip to Asia to attend a client reception to celebrate the opening of a new office location there. He was busily planning his trip and looking forward to the event. His spouse said to him, "You know you're not going, right?" Malley told her that he would plan to go but would see how things unfolded. Days later, the event would be canceled.

By the last week of January, the first COVID-19 cases would be identified in Seattle and Portland, Oregon, where Perkins Coie also had offices. At the time, Malley was traveling through the law firm's several offices on the West Coast, attending in-person meetings, going to firm dinners afterward, with "not a care in the world about COVID"—until he received word one evening in late February that the first cases had been identified on the west coast, and they happened to be in Portland and Seattle. By the end of the first week of March, attitudes about COVID-19 had shifted dramatically. After attending a lunch meeting in Washington, DC, where fifty people were in the same room to hear a speaker, Malley remembers asking himself, "Should we be doing this?" He then went home, took what he needed, and said to himself, "That's it, I'm done. I'm working from home." He realized the whole firm was about to go fully remote.

The first domestic office that Perkins Coie would close was its largest and oldest one, in Seattle, where early COVID cases spiked. In that city, many of the local businesses, like Microsoft and Amazon, had already sent their employees home, and, as Malley recalled, "there was a sort of echo chamber," with many other businesses following suit. As they started to see the threat rising in other cities as well, the firm decided to start closing other offices. While Malley had sent a few firmwide emails to convey to people what measures the firm was taking to respond to the rising public health concerns regarding the pandemic, he felt it was important at this point to try to connect with people but to do so in a way that kept everyone safe. He filmed himself on his iPhone doing a quick video message from his porch at home, telling everyone that "this is Day One of remote working" and that it was a "hard moment" but that the firm was going to "get through it."

Ali Frick's COVID experience was a bit different from Malley's and the attorneys at Perkins Coie. Working at a small (by New York City standards) civil rights litigation firm in the fall of 2019, she and some of her coworkers decided that they wanted to branch out and start their own firm.[15] In mid-February 2020, they told their employers, who they enjoyed working for, that this group of four would soon leave to start their own firm, Kaufman, Lieb, Lebowitz & Frick. They gave four weeks' notice and expected their new firm would open its doors in mid-March 2020. As it turns out, Frick and those who were leaving with her spent their last two weeks at their former firm working remotely, after which they opened the doors of their new firm, although there really were not doors to open. Although the firm had rented space, they went fully remote for the first six months or so of the pandemic. What is more, many of the lawyers at the new firm, including Frick, had young children at home. Frick and her spouse, also a working professional who was stuck at home, would split up the day, with each of them watching the children for half the day. Frick and her children would walk to Central Park during the day, which, as she explains it, they would have practically to themselves in the earliest days of the pandemic.

These sorts of experiences occurred in firm after firm, in government offices, in corporations, and in nonprofit legal services providers throughout the United States.[16] But pandemic protocols affected not just law offices' internal functions. They also impacted the ways lawyers practiced and interacted with individuals and institutions outside their offices as well. Courts, to the extent they were able to function, worked mostly remotely, with all but emergency functions provided online.[17] Frick's work involves almost exclusively litigation. In the two and a half years since the outbreak of the pandemic, she appeared in court once, for a one-day trial before a judge, and conducted no depositions in person in that time. She says that she "would have to think about what is the circumstance in which it really is important to be in person," and she doesn't "really know what that would be." She added that, because she is typically only seen from the waist up on video, it is "great not to have to wear a full suit. I love that."

One group of practitioners that was at the forefront of the work-from-home revolution sparked by the pandemic are those who practice as solo practitioners or those in small firms, many of whom have had home offices since they first began their personal practice. Indeed, throughout the nineteenth century, many lawyers, solo practitioners almost exclusively, probably worked out of their homes in their community's county seat more than in any other setting. Today's solo practitioners, long before COVID-19, have been leading the way in terms of operating more accommodating work arrangements. In fact, solo practitioners and those in small firms who have already worked out many of the kinks of remote work—and the technology that enables it—may find that the general movement to remote technologies in the practice of law makes their niche in the market more secure, not less. What is more, remote work is no longer frowned upon by the profession. As Carolyn Elefant, who has had a solo practice for several decades, explains, in the early days of her practice, after the rise of big tech and the notion that companies might get started out of a founder's garage, working from home "started to become more acceptable," at least to a degree. The pandemic has "eliminated all barriers" to the normalization of remote work. For example, "nobody bats an eye if the dog walks in the background, or if you see the kids poking through the screen" while someone is in a video meeting.[18]

Across the country, client meetings, depositions, contact with adversaries, and research (which had mostly been online already in many respects) all went virtual.[19] This turn of events certainly made it more difficult for some to assert claims or defend their rights. For those who did not have a means of connecting with their lawyers or the courts, this made it more difficult to obtain legal redress for harms they may have suffered or were still suffering. For example, the housing courts in New York City were rendered largely inaccessible if a tenant wanted to bring their landlord to court for housing code violations;[20] the family courts there deemed custody, visitation, and guardianship and new child support matters as "non-emergencies," and they did not schedule such cases for roughly a year from the start of the pandemic.[21] Without an ability to enter virtual court sessions due to a lack of access to the internet or mobile technologies, many low-income clients fell through the cracks of a system that did not serve them well before the pandemic. Inside law offices, junior lawyers missed out on valuable mentoring opportunities that might have arisen in in-person settings that were hard to replicate in an online format.

At the same time, for lawyers and clients alike, pandemic protocols reshaped the practice of law and the functioning of courts in new ways that proved quite beneficial.[22] The most significant change to how law offices functioned was the location where most legal work occurred.

Most law offices operated in a remote format, which meant that the lawyers and legal staff were able to work from home.[23] This meant fewer hours commuting, an ability to work around the needs of one's family, and more control over their time.[24] Of course, it likely made it more difficult for some to manage work and family obligations, or it left them with the sense that they were always "on" and merely living at work and not working from home.[25] Pre-pandemic, a lawyer might lament that they "lived at the office" given how much time they spent there. Now that was literally true; it's just that the office moved to the lawyer's home and not the other way around.

In a profession that, pre-pandemic, often equated hours in the office (and hours billed to the client) with commitment to the success of the firm, those who had fewer obligations at home could excel. Under pandemic protocols, the profession no longer had that metric by which to gauge their employees.[26] At least for some lawyers, having the flexibility to work when they were able, to dedicate less time to commuting, and to manage how they worked proved beneficial and more humane than pre-pandemic practices.[27] For those with mobility impairments, social anxiety disorder, or issues that made it difficult to commute or work long hours in a formal work environment, remote work made it easier for them to focus on their professional obligations and not have to also struggle with overcoming the barriers they otherwise face when working in a traditional law office setting.[28] While supervision and mentoring had to be more intentional in terms of when and how it occurred, lawyers found ways to connect with each other to make sure they were working toward the same goal and providing competent service to their clients.[29] While some newer attorneys might feel they missed out on opportunities to receive more hands-on guidance and supervision, when considering the benefits of virtual work many lawyers new to practice are saying they prefer the greater flexibility and opportunity that remote work affords them. And many do not want to go back to the pre-pandemic approach to law practice.[30]

Apart from some of the challenges clients faced by not having full access to their lawyers and the courts due to those clients' inability to participate in remote communications, for many clients the pandemic protocols had some positive effects. Instead of feeling silenced in judicial settings, there was a democratic aspect to remote court hearings. When everyone is reduced to a tiny square image on a computer screen, there is less hierarchy, with lawyers, clients, parties, and witnesses all on somewhat equal footing. In courts where low-income clients are not typically represented by counsel, as in housing court or small claims court, virtual court hearings had a leveling function, creating a degree of parity between parties and lawyers; of course, for low-income clients or those in rural communities with poor access to broadband, the courts' reliance on technology might close even the virtual courthouse door to them. Nevertheless, where lawyers could conduct client meetings and brief court appearances through remote technologies, they did not need to bill clients for the expense of travel; and legal aid lawyers, particularly those serving rural communities, could avoid driving to far-flung locations to attend a brief court appearance, freeing up resources to serve other clients. Where a court could conduct a fifteen-minute court appearance halfway across the country in a virtual format, it would save the lawyers involved with the matter hours of travel time; billing by the hour, that translated into considerable savings for the client and more time available to the lawyer to assist others or to spend that reclaimed time with family.

While remote court appearances have the potential of making litigation more accessible, and perhaps a little less intimidating, for litigants, there are things to keep in mind when considering what types of reforms courts should preserve once the "return-to-court" protocol is fully underway. Jim Sandman, former president of the U.S. Legal Services Corporation, which provides funding to nonprofit legal services providers across the country, believes that court systems could adopt some best practices that would make them more accessible. He points out that, even with a court system that is sometimes slow to change, because of COVID "[n]ecessity drove innovation at a pace few would have thought possible."[31] The response to the pandemic also showed that court system adaptations occurred without major legislation or significant changes in court rules. Indeed, it showed that "existing court rules have much more inherent flexibility than we might have thought."[32] He would add that we need to "retain and build on this spirit of innovation, adaptability, and user-service focus to improve access to justice post-pandemic. We need to resist any urge to get back to the way we used to do things."[33]

Even as we start to see courts and law offices attempting to institute return-to-court and return-to-work guidelines, it is important to assess whether the pre-pandemic fears of remote work materialized once courts and law offices changed their approach to practice. The most important question for remote law office work is whether it negatively impacts the ability of lawyers to practice competently. While it is difficult to gauge with certainty whether remote settings led to actual malpractice due to the constraints of remote practice, there have been few formal complaints filed by clients against lawyers charging them with misconduct due to pandemic protocols: that is, there are few, if any, recorded cases of clients claiming their lawyers failed to reach the standard of care owed the client because those lawyers were providing their services through remote technologies. Sure, there are instances where lawyers seemed incapable of managing those technologies themselves, as when a lawyer, in a court appearance over a virtual platform, was unable to remove a filter his child had installed on his computer that made that lawyer appear through the image of a cat,[34] or where lawyers failed to comply with a court deadline because they were unfamiliar with the document production software they were obligated to use by virtue of their collaborating remotely.[35] Despite the high-profile, viral, and notorious nature of these instances generating a potential perception that pandemic law practice led to instances of incompetence, the reality is that, when it comes to lawyers' ability to meet the standard of care and to preserve client confidences despite working remotely, it seems clear that the pandemic and the remote-work protocols it required lawyers to institute have not led to a flood of cases against lawyers claiming that they have not been able to uphold their professional obligations to their clients. What is more, by making law practice easier for those who, previously, might have found it difficult to manage a mobility impairment or juggle family obligations, the pandemic has proven beneficial to many, making the practice of law more inclusive while not seeming to sacrifice lawyers' professional obligations.

When it comes to courts, particularly those handling "high volume, high stakes" cases, like housing court, Sandman recommends that courts begin to differentiate between appearances that need to be in person and those that could be managed well through remote technology.[36] In addition, courts could institute staggered, scheduled times when a particular case is to be heard.[37] Instead of expecting a low-wage worker to spend a whole day in court for a five-minute court appearance, losing a day's wages as a result, the court could schedule a specific time slot during the day when that case would be heard; the litigant could join remotely only at that time. Because of the digital divide, though, which impacts low-income and rural communities disproportionately, courts and legal aid offices should provide technology assistance and create accessible physical spaces that litigants can access in person to attend court appearances via remote login.[38]

Thus, it would seem that the values of access to justice and the rule of law are advanced by making courts more accessible. Another aspect of the value of professionalism that is harder to gauge is whether law practice has suffered due to virtual work in terms of whether lawyers working in remote settings—particularly newer lawyers—are receiving the mentoring and guidance they require to develop as attorneys in their field. Once again, there do not appear to be any recorded instances of lawyer supervision failing because of remote work. In fact, senior lawyers seem to have made some of the high-profile mistakes (described above) that centered around an inability to utilize remote technologies. Still, it is possible that junior lawyers are not receiving the hands-on guidance and professional acculturation that comes with being present in an office and observing a more senior lawyer go about their business.

For Malley, the profession has been so geared toward the in-person supervision of newer lawyers that even the language that surrounds supervision and mentoring assumes that they will take place in person. "Think about the words that you would use to describe management techniques," he explains. The profession uses such terms as "management by walking around"; managers tend to "walk the halls"; they maintain an "open door policy"; and so on. For Malley, these descriptions "all manifest a physical presence." At the same time, they are "all gone from your toolbox" as a manager and supervisor when remote working becomes widespread. At Perkins Coie, which has long had multiple offices and teams that are made up of attorneys spread throughout the world, Malley explains that the firm has been good at remote collaboration, and clients themselves are often communicating with the lawyers using remote technology. There might be situations where the firm is working on a complex lawsuit and everyone preparing for that work needs to be in the office, but Malley does not necessarily think everyone has to come in to the office all the time to be good at their jobs. At the same time, there are some things that are lost in remote work settings, like "soft skill development," particularly for newer lawyers. He feels that a gap in the development of these skills will not necessarily appear immediately, but it might show up in the long term. In addition, developing personal bonds with coworkers that both foster and strengthen trust is sometimes harder to develop in remote settings, and it is that kind of trust that can help individuals and teams weather challenging situations better than if that trust does not exist.

Frick echoes these sentiments and thinks that something is certainly lost by not having "social lubricants" at work, like seeing each other in the hallways or at the office refrigerator. Frick always enjoyed being in the office and would routinely go door-to-door pre-pandemic for guidance, to get a reality check on a case, or to run a theory by a coworker. While she simply enjoyed the social aspects of it and the camaraderie, she also knew that, as a newer attorney, she could pick up a lot from the more senior lawyers with whom she worked, even in casual conversations. For example, she might be chatting with one of her colleagues informally and the colleague would explain that he had been preparing his opening for an upcoming trial all weekend. She would then file away this information: this experienced lawyer "has been practicing for thirty years, and they practice their opening. I should practice my opening. It's not actually something that when you're really good, you wing it."

Going into the office, Frick believes, where she can have these sorts of informal conversations, helps make her a better lawyer, "because in those personal conversations and those personal relationships you hear inevitably about the stuff that people are working on, and the legal issues that they're facing, or even just if you hear somebody griping about an aggressive conversation they had with the opposing counsel. All of that gets filed away." It helps the person, because when they face a similar situation they will know how their colleague handled it. These sorts of exchanges typically cannot happen over platforms like Slack or a group chat: they happen "over lunch or in the kitchen getting coffee." Today, Frick likes to go to the office and continues to do so, as often as four and sometimes five days a week. She describes herself as someone who "needs the energy of other people," but she realizes that some of her colleagues, "all things being equal," might prefer to work from home more than she does, particularly the newer attorneys. But, as one experienced lawyer, Deborah Enix-Ross, cautions, for newer lawyers, "you have to be in control of your career, to manage your career." As a result, such lawyers need to be doing all that they can to "maximize the options for working at home but also networking and figuring out what you need to do in your own law firm or workplace culture to keep in touch," regardless of the work setting, whether it is "completely remote, hybrid, or completely in person."

I spoke to Enix-Ross, a partner at the international law firm Debevoise & Plimpton, when she was president of the American Bar Association. She explains how the legal profession "needs to take the best of the virtual world, retain that, build on it, and then build the new normal," because the legal profession is not likely "going back completely to the old ways."[39] At her firm, leadership encourages the lawyers to come in at least three days a week but also to have "anchor days"—where different practice groups try to come in to the office on the same day of the week. She calls this "presence with purpose," where the lawyers are intentional about reaping the benefits of being physically in the office while preserving a degree of flexibility to allow for remote work as well.

So how does the legal industry try to balance the benefits of in-person work and those that remote work clearly brings as well? Since before the pandemic, one nonprofit group has shown how to function effectively through remote settings, and it is also sharing those experiences with other advocacy groups to support them as they operate remotely. The founders of the Asylum Seekers Advocacy Project (ASAP) got their start working to provide legal assistance and guidance to those applying for asylum during the border crisis in 2015. As law students, Conchita Cruz, Swapna Reddy, Dorothy Tegeler, and Liz Willis all volunteered in-person at Texas border towns and remotely from their perch as law students at Yale Law School in Connecticut. They initially provided direct legal assistance to those held in migrant facilities in places like Dilley, Texas. Taking time during breaks in school to visit border facilities, the group represented a small number of migrants pursuing asylum cases. Many of the hearings in these cases were conducted remotely, even in 2015, with judges, lawyers for the government, and the law students and lawyers representing the asylum applicants appearing either in a courtroom or over video links.[40]

After many of them graduated from law school in May 2016, the founders of ASAP knew that the students did not intend to all live in the same area, so ASAP had to come up with a way to collaborate from a distance. They would find a functional organizational home in the nonprofit Urban Justice Center, which is based in New York, but none of the ASAP staff would work there physically. Some were based in Chicago, others in Washington, D.C.; all of their clients were in migrant detention facilities along the United States–Mexico border, at least to start. After winning their initial hearings, as almost all of ASAP's first clients did, the clients were then able to relocate throughout the United States while awaiting a full asylum hearing. ASAP's founders knew that they could not possibly have offices wherever their clients ended up settling pending their hearings, and they also knew they could never provide full assistance to everyone seeking asylum in the United States. They then began to shift their model from one that provided direct legal services to one where their goal was to provide some support and guidance to anyone seeking asylum who wanted assistance. ASAP's leadership and staff have learned a great deal from working in such a diffuse, decentralized way, as their staff are located throughout the United States, and have been working in this fashion since they first opened their proverbial doors. They have also tried to distill some of these lessons into written guidance that they have shared with other legal practitioners,[41] many of whom had to adjust to a remote style of work for the first time in the face of pandemic protocols.

ASAP's guidance provides information on how lawyers can improve collaboration in remote settings with each other and with clients. Among coworkers, ASAP recommends using tools for communicating, like the Slack platform, provided whatever service the organization uses offers a "transparent, accessible, and organized remote workplace" and includes "in-app video calls and screensharing."[42] Within Slack, ASAP has set up multiple "channels" for different purposes, and for different teams and departments, including one for managers. Those who have a need to be in a particular channel can access it. There is also a separate "news and resource channel that staff can intentionally access or avoid depending on what best supports their mental health."[43] They recommend defaulting to video calls whenever possible, as opposed to just phone calls or email exchanges. They suggest that organizations have regular all-staff video calls and that, during those calls, participants should dedicate a portion of them to "all-staff social interaction as opposed to substantive agenda items."[44] They also "schedule regular, optional hangout calls that staff members can join while they eat lunch, or just to chat."[45] They encourage sharing calendars with each other and recommend that staff members block out times when they are working on a project and do not want to be disturbed; staff is also encouraged to identity "office hours" when they welcome an invitation to join a video call. They also utilize shared "to-do" list software that enables them to collaborate and stay on task for larger projects.[46] Finally, they recommend that all staff members have an adequate work-from-home space in terms of technology, supplies, and furniture.[47]

They also recognize that remote work with community partners and the members they serve can be both challenging as well as beneficial. For ASAP, "[r]emote representation makes it easier to accommodate clients' busy schedules with work and childcare and means that they do not have to find a way to travel to a physical office." Remote contact with clients can make it "easier to have multiple follow-up conversations with a relatively short period of time, breaking up difficult or heavy conversations and building rapport gradually."[48] But it is also important to meet clients where they are, to ask them the best way to communicate with them, what technology is available to them, and the ways in which they prefer to be contacted and communicated with.[49] Finally, in order to ensure that staff can try to build a relationship of trust with those they serve, ASAP recommends videoconferencing where possible because it is easier to pick up on and convey nonverbal cues. They also recommend that the advocate explicitly acknowledge with the client the barriers such technologies can impose when it comes to building trust between that advocate and the client and in the provision of trauma-informed services.[50]

What the ASAP guidance suggests, along with the experiences of law firms like Malley's, Enix-Ross's, and Frick's, is that lawyers are adapting, and must adapt, to a new normal in the practice of law. They must recognize the ways in which remote and distance communications must be intentional to reclaim at least some of the benefits of in-person work. When lawyers are physically present, they must utilize time really effectively to achieve the benefits that face-to-face interactions can generate: presence with purpose. This also means that, in the legal industry, as in most sectors of the economy, the transformation of the practice of law can actually have positive effects.

The question then becomes: How can lawyers garner some of the benefits of remote work while not missing out on key skills development, mentoring, supervision, and support? In addition, while all lawyers must ensure that they provide competent service to clients, this is truly the least common denominator, the floor below which lawyers must not fall. At the same time, lawyering generally requires more than mere competence. It requires genuine skill, creativity, ingenuity, and grit. Working in isolation is not always conducive to effective lawyering. And a group of professionals can often reach a better solution than an individual working alone. In fact, teamwork is a critical part of problem-solving skills and one of the core skills that effective lawyers must exhibit.[51] But does that teamwork always require that the team members must be in the same place physically at the same time? There is certainly something to productive brainstorming sessions where groups of people with diverse insights and experiences are able to come up with creative solutions that they would not have reached as individuals.[52] At the same time, there is a value to separation, to allowing ideas to germinate, to working in an isolated fashion to come up with the ideas, to drafting the memorandum, or to thinking up a strategy—all of which can be brought to the team later. This sort of "deep work," as author Cal Newport calls it, is often dreamed up in the spaces in between, when we are not necessarily bombarded by the crowd, no matter how secure we might feel in their presence.[53]

There certainly is something to the importance of in-person collaboration for improving the work product of the group, and in the legal profession there is certainly a degree of professional training that comes from being in the presence of a highly effective and experienced lawyer going about their business. But there are significant benefits to separation as well, to having time to reflect and think. Moreover, diverse teams generate better, more creative ideas,[54] and we might be able to form such teams because we are more flexible in how we permit them to work. At the end of the day, the ability for remote work is likely a net positive. A combination of looseness and support, collaboration and independence—all fostered by a workplace culture that permits teamwork but also fosters solitary, deep work—is likely the type of approach that will generate the best, most creative, most impactful work product.[55]

What is more, what the legal profession has shown is that, in a relatively short span of time—just three years—it has transformed itself in dramatic ways to respond to the needs of clients, courts, and members of the profession itself. With the lawyer's ethical obligations always as a backdrop, the profession showed that it could still operate effectively while ensuring professional responsibility or professionalism. It also worked to continue to serve clients and provide access to the legal system to those clients (at least when the legal system itself was not closed). It also proved that it could operate in an inclusive way, accommodating the needs of a range of its members. An industry hesitant to change found that it could do so, although it took a global health pandemic. It found ways to promote the values of professionalism, access, and inclusion in addressing and shaping the delivery of legal services in effective and efficient ways. But the profession also faces another crisis, and its ability to address that crisis in a meaningful way is another challenge it must address to shape itself to the needs of the community and affirm the values of professionalism, access, and inclusion.

The Ongoing Crisis of Exclusion

The pandemic forced the profession to address some of its inequities, especially those that privileged individuals able to work long hours in an office with little control over their schedule. Due to the fact that remote work helped make work a little easier and more flexible for many—lawyers and clients alike—it made the practice of law more inclusive and more accessible for clients without any measurable decline in professionalism: clients were served well, more efficiently, and possibly even more effectively. The transformation that the legal profession experienced did something else: it proved that the profession—one that strives to adhere to precedent, prefers path-dependent approaches to problem-solving, and supports a structured hierarchy—could change and evolve when the needs of the broader community required it. Perhaps this offers some hope that, in other areas, as with issues of inclusion and access more generally, the profession can overcome the structural, cultural, and historical practices and institutions that have led to the profession we have, one in which the ranks of the profession generally, and of its leadership in particular, fall far short of reflecting the demographic makeup of the nation as a whole. There are historical and institutional reasons for these discrepancies. In order to get a sense of the scope of the problem, I will first review the demographics of the profession, from practicing lawyers to law faculty and the judiciary.

As discussed in chapter 4, in the early 1900s the profession institutionalized its values into norms and the organizations where they would be realized: creating rules of ethics, forming and expanding law schools to teach those who aspired to join the profession, forming law firms, and creating bar associations. Virtually all of these institutions played a significant role in making the practice of law an exclusive endeavor, sometimes for perfectly legitimate reasons, like the desire to ensure that consumers of legal services were not being taken advantage of by unscrupulous and poorly trained lawyers. All too often, however, it did so for illegitimate, invidious reasons. Sometimes, good intentions inspired efforts to promote consumer protection by raising standards for admission not just to law school but also to the practice itself. Yet it is hard to come to any conclusion other than that such claims of consumer protection were, at least for some, thinly veiled attempts to accomplish other goals as well, including the preservation of the privileges of white males as they relate to entry in the profession and advancement and success within it.

Historically, many of the institutions described in chapter 4, including the profession as a whole and the ABA itself, have operated as exclusive clubs, at first keeping out all but white males, then opening up their ranks only when it no longer seemed tenable (or legal) to exclude women, Blacks, and other groups from the profession.[56] While some may say that decades may have passed since explicit racism was rampant in the profession, it is difficult to say that we have made significant progress toward diversity, equity, and inclusion (DEI) in the profession. Firms across the country certainly have issued DEI statements, undertaken programs designed to promote diversity, and sought ways to become more inclusive, all in an effort to make those terms mean more than just hollow words on a page. Still, much work needs to be done, and a snapshot of the profession and its institutions reveals just how far we still have to go to ensure that the profession operates in an inclusive fashion, from top to bottom, at its entry point and throughout the lives and careers of practicing lawyers.

In 2020, the percentage of practicing attorneys in the United States who identified as male was 63 percent, with 37 percent identifying as female.[57] That is a bit of an improvement over 2010, when the profession was 69 percent male and 31 percent female.[58] In 2019, women made up just 21 percent of equity partners at law firms; 31 percent were nonequity partners and 47 percent were law firm associates. Just 24 percent of those associates were women of color.[59] Only 4 percent of associates and 2 percent of equity partners self-identified as LGBTQ+.[60] Only 9 percent of equity partners were lawyers of color.[61] Individuals with disabilities represented less than 1 percent of equity partners.[62] In 2011, the ABA reported that 7 percent of its members self-identified as having a disability,[63] with 41 percent of ABA-related entities reporting having a lawyer with a disability in a leadership position.[64]

When it comes to race and ethnicity, in 2020, 86 percent of attorneys were Caucasian/white, 5 percent were African American, 2 percent Asian, 5 percent Hispanic, and 2 percent multiracial.[65] These numbers have remained fairly constant for about a decade.[66]

As of 2019, a study of the federal judiciary revealed that 73 percent of federal judges were male, 27 percent female, 80 percent white, 10 percent Black, 6 percent Hispanic, and less than 3 percent Asian American.[67] Less than 1 percent of federal judges self-identified as LGBTQ+.[68]

When one looks at the demographics of those who have attended law school in recent years, it is possible to see slight shifts in at least some of these demographic metrics. In 2020, more than half of the 38,202 students enrolled for the first year of law school in the United States were female (20,829, or approximately 55 percent); 17,206 were male (approximately 45 percent), and 167 identified as "other" (less than 1 percent).[69] Among all students, 12,471, or roughly 32 percent, identified as minorities;[70] 5,084 of these first-year students identified as Hispanic (2,123 male, 2,948 female, and 13 identified as other), representing approximately 13 percent of all first-year students.[71] There were 2,551 Asian first-year law students in 2020 (958 male, 1,586 female, and 7 identified as other), representing nearly 7 percent of all first-year students.[72] In this group, 2,975 first-year students identified as Black (1,004 male, 1,964 female, and 7 identified as other), or nearly 8 percent of all first-year students at that time.[73] While the number of students with a disability is not clearly tracked, the National Association for Law Placement estimates that approximately 3 percent of law school graduates self-identify as having a disability.[74]

In law schools, many students are first exposed to the values of the profession and get to see leaders from within the profession either sharing demographic or life experiences that are similar to their own or not. By almost any measure, law schools have a long way to go before they can offer students role models that can inspire them to go on to fill the leadership roles in the profession themselves. In 2013, law faculties in the United States were roughly 64 percent male and 36 percent female,[75] with 79 percent identifying as non-Hispanic white, 10 percent Black, less than 5 percent Asian American/Pacific Islander, less than 5 percent Hispanic, and less than 1 percent Native American or self-identified as two or more races.[76]

At the same time, there is some hope the situation might be improving. Mark Alexander, dean of Villanova University's law school and president-elect of the American Association of Law Schools when I spoke to him, pointed out that there is a "striking" number of new law deans who are African American women.[77] This is likely to have a ripple effect throughout law schools and the legal industry as a whole. There are many ways that the visibility and leadership of administrators and faculty of color in the legal industry can inspire and support growing diversity in the profession. Alexander, who is African American, can credibly attend a meeting of the Black Law Student Association at his school and say he has been a member of the group since 1989 and that "he hasn't been kicked out yet." Alexander believes that this sort of visibility in law school leadership is going to make a difference over the next five to ten years: "When you see somebody who looks like you, you can say, 'Aha! That is possible.'"

Danielle Conway, also an African American law dean, is one of the founders of the American Association of Law School's Law Deans Antiracist Clearinghouse Project, which is designed to provide law schools and the legal profession as a whole tools to eliminate racism in the profession in all its forms. This racism is described as "a scourge that threatens both our democracy and the rule of law."[78] For Conway, the antiracism project goes beyond merely promoting diversity, equity, and inclusion: "Anti-racism speaks about the fundamental constitutional tenant not to oppress people. That's what the Fourteenth Amendment is there for."[79] It stands for "anti-subordination and anti-oppression because otherwise it has absolutely no legitimacy." What is more, this effort to combat racism has a critical rule-of-law function for Conway, one that is closer to the "thick" version of the rule of law that I described earlier. This is in stark contrast to a vision of the rule of law where "those who see themselves in the sphere of whiteness and part of the beneficiary group of white hierarchy" also believe that the rule of law does not "belong[] to everyone." For Conway, antiracism is connected to this thick version of the rule of law: "If the legal academy, the legal profession and legal institutions writ large are fulfilling their obligation to the rule of law[,] then they would best serve that obligation by directly and intentionally acknowledging, addressing, and then responding swiftly to systemic racial inequality, intersectional injustice, oppression, and subordination." If the profession as a whole does not do so, "it will remain complicit in subordinating oppressing and racializing our society to a point where we will no longer be legitimate in claiming to be democratic institutions." Conway argues that "law scaffolds society," and when a society "is only formed and defined by one perspective, that is the perspective that is going to be served whether intentional or unconscious."

And the profession still has a long way to go. Just as examples of diversity in the upper echelons of practice can have positive and inspirational effects, when the judiciary, law firms, and law schools continue to fall far short in terms of matching the demographic makeup of the American population as a whole, particularly in positions of leadership, we see the deleterious effects of this mismatch. This is perhaps most clear in the courts, where women, immigrants, and litigants of color in particular are often treated poorly by lawyers, judges, and court personnel. A recent report, prepared on behalf of the courts of the state of New York by a team led by Jeh Johnson, former secretary of the Department of Homeland Security, reviewed "existing policies, practices[,] and organizations within the [New York State] court system that are intended to address racial bias and recommend any changes or expansion of those policies, practices[,] and organizations."[80] The study found that many of those the researchers interviewed described New York courts as "under-resourced" and "over-burdened." Court practices had a "dehumanizing effect" on those who appeared there, particularly people of color.[81] The report describes incidents where judges used racial slurs to refer to litigants of color.[82] Court officers presented particular problems, with the researchers finding that this group of court personnel engaged in behavior that provided evidence of "broader institutional acceptance of racist behavior,"[83] including denigrating interpreters, sharing racist memes on social media, and referring to court officers of color with racist slurs. One criminal defense attorney recounted an experience of being with their clients, who were young African American teens, in an elevator with several white court officers. One officer turned to the lawyer's clients and said, "'Keep running your mouth. You'll always be a [n——r].'"[84] In a separate incident, one white court officer told an African American court officer he was "'one of the good monkeys.'"[85] In addition, attorneys of color faced bias in the court system, including being mistaken for criminal defendants.[86] The team recommended that leadership of the courts should "embrace a 'zero tolerance' policy for racial bias, along with an expression that the duty to uphold this policy extends to all those workings within the [New York state] court system."[87]

Lillian Moy, a recently retired lawyer who worked in legal aid organizations for over forty years, saw this sort of mistreatment of attorneys of color and women throughout her years of practice. As an Asian American woman practicing law in rural Georgia at the beginning of her career, perhaps she expected such treatment, but forty years later "lawyers of color are still going to court, the first, second, third time, and they're asked 'are you a lawyer?' or 'you must be the client,' or 'you must be an interpreter' or 'you're the defendant, right?'" Young women of color still face this kind of treatment in court, and young female colleagues "still face sexual harassment, by adverse parties, by court officers, and maybe by clients."[88]

For fifteen years, I practiced in a New York City housing court, where litigants of color constituted a majority of the defendants. In housing court, low- and middle-income persons (and an occasional wealthy person) faced eviction. Many of the tenants were women of color, and my colleagues of color were repeatedly treated by judges as if they were defendants, not attorneys. When the judge reviewed a court file and noted that an attorney had appeared in the case, the judge would turn to my colleague and say: "[W]here is your lawyer? Your. Law. Yer." This would never happen to me, even as a twenty-six-year-old lawyer just out of law school. But I am white and male.

Deborah Enix-Ross, as a young Black woman representing low-income tenants of color in housing court as a legal aid attorney, was often on the receiving end of this type of treatment. As she describes it, in the early 1980s, when she was fresh out of law school, several outward characteristics she possessed tended to invite demeaning treatment—what she says might be described as "microaggressions" today. She was young, Black, and female, and judges might consider her a litigant and not a lawyer, or they might reference her appearance in some way. Sometimes even her clients would ask if they could have a white lawyer. As Enix-Ross describes it, because of her youth, gender, and race, she had "three layers of convincing" to do to help her clients overcome their concerns about her competence. And members of the judiciary were no better. In one instance she recalls, a judge asked her how old she was. Enix-Ross admits that a more experienced attorney might have said, "'Don't harm your client by mouthing off to the judge.'" But, as she explains, "I was young, and I was a New Yorker, and I was bold," so I told the judge that he had no business asking that. To the judge's credit, he agreed and moved on. In the end, her response generated respect not only from the judge but also from the client and even opposing counsel. Still, for Enix-Ross, she did not "know of any man that would have been asked that question."

Once again, with my own experiences in housing court, I would often witness court officers berating and belittling low-income tenants, particularly immigrants who might not speak English well—or were at least *perceived* as not speaking English well. One courtroom that would handle hundreds of cases a day during a long calendar call started a practice of hearing the cases of litigants with small children in tow out of turn so that those litigants could move more quickly through the process. One court officer tasked with carrying out this practice would use it as an opportunity to flex and abuse his power. He would seek out the women with small children who he thought, by their appearance, did not speak English (and I cannot recall a single instance in which this officer identified a man for this treatment). He would then stand over them in an intimidating fashion and bellow at them: "*Dame sus papeles!*" (Give me your papers). Without explaining the purpose of this request, he would then take note of the case number and stomp away, leaving the litigant unaware of why she was being singled out for this treatment. Instead of serving as a means of accommodating the needs of parents with young children facing an eviction, as it was intended, this practice became yet another opportunity for court officers to make the court system more brutal, not less.

While the Johnson report, Moy's and Enix-Ross's experiences, and my own observations reflect conditions in the courts in New York, the sorts of issues are common in courts across the nation. Legal systems are neither diverse nor inclusive.[89] Historically, attorneys of color, women attorneys, women attorneys of color, disabled attorneys, and attorneys who identify as LGBTQ+ have experienced indignities such as these. They are the products of both implicit *and* explicit bias. Such biases manifest not just in slights and slurs but also in decisions related to admission to law school as well as in hiring, promotion, and compensation once the lawyer enters the profession.[90] And these sorts of experiences are not relics of a past, more abusive time. In July 2022, a male lawyer was referred to an attorney disciplinary committee after utilizing the phrase "See you next Tuesday" in open court when referring to his female adversaries, a thinly coded phrase meant to demean and insult women, not unlike "Let's go, Brandon," which is used to insult the sitting president.[91]

As we saw in chapter 4, the structures the profession put in place in the early twentieth century were designed, at least in part, to *institutionalize* exclusion. The institutions within which such exclusion was embedded have subsequently shaped the profession in myriad ways: determining who to train, who to admit, who to tap for leadership and prestigious positions within the profession, and who to recruit to educate the next generation. For the first fifty years in these institutions, these elements all worked together to generate a profession that was overwhelmingly cisgender, white, and male. Culturally, this had the effect of creating institutional values that reflected the perspectives of those in the dominant group, and it converted discriminatory treatment into a values orthodoxy that meant the profession advanced expectations regarding quality, potential, skill, and leadership that matched those that most aligned with the capacities and characteristics of the dominant group. The well-worn path, the "best" upbringing and education, led to admission in the most prestigious schools, which led to the most enriching and prestigious opportunities in the profession. In turn, those who traveled this path held expectations for those who they would seek out to recruit to follow in their footsteps, who often did just that: from the frat house, to the clubhouse, to the courtroom, and to judges' chambers.

These forms of dominance perpetuated barriers to entry and shaped the roads to success in the profession; those who could not count themselves as members of the dominant group found that they were often denied entry to the halls and levers of power.[92] By limiting access to the means of changing the system, that system replicates itself, perpetuating exclusion.[93] As Danielle Conway explains, for the first decades of the twentieth century, exclusion from the profession was the rule. And with passage of civil rights protections in the 1960s, three generations of lawyers had already been educated in a system that institutionalized exclusion. What is more, the pathways to the profession that enabled aspiring lawyers to get an effective education, for example, prevented a "more full and robust pipeline to be created." For Conway, "what you see [now] are vestiges of exclusion . . . that work together to conspire against the lifting up of black people, women, those with intersectional identities, those who are routinely oppressed, [and] the impoverished." While there are outliers who have reached the highest pinnacles of the profession, the institutionalized and entrenched nature of structural exclusion remains, and the results of half-hearted efforts to promote inclusion over the last fifty years show some degree of progress, but the structural inequalities remain.[94] This is where representation truly matters, but in terms of representation in the upper echelons of the profession, or lowercase r representation. But there is also capital R Representation: the formal representation of communities historically marginalized by the legal profession by individuals who are, as Conway explains it, "fluent" in representing those communities.

Conway has long had to navigate within corridors of power dominated by whites. As an African American woman and lawyer who retired from years of service in the military with a commission as a lieutenant colonel, she understands how to operate within those systems. Similarly, having practiced in Hawaii, where she served many clients of Asian descent, she developed a fluency for working within that community. As a result, she describes herself as "multilingual." What is more, "until white people become fluent" in individuals from different backgrounds, capital *R* Representation matters (clients have lawyers who represent them who understand the challenges they face in their lives), just as lowercase *r* representation matters (the notion that the legal system must reflect the demographics of the nation much more than it does today, where the halls of power are overwhelmingly white).

Many thoughtful scholars and leaders have recommendations for bringing greater diversity, equity, and inclusion into the practice of law to make sure all within the profession are treated with dignity and respect and are offered the same opportunities as those lawyers who benefit historically from systems of exclusion.[95] One of these scholars, Meera Deo, offers strategies that law schools, in particular, can deploy to promote greater diversity within their faculty and administration in terms of ensuring women of color can succeed in the legal academy.[96] "Because intersectional discrimination, implicit bias, and gender privilege are institutional rather than purely individual problems," she argues, "only structural solutions can truly ameliorate them."[97] Such solutions must involve "allies in the administration who are aware of the obstacles facing women of color and proactively work to overcome them."[98] Schools have to "stock the pipeline[] to prepare greater numbers of nontraditional students for careers in legal academia."[99] Because subjective hiring practices often stand in the way of the recruitment of diverse faculty, schools must "think outside the box, with regard to recruitment, retention, and leadership potential."[100] Because "faculty diversity and inclusion can transform legal education only with perseverance and persistence," Deo argues that law schools "must invest time, money, and effort in this endeavor to improve our unequal profession."[101]

In the wake of the Black Lives Matter protests in 2020, many law firms claimed to take a hard look at their hiring practices and the lack of diversity within their own ranks. They professed a commitment to greater inclusivity with respect to marginalized groups, especially lawyers from communities of color.[102] A group of law school deans created the Law Deans Antiracist Clearinghouse Project described earlier to raise the "collective voices" of several law school deans who would assist them to engage their "institutions in the fight for justice and equality" and "strive to focus [their] teaching, scholarship, service, activism, programming, and initiatives on strategies to eradicate racism."[103] Similarly, a group of law firms from across the country have created the Law Firm Anti-

Racism Alliance, which is committed to "leveraging the resources of the private bar in partnership with legal services organizations to amplify the voices of communities and individuals oppressed by racism, particularly anti-Black racism, to better use the law as a vehicle for change that benefits communities of color and to promote racial equity in the law."[104] One commentator has advocated for a new ethical rule requiring every lawyer to "undertake affirmative steps to remedy de facto and de jure discrimination, eliminate bias, and promote equality, diversity[,] and inclusion in the legal profession."[105] In addition to such efforts, clients will need to demand that the legal teams assisting them are diverse, as Malley explains is happening more and more. Newly minted lawyers just coming out of law schools, or those looking to leave law firms that are less flexible, accommodating, and inclusive, will demand that the places where they work are more humane—and diverse—than the law offices of prior eras. As Swapna Reddy from ASAP reports, that organization is already seeing that flexibility in terms of where and how their teams work has been a real draw when it comes to recruiting and retaining a highly diverse legal team.

I have tried to take the long view here and not just consider where we are today. I also look backward and forward to see the institutions of the profession as systems the elite lawyers put in place at the beginning of the twentieth century as well as the shadows they have cast since. Just as today's efforts at reform are creatures of our imperfect moment, those institutions were likewise the product of a time of de jure, institutionalized racism, classism, sexism, and heteronormativity. The values baked in to those institutions have shaped and distorted the profession for a century. While there have been attempts to represent more inclusive values over the years, the ethos of exclusion continues to taint the profession in ways seen and unseen, acknowledged and unacknowledged. How we view excellence, who we cultivate as leaders, who we promote, whose skills we value, whose scholarship we recognize, what educational and experiential backgrounds we appreciate: these are all the products of a century-long struggle with the fruit of the extractive and exclusive institutions the profession put in place one hundred years ago. Changing those institutions will be difficult and requires a commitment to diversity, equity, and inclusion, not as buzzwords but as systemic values that the profession must institutionalize.

When considered in light of the values framework supplied in chapter 5—which looks to promote professionalism, access, and inclusion—the legal profession in this context must take aggressive efforts to promote a more inclusive profession that welcomes, supports, and advances greater diversity, equity, and inclusion, not as mere marketing terms but as core institutional principles that should inform everything the profession does moving forward. *Legal* professionalism that *fits* within a multiracial democracy means that core values like equal treatment before the law and equality of opportunity within the profession are reflected in judiciaries, law firms, public interest organizations, and law schools where the members of those institutions do not just reflect but also treat with dignity and respect minoritized groups. As Enix-Ross explains, "You cannot have confidence in the legal profession and in a legal system if you are participating[] and don't see people who look like you." Because of this, for Enix-Ross, it is "of paramount importance that we continue to . . . not just promote but do all that we can to make sure that we have a legal system that is reflective of society."

Representation matters: on law faculties, on the bench, and within the practicing bar. It makes for a more inclusive profession, and it results in a legal system that is more accessible to litigants from minoritized groups, to law students from such groups, and to practitioners who are members of such groups who not just seek to succeed within the profession but also wish to pursue leadership roles within it.

When it comes to the access value, we must provide access to the profession to those who seek it and who have what it takes to carry out the duties of membership (without relying on outdated and biased metrics for determining who can practice in a competent way). Expanding access to the profession, particularly for minoritized groups who will then make the legal system less "otherized" for minoritized communities— meaning for such groups the legal system will not appear as for, of, and by dominant groups—will have critical access-to-justice implications, issues I will return to in chapter 8. In terms of the value of inclusion, it should be obvious that a more diverse profession is a more inclusive profession and that promoting diversity, equity, and inclusion will necessarily render the profession more inclusive. Once within the profession, though, otherwise marginalized groups will also need to feel a sense of belonging within the profession: access alone will not render the profession inclusive. Support for individuals from minoritized groups to gain access to the profession, equal treatment once such individuals are members of it, and equal opportunity for advancement within it are all central to creating a fully inclusive legal profession, one that will advance and embody the core values of professionalism, access, and inclusion and realize them in the institutions of the profession. The U.S. Supreme Court has already begun to make such efforts more challenging. That does not mean the profession should halt the progress it has made in recent years in advancing what should be its core institutional values.

7

A Serpent in the Ear of the President

As Vice President Mike Pence was preparing to fulfill his duties to certify the results of the presidential election of November 2020, a short distance away President Donald Trump was speaking at the Ellipse beside the Washington Monument at a rally dubbed the "March to Save America" designed, purportedly, to "stop the steal" of that same election.[1] President Trump would proclaim: "We're going to walk down to the Capitol, and we're going to cheer on our brave senators and congressmen and women, and we're probably not going to be cheering so much for some of them."[2] He added: "[Y]ou'll never take back our country with weakness. You have to show strength, and you have to be strong."[3] For many in the crowd, a previous Tweet sent by the president had urged them to attend, exhorting them as follows: "Be there, will be wild."[4] Rudy Giuliani would egg on the crowd further: "If we're wrong, we will be made fools of, but if we're right a lot of them will go to jail. Let's have trial by combat."[5] A large group from the rally then marched on the Capitol.[6] Once the crowd of thousands reached the Capitol, as the joint session of Congress had convened to certify the vote results, the rally's participants would overwhelm the security force responsible for defending the building and protecting the vote certification process.[7] It would take hours to clear the violent crowd from the Capitol.[8] Once the building was secure, Congress reconvened and certified the election, with more than a hundred Republican representatives and a few senators objecting to the process.[9]

As legal scholar Richard Fallon has argued, "mob rule" is the "antithesis" of the rule of law.[10] What is more, according to another legal scholar, Richard Levy, "the legal profession has a special obligation to respect, preserve, and nurture the rule of law, especially because once the rule of law is lost, it is not clear how it can be regained."[11] What role did lawyers play, if any, in the crowd's actions on January 6? The storming of the Capitol was not an isolated event. Rather, it was the culmination of a nearly two-month-long process to challenge the results of the 2020 election. That process not only had lawyers at its center, but, in many ways, the legal minds involved in the effort concocted a witch's brew of dubious legal claims and utterly unsupported and, at times, purely fantastical factual assertions. They served this slurry of advice and exhortation to a president eager to cling to power, regardless of the consequences or the fate of the nation's democratic institutions.

The history of the relationship between social and political movements and their lawyers is long and varied. At times, such movements are guided by lawyers. At others, legalistic concerns can stifle an otherwise spontaneous outpouring of popular support or opposition to an incident or situation. At still others, movements can take action that disregards the advice of their lawyers. In the events that led to the insurrection of January 6, the loyalist Trump lawyers and their arguments were inextricably intertwined with the violent riots on that day. The lawyers gave the president, and, in turn, the mob, a framework for arguing that the results were fraudulent and a legal maneuver was available—that is, that the vice president could singlehandedly overturn the election—that served as a centerpiece of and the pretext for the invasion of the Capitol. When their legal challenges failed miserably, and the vice president showed no sign that he would listen to the siren song that he had unchecked authority to dispense with the votes of tens of thousands of American voters, all that was left was a resort to the mob. But without the loyalist lawyers, and the Silly Putty–and–string arguments they cobbled together, it is quite possible that the assault on the Capitol, and democracy itself, never would have happened.

In this chapter, I will explore the events following the 2020 presidential election and the role of lawyers in seeking to overturn it. The brazen effort to undermine the rule of law had lawyers at its center. While the institutions of democracy and professional ethics held, to a certain extent, what is to stop lawyers from engaging in similar conduct in the future? As such, this force—the notion that lawyers might act in ways that undermine the rule of law—is one the profession needs to check. In this chapter, I explore the conduct of several lawyers in the events following the election of 2020. I not only examine the ways in which our institutions held in the face of these threats but also explore ways to strengthen those institutions in the future. Although it is rare to have the opportunity to assess the inner workings of lawyers' minds, methods, motives, or strategies, we actually do have a great deal of information—memos from lawyers advising the president, discussions recounted from strategy sessions, emails—that provides insights into the thinking behind the arguments the loyalist lawyers were making and the ways in which other, responsible lawyers ended up pushing back against them. What I hope to show is not just the extent to which lawyers were at the center of the events of January 6 but also the ways in which we have to shore up our institutions, and aspects of the profession itself, to ensure we do not have another desperate challenge to American democracy and the rule of law.

Even as the votes were still being counted in several states, including Arizona and Georgia, President Trump's supporters could see the writing on the wall, and it looked increasingly like Joe Biden would ultimately prevail, both in the popular vote and in the Electoral College, denying Trump a second term. According to reporting by *Axios*, the leadership of the Trump campaign believed it had two options.[12] The first involved attempting to secure enough votes in Arizona and Georgia to win those states and then turn to challenge the results in Wisconsin.[13] A second, promoted by Rudy Giuliani, Sidney Powell,[14] and others, involved claims of a globe-spanning conspiracy to manipulate voting machines that apparently employed satellites, servers in foreign countries, and even thermostats in homes that could flip votes.[15] According to the *Axios* report:

> The[] meetings [involving the teams] would begin with official staff raising plausible legal strategies. Then Giuliani and Powell, a lawyer with a history of floating "deep state" conspiracy theories, would take over, spewing wild allegations of a centralized plot by Democrats—and in Powell's view, international communists—to steal the election.[16]

The strategy ultimately adopted was a bit of a hybrid of the two approaches: make some of the more outlandish allegations in the media and the somewhat more straightforward ones in actual court filings.[17] While some of the allegations made in courts throughout the country tended to depart from the greater conspiracy theories being spun out in the press, nevertheless, in over sixty lawsuits filed on various grounds to challenge the results of the election, the lawyers proceeded to lose virtually all of them. While none of the cases seemed to raise claims asserting that "little green men"[18] had changed the vote totals, a few came close. At least one complaint explicitly referenced the mythic land of Gondor from the epic fantasy trilogy *The Lord of the Rings*.[19] The lawyers in that case argued that, as a result of the alleged fraud in the 2020 election, the federal courts had to place the other branches of the federal government—the U.S. Congress and the presidency—"into a state of stewardship" as in the mythic land of Gondor. There, according to this work of fiction, a line of stewards managed the nation for generations because the hereditary line of ancient kings had been broken by the apparent end of the royal line without heirs. A federal court was asked to do the same thing: place the nation in a stewardship until the results of the election could be sorted out. While such an approach might have served the White City in Middle Earth, no such mechanism was available to a U.S. court. In the end, Trump supporters filed over sixty cases in state and federal courts, trial courts, appellate courts, and even the Supreme Court,[20] with many of the cases summarily dismissed, even the one seeking direct relief in the highest court in the land.[21]

But the judges adjudicating these cases did not simply toss them out of court because they were without merit. Those judges also criticized many of the lawyers bringing them because there were no factual bases for their claims.[22] One federal district court judge reviewed the conduct of the lawyers bringing such claims.[23] After noting that he would have to overturn recent Supreme Court precedent, including *Bush v. Gore*,[24] to rule in the plaintiffs' favor, Judge James Boasberg, a U.S. district court judge from Washington, DC, noted that the plaintiffs had failed to "explain how this District Court has authority to disregard Supreme Court precedent." He also criticized them for waiting "until seven weeks after the election to bring this action and seek a preliminary injunction based on purportedly unconstitutional statutes that have existed for decades—since 1948 in the case of the federal ones."[25] He would conclude that it was "not a stretch to find a serious lack of good faith here."[26] He stressed that the courts "are not instruments through which parties engage in such gamesmanship or symbolic political gestures."[27] In a later decision, Judge Boasberg referred the lawyer for the plaintiffs in the action to local disciplinary authorities for his conduct, stressing the extraordinary relief the lawyer sought on behalf of his clients:

The Court ends by underlining that the relief requested in this lawsuit is staggering: to invalidate the election and prevent the electoral votes from being counted. When any counsel seeks to target the processes at the heart of our democracy, the Community may well conclude that they are required to act with far more diligence and good faith than existed here.[28]

Another judge, Judge Stephanos Bibas of the Third Circuit Court of Appeals, was nominated to the federal bench by President Trump early in his term.[29] Writing for a unanimous panel of that court regarding a challenge to voting procedures in Pennsylvania in the 2020 election, Judge Bibas found as follows: "Free, fair elections are the lifeblood of our democracy. Charges of unfairness are serious. But calling an election unfair does not make it so. Charges require specific allegations and then proof. We have neither here."[30]

The conduct of several of the lawyers, including Giuliani, Powell, John Eastman, and Jeffrey Clark (see below on the actions of the last two), became the subject of disciplinary complaints filed against them in several jurisdictions where they are admitted to practice law. Rudy Giuliani has already been suspended, while the complaint filed against him in the state of New York is being considered by disciplinary authorities.[31] That complaint alleges that Giuliani filed frivolous claims, proffered evidence he knew was false, and that his actions violated several rules of ethics. These included that he engaged in conduct that "involv[es] dishonesty, fraud, deceit or misrepresentation," was "prejudicial to the administration of justice," and "adversely reflects on the lawyer's fitness."[32] It alleged further that Giuliani "publicly and in front of multiple tribunals[] alleged that Democrats engaged in a grand conspiracy of election fraud, while failing to produce any facts to back up his assertions."[33]

The litigation and extrajudicial efforts to overturn the results of the 2020 election (such extrajudicial efforts included speaking at rallies, including the March to Save America and press conferences, and before legislative tribunals), it is hard to conclude anything other than that the baseless allegations and unsupportable claims, none of which have been upheld by any court in any significant way, not only propped up the president's quixotic effort to overturn the results of the election but also fueled the sentiments that motivated the rioters on January 6, 2021.[34] A deeper analysis of some of the efforts of the loyalist lawyers, as I have called them, which we now have at our disposal, reveals the depth of their willingness to put aside professional ethics in the service of political ends, regardless of the consequences. What is more, their advocacy would give a framework and a vocabulary to the mob.

In addition to Giuliani and Powell, several lesser-known lawyers were able to vault themselves from relative obscurity to serve as key advisers to the president, perhaps because they were telling him what he wanted to hear. The first of these loyalists lawyers who was able to whisper in the ear of the president was Jeffrey Clark. Clark was an environmental lawyer in the Justice Department who prepared what he called a "Proof of Concept": a memorandum that he drafted for the acting Attorney General, Jeffrey Rosen, to send to public officials in Georgia in late December to get them to halt the transmittal of electors pledged to Biden. This draft memorandum opens with the following passage:

> The Department of Justice is investigating various irregularities in the 2020 election for President of the United States. The Department will update you as we are able on investigatory progress, but at this time we have identified significant concerns that may have impacted the outcome of the election in multiple States, including the State of Georgia.[35]

Because of these "irregularities," as Clark's draft memo explains, "the Department recommends that the Georgia General Assembly should convene in special session so that its legislators are in a position to take additional testimony, receive new evidence, and deliberate on the matter consistent with its duties under the U.S. Constitution."[36] He would add that "[t]ime is of the essence" due to the impending certification of the votes on January 6, 2021.[37] According to the memorandum, the "purpose" of such a special session was for the legislature to "evaluate the irregularities in the 2020 election . . . [and] determine whether those violations show which candidate for President won the most legal votes . . . and . . . whether the election failed to make a proper and valid choice between the candidates," so that "the General Assembly could take whatever action is necessary to ensure that one of the slates of Electors cast on December 14 will be accepted by Congress on January 6."[38] Clark believed that if Rosen would not circulate this memorandum to Georgia officials, then Rosen should be removed from his position by the president and Clark put in his place. Once installed as Attorney General, Clark would advance the ideas in the memorandum and start pressing states to consider alternate slates of electors. Putting aside that the scheme was ultimately rejected by Rosen, as Trump relented when most of the top Justice Department officials said they would resign if Rosen was removed, the factual predicate of the Clark memorandum simply did not exist.[39] The Justice Department was not, in reality, "investigating various irregularities in the 2020 election for President of the United States," nor had it "identified significant concerns that may have impacted the outcome of the election in multiple States, including the State of Georgia." Moreover, just days before, William Barr, still Attorney General at the time, had made it clear that there simply was no widespread fraud in the election: in fact, as he testified before the U.S. House of Representatives Select Committee to Investigate the January 6th Attack on the United States Capitol, the claims of fraud were "bullshit."[40]

Another rather obscure figure, William Olson, a lawyer in private practice in Washington, DC, wrote a memorandum for the purpose of convincing President Trump to take action the Department of Justice and the White House counsel's office would not take, including filing a case directly in the Supreme Court. On the morning of December 28, 2020, the date the letter was prepared, Olson wrote that he "assum[ed] that the Attorney General is attempting to discourage filing such an action[] or is slow-walking his response to you."[41] Olson would stress that, although "the time was short when we spoke on Christmas Day, *time is about to run out*."[42] He recounted a conversation apparently between an attorney from the White House counsel's office and the president in which Olson claimed he could "hear the shameful and dismissive attitude of the lawyer from [that office] toward you personally—but more importantly toward the Office of the President of the United States itself." In Olson's opinion, not only was that lawyer not "offering [the President] any options, but . . . he was there to make certain you did not consider any."[43] He would add: "But you do have options."[44] Olson argued that a lawsuit before the Supreme Court could possibly invalidate electors "selected by processes not authorized by state legislatures."[45] But even if such a lawsuit "results in another loss in the Supreme Court," it would "serve an important function in exposing to the diminishing number of Americans who still have faith in government, the true depth of the corruption."[46] Moreover, if the Supreme Court failed to take action, "the deep corruption of that institution again would be laid bare for all to see—confirming what the People learned when the [case filed by Texas in the Supreme Court] was dismissed." As a result, "filing the case is a 'win-win' with the overwhelming number of Americans who just voted for you." He would continue, ominously: "As you said, all you have is the People and the votes." Olson would then argue that the White House counsel should be fired and a new one appointed; that the president should return to Washington from Mar-a-Lago, his residence in Florida, to "take charge at the White House"; and order that the Department of Justice file suit in twenty-four hours or else the president would appoint a new Attorney General.[47] Moreover, the president should "task" the new White House counsel "with identifying how the powers of the Presidency can be used to ensure that the People receive a fair election count."[48] He would assert that "[o]ur little band of lawyers is working on a memorandum that explains exactly what you can do."[49] While "[t]he media will call this martial law," he would add that "that is 'fake news'—a concept with which you are well familiar."[50]

The most egregious example of a disregard for law, facts, and, ultimately, the rule of law is seen in the acts of John Eastman, a law professor who found himself advising a president. Eastman had a plan for overturning the results of the election, and it had to do with ensuring the vice president would disregard the votes of seven different states on January 6. The Eastman memo describes what is called the "January 6 scenario" and opens with the following sentence: "[Seven] states have transmitted dual slates of electors to the President of the Senate."[51] It then sets forth his plan in clear steps, even with bullet points. First, as the vice president began to review the state certifications on January 6, he would announce that, starting with Arizona, "he has multiple slates of electors[] and so is going to defer decision on that until finishing the other States."[52] He would then announce that there were "no electors that can be deemed validly appointed in those States."[53] Disregarding the votes of such states—which, as fate would have it, just happened to be votes from states in which Trump had lost—would reduce the overall number of valid electors. When one eliminated the electors from the seven states Biden had won, it would—*presto chango!*—put Trump in the lead: "There are at this point 232 votes for Trump, 222 votes for Biden.

Pence then gavels President Trump as re-elected."[54] He would continue: "Howls, of course, [will arise] from the Democrats, who now claim . . . that 270 [Electoral College votes] is required."[55] In response, Eastman explains: "So Pence says, fine." This would mean that no candidate "has achieved the necessary majority" which, according to the Twelfth Amendment to the U.S. Constitution, throws the election to the House of Representatives: there, each state has a single vote, and that vote is cast according to how each state's delegation votes.[56] Since, as Eastman explained, "Republicans currently control 26 of the state delegations," this was "the bare majority needed to win the vote." Accordingly, "President Trump is re-elected there as well."[57]

Because of the litigation sparked by Eastman's fight to withhold information from the House Select Committee, we have learned of a heated and emotional email exchange between Eastman and Gregory Jacob, a lawyer in the vice president's office, some of it occurring as the events of January 6 unfolded and as Jacobs's life was in danger within the Capitol. Jacob, responding to Eastman, wrote as follows:

> I respect your heart here. I share your concerns about what Democrats will do once in power. I want election integrity fixed. But I have run down every legal trail placed before me to its conclusion, and I respectfully conclude that as a legal framework, it is a results oriented position that you would never support if attempted by the opposition, and entirely made up.
>
> *And thanks to your bullshit, we are now under siege.*[58]

Some time later, Eastman would reply:

> My "bullshit"—seriously? You think you can't adjourn the session because the [Electoral Count Act] says no adjournment, while the compelling evidence that the election was stolen continues to build and is already overwhelming. The "siege" is because YOU and your boss did not do what was necessary to allow this to be aired in a public way so that the American people can see for themselves what happened.[59]

Jacobs would apologize for using the term "bullshit," saying that it was "unbecoming" of him, but using that term was, as Jacobs replied, "reflective of a man whose wife and three young children are currently glued to news reports as I am moved about to locations where we will be safe from people, 'mostly peaceful' as CNN might say, who believed with all their hearts the theory they were sold about the powers that could legitimately by exercised at the Capitol on this day."[60] He would continue: "But the advice provided has, whether intended to or not, functioned as a serpent in the ear of the President of the United States, the most powerful office in the entire world. And here we are."[61] He would continue as follows:

> Respectfully, it was gravely, gravely irresponsible for you to entice the President with an academic theory that had no legal viability, and that you well know we would lose before any judge who heard and decided the case. And if the courts declined to hear it, I suppose it could only be decided in the streets. The knowing amplification of that theory through numerous surrogates, whipping large numbers of people into a frenzy over something with no chance of ever attaining legal force through actual process of law, has led us to where we are.
>
> I do not begrudge academics debating the most far-flung theories. I love doing it myself, and I view the ferment of ideas as a good and helpful thing. But advising the President of the United States, in an incredibly constitutionally fraught moment, requires a seriousness of purpose, an understanding of the difference between abstract theory and legal reality, and an appreciation of the power of both the office and the bully pulpit that, in my judgment, was entirely absent here.[62]

There is no question that the Electoral Count Act (ECA) of 1887 is difficult to parse and to understand.[63] It was drafted in the late nineteenth century to correct for the confusion that emerged in the wake of the disputed election of 1876.[64] The type of opaque language found in the ECA is often seen in other contexts as fodder for lawyers who can try to make novel arguments about the language found in the legislation and the purposes behind it. In fact, the confusing nature of the ECA itself would likely lead even the most conscientious lawyer to harbor doubts about their reading of the statute in advising a client impacted by it. And certainly, loyalist lawyers like Eastman could muster somewhat plausible legal arguments about how the law should be applied. But such an admission ignores the reality that the facts as Eastman explained them in his memorandum, and from which his entire legal argument flowed, were simply untrue. Again, he opened this memorandum by saying that seven states had "transmitted dual slates of electors to the President of the Senate."[65] This was false. This same sort of factual inaccuracy plagues Clark's "Proof of Concept," where he tried to strong-arm the Department of Justice by stating that it is in the process of "investigating various irregularities in the 2020 election for President of the United States."[66] Again, that simply was not true. What is more, the factual predicate of the entire "stop the steal" movement, which was embraced by lawyers in courtrooms, in statehouses, in press conferences, and in the streets, was that there was massive voter fraud in the 2020 election. To this day, despite wild allegations of Italian computer servers and satellites, Nest home thermostats, a dead national leader from Venezuela, Sharpie pens changing votes, the destruction (and fabrication) of ballots, and the manipulation of voting machines, no one has produced a whiff of proof for any of these theories. And no one ever will.

Making up false claims is bad enough—and it certainly is bad. But the loyalist lawyers continued to press such claims, to concoct legal theories based on lies with no factual support, and then to advocate for them with the express purpose of disrupting the certification of the vote to, in the words of John Eastman, commit a "minor violation of the law" so as to delay certification to buy time for state legislatures to fabricate false slates of electors.[67] They did so despite knowing that such conduct was leading to violence and even continued to advocate this position while rioters stormed the Capitol: such behavior is morally bankrupt. But is it also unethical under the rules governing the practice of law? And are the rules currently in place that might address such lapses, and the types of penalties available for their violation, calibrated to appropriately punish such conduct and deter it from happening in the future?

In an opinion piece for the *New York Times*, legal scholar Tim Wu argued that the institutions held in the face of this onslaught because of "civic virtue"—institutional norms that motivated individuals to act according to professional norms and the dictates of personal conscience:

> The survival of our Republic depends as much, if not more, on the virtue
> of those in government, particularly the upholding of norms by civil ser-

vants, prosecutors and military officials. We have grown too jaded about things like professionalism and institutions, and the idea of men and women who take their duties seriously. But as every major moral tradition teaches, no external constraint can fully substitute for the personal compulsion to do what is right.[68]

As an example of this, lawyers at the Department of Justice reportedly opposed President Trump's efforts to replace the acting Attorney General with a lower-level official who was inclined to assist Trump's efforts to undermine and overturn the results of election.[69] Despite these institution-supporting efforts, as Sherrilyn Ifill, then the executive director of the NAACP, would argue, given the outsized role that lawyers played in efforts to undermine the election and, by extension, the rule of law, it is appropriate to review the relevant institutional norms to ensure they are as strong as they can be to avoid similar behavior repeating itself in the future.[70] As she would write: "Just as the president, members of Congress, and insurrectionists must be held accountable for their actions, the legal profession must urgently take collective stock of why so many prominent legal institutions and leaders were embroiled in supporting one of the most corrupt and destructive presidencies in our history."[71]

Such an accounting is necessary, and I think it will show that civic virtue alone is a slender reed on which to rely to deter future misconduct, especially when the stakes are so high. Personally, I would prefer stronger rules, clearer guidance, and a robust enforcement regime. As one state's disciplinary authority has explained, the purposes of a disciplinary proceeding are punishment for unethical conduct, "purification of the legal profession," protection against "substandard practitioners," and "deter[rence of] future misconduct."[72] Accordingly, we must undertake a proper assessment of the efforts that are needed to deter such future misconduct.

Much of what the loyalist lawyers did certainly falls within the purview of the rules and qualifies as unethical conduct. They raised claims without any basis in law. They asserted factual contentions without any foundation. They took to social media and cable news, attended press conferences, and threw gasoline on the fire on January 6, and not simply to gain some tactical advantage in a slip-and-fall case or to wring a few more dollars out of a transaction for themselves or their client. The lawyers who promoted what has come to be known as the "Big Lie" had designs on democracy and the peaceful transition of power; they took actions that undermined the core of legal professionalism: defense of the rule of law. The rules that govern the legal profession are mostly considered "trans-substantive": they should apply to all lawyers regardless of the type of law they practice or the sector in which they find themselves. In some ways, this is helpful, because it means that all lawyers must hold themselves to the standards set forth in the rules. At the same time, those rules do not differentiate between a simple and straightforward act of misconduct and one that strikes at the heart of our democratic institutions and undermines the rule of law itself. Given this trans-substantive and general nature of the ethics rules, and the fact that they do not have more specific guardrails related to attorney misconduct that consists of flagrant disregard for the rule of law, it is worthwhile to consider whether the rules governing lawyer ethics should include more explicit reference to such violations. In addition, the profession should consider strengthening the tools available to punish such violations.

Baked in to the rules are what might be considered provisions that reflect a bias in those rules toward preserving the rule of law, like prohibitions against ex parte communications among lawyers, judges, and jurors.[73] The preamble to the Model Rules of Professional Conduct (hereinafter the "Model Rules") also provides as follows: "A lawyer, as a member of the legal profession, is a representative of clients, an officer of the legal system and a public citizen having special responsibility for the quality of justice."[74] Lawyers have to comply with the law generally[75] and may not engage in acts "prejudicial to the administration of justice."[76] They should also not engage in actions involving "dishonesty, fraud, deceit[,] or misrepresentation"[77] and refrain from making "false statement[s] of material fact or law to a third person."[78]

In addition, in the litigation context, the rules provide as follows: "A lawyer shall not bring or defend a proceeding, or assert or controvert an issue therein, unless there is a basis in law and fact for doing so that is not frivolous, which includes a good faith argument for an extension, modification[,] or reversal of existing law."[79] A lawyer shall also not present evidence in court the lawyer knows to be false[80] and, if they should later come to know of its falsity, must correct the record.[81]

This disclosure requirement kicks in when the lawyer has "actual knowledge" that the evidence is false, but disciplinary authorities reviewing the lawyer's conduct after the fact can "infer" such knowledge from the "circumstances" surrounding the lawyer's actions.[82]

Similarly, and also in the litigation context, Rule 11 of the Federal Rules of Civil Procedure (FRCP), which applies in the federal trial courts but has corollaries in most states' procedure rules and those of appellate courts, states that when a lawyer presents a "pleading, written motion, or other paper—whether by signing, filing, submitting, or later advocating it,"[83] they are certifying that, "to the best of the person's knowledge, information, and belief, formed after an inquiry reasonable under the circumstances,"[84] the document "is not being presented for any improper purpose, such as to harass, cause unnecessary delay, or needlessly increase the cost of litigation."[85] The lawyer's signature on the document serves as a certification by that lawyer that the "claims, defenses, and other legal contentions are warranted by existing law or by a nonfrivolous argument for extending, modifying, or reversing existing law or for establishing new law."[86] It is also an attestation that the factual contentions contained in that document "have evidentiary support or, if specifically so identified, will likely have evidentiary support after a reasonable opportunity for further investigation or discovery."[87] Like with the rules generally, prohibitions on frivolous court filings are also trans-substantive—that is, they do not differentiate between the type of case the lawyer is litigating.

Although the applicable rules themselves do not make explicit reference to any type of case, or suggest that claims that threaten to undermine the rule of law itself warrant special attention by the courts, in the litigation following the 2020 election that did not stop courts from considering the gravity of the claims and the threats they posed. In one case challenging the results of the 2020 election in Michigan, *King v. Whitmer*,[88] the plaintiffs offered no evidence to support their claims. Accordingly, the court found that the lawyers who filed the case "abused the well-established rules applicable to the litigation process by proffering claims not backed by law; proffering claims not backed by evidence (but instead, speculation, conjecture, and unwarranted suspicion); proffering factual allegations and claims without engaging in the required prefiling inquiry; and dragging out these proceedings even after they acknowledged that it was too late to attain the relief sought." The court went on to rule as follows, with the italics in the original: "*And this case was never about fraud—it was about undermining the People's faith in our democracy and debasing the judicial process to do so.*"[89] The court would add that the lawyers and advocates had many "arenas," including "print, television, and social media," where they could advance their "protestations, conjecture, and speculation"; such communications "are neither permitted nor welcomed in a court of law." Indeed, "the sanctity of both the courtroom and the litigation process are preserved only when attorneys adhere to this oath and follow the rules, and only when courts impose sanctions when attorneys do not. And despite the haze of confusion, commotion, and chaos counsel intentionally attempted to create by filing this lawsuit, one thing is perfectly clear: Plaintiffs' attorneys have scorned their oath, flouted the rules, and attempted to undermine the integrity of the judiciary along the way."[90]

But there is nothing explicit in these rules or the supporting commentary that suggests that heightened punishment is appropriate given the nature of the offense, particularly one that is designed to undermine democratic institutions or the rule of law itself. Courts might find themselves able to shoehorn in more serious penalties for such offensive conduct if they found it "willful," and it almost certainly will be in many instances. Still, the framework available to judges in punishing such offenses does appear to resemble a thin version of the rule of law, one that is purely procedural and looks less to substantive outcomes. Accordingly, those drafting procedural rules should consider incorporating not just explicit prohibitions on actions designed to undermine the rule of law but also stiff penalties for those lawyers who engage in them.

The Rule of Law and the Role of Lawyers

I will explore in chapter 9 some of the ways in which judges might have some flexibility to exact more serious punishments for violations of the rule of law; for example, the rules themselves and the procedures surrounding litigation should specify that it is a clear act of misconduct to take action that undermines the rule of law. Accordingly, one possibility would be to amend Model Rule 8.4, which relates to attorney misconduct generally, to provide as follows: "It is a professional misconduct for a lawyer to engage in conduct that is knowingly designed to undermine the rule of law." Amending the rules in this way would represent an embrace of the thick version of the rule of law rather than a thin one that is more procedurally focused. It would recognize that rule-of-law violations can serve as acts of misconduct on their own, as opposed to having to arise as a violation of some other rule or standard of practice.

At the same time, it is important to differentiate between actions that undermine the rule of law and legitimate forms of legal actions that have been the bread and butter of cause lawyers for over a century. Courts and disciplinary committees should make sure the prohibition on actions undermining the rule of law is not weaponized to chill appropriate forms of advocacy and creative claims, particularly those raised by marginalized or disfavored groups. There is precedent for this sort of abuse. After amendments to FRCP Rule 11 in 1983 made it easier to seek sanctions, courts appeared to have applied them disproportionately against civil rights litigants.[91]

There is no question that a group of loyalist lawyers with designs on overturning the results of the 2020 election for president of the United States seemed unconstrained by the limits of legal professionalism when they raised baseless claims and filed case after frivolous case in an effort to achieve their political goal. Such actions were certainly designed to undermine faith in our democratic institutions, if not destroy them altogether. They also threaten to undermine faith in the institution of the legal profession itself. We know the crisis of professionalism that this effort represents. As this book goes to print, former President Trump has been indicted several times for the events leading up to, during, and even after January 6th. It is quite shameful for the profession that over a dozen lawyers are either indicted or unindicted co-conspirators in those proceedings.

It is not clear whether existing institutions will withstand this onslaught on the rule of law. To date, they have largely held. At the same time, there are clear cracks in those institutional pillars, and this chapter has presented some ideas by which the profession might overcome the weaknesses. But even if we were to fully insulate the profession, and society, against such threats to democratic institutions, other threats remain. In chapter 8, I examine two of those threats and some potential responses.

8

The Access-to-Justice Crisis and the Rise of Legal Technology

Every day, in courthouses, government buildings, and the offices of small businesses throughout the country, Americans struggle with the ability to find representation to help them address their legal needs, mostly because of the high cost of legal services. Due to this cost, the inability to secure representation is felt most acutely in low- and moderate-income communities, where tens of millions of Americans face their legal problems without a lawyer. Making matters worse, because the legal system is difficult to navigate without the benefit of a lawyer, it can lead to mistrust and fear of that system. In turn, this leads to lawlessness or disaffection or both, prompting individuals to seek to resolve their disputes, if they try to resolve them at all, outside the legal system or to permit their rights to languish. At the same time, the broken state of the legal market has created an opportunity for innovation, and technological change is leading to new ways through which many Americans get information about their legal problems, locate a lawyer to represent them, or perhaps even find a solution to their problem, often at a fraction of the cost of what a traditional lawyer would charge.

As I have laid out in previous chapters, together with some of the other forces the legal profession faces at present, there is a twin set of additional challenges it must address as well. First, the fact that too many Americans face their legal problems without a lawyer means that the legal community is failing to meet the needs of millions of Americans. And what is the point of the legal profession other than to meet the needs of the community it is supposed to serve? Unless we are to say that the point of the American legal profession is to serve only a percentage of Americans, or that it exists to give its members jobs and protect their monopoly on the delivery of legal assistance, it would seem that there is poor institutional fit between what the profession is doing and what it is supposed to do. The second of these challenges is actually related to the first: the failure of the legal profession to meet the needs of many Americans, coupled with advances in technology, means that new modes of obtaining some form of legal assistance are becoming available, and they are threatening to disrupt the market for legal services. These two, connected forces pose a continuing threat to the legal profession. When these challenges are viewed together, and refracted through the values-based prism of professionalism, access, and inclusion, it is possible to see opportunity in these challenges. That opportunity is the focus of this chapter.

Access to Justice and the Thick View of the Rule of Law

Current research on the legal needs of low- and moderate-income Americans shows the extent of the access-to-justice crisis, a crisis made worse by the COVID-19 pandemic.[1] According to a study carried out on behalf of the U.S. Legal Services Corporation (LSC), which provides funding to a network of nonprofit legal services organizations that serve low-income communities across the nation, the current "justice gap"—the difference between the number of Americans who need legal services to address specific needs and those who are able to secure that representation—is vast. For low-income American households, which the LSC describes as those with incomes at 125 percent of the federal poverty rate, roughly three out of four of them experienced at least one civil legal problem in the previous year, including problems related to consumer debt, access to health care, and housing.[2] Once beset with these problems, only one-quarter of low-income Americans who face such problems seek out legal assistance to address them, and half of those who chose not to seek legal assistance at all did so because of the expense associated with retaining a lawyer.[3] In the end, the overwhelming majority of those in need of legal assistance were unable to meet their legal needs. As the report concluded, for those with such needs, "they do not get any or enough legal help for 92% of the problems that have had a substantial impact on them."[4] Even for those prospective clients who do find their way to LSC-funded organizations, such organizations "are unable to provide any or enough legal help for an estimated 1.4 million civil legal problems (or 71% of problems) that are brought to their doors in a year."[5] Apart from the very real impacts that can befall a family that does not have legal representation, including homelessness, bankruptcy, or loss of a job or access to health care, the lack of representation also has political effects. The study showed that individuals with incomes at 400 percent or above the federal poverty rate were roughly 50 percent more likely to feel "confident that they could find and afford a lawyer if they needed one than those with lower income (73% to 45%)."[6] It is no coincidence, then, that those wealthier individuals are also roughly 50 percent "more likely to believe that they can use the civil legal system to protect and enforce their rights (59% to 39%)."[7]

Similarly, a 2014 study conducted on behalf of the American Bar Association and led by researcher Rebecca Sandefur found that residents of one representative American city did not seek the assistance of a lawyer to address their civil legal problems for a range of reasons, even though these issues could lead to harms to physical and mental health, harassment, assault, a decrease in income, and harm to the respondents' relationships.[8] While this study showed that many did not access a lawyer to solve their legal problems because of the cost associated with doing so, there were other reasons as well, including that they did not know they needed a lawyer, did not know how to access one even if they wanted representation, thought they could handle the matter on their own or with the assistance of a lay third party like a family member or friend, or chose to ignore the problem altogether.[9]

The access-to-justice crisis facing Americans with low and moderate incomes means that millions of families face their legal problems—like eviction, consumer debt, and wage theft—without the benefit of a lawyer. As economist Gillian Hadfield has described it, we exist in a "law-thick" world,[10] and, as a result, access to legal assistance is a fundamental necessity to resolve disputes, defend one's rights when they are in jeopardy, and assist individuals in the ordering of their lives with the knowledge that those rights will be protected. If one of the main reasons that so many Americans face their legal problems without the benefit of legal assistance is the prohibitive cost of that representation, and that cost is largely a function of the barriers to entry to the profession, the cost to overcome those barriers that prospective lawyers must absorb to enter the profession, and the fact that lawyers can charge what they do because of the monopoly lawyers enjoy with regard to the ability to provide legal representation, then these institutional features of the profession—

the barriers, the monopoly, the cost of representation—reflect their distinctly extractive qualities. What is more, in an adversarial setting, where only one party has representation, that party clearly has a distinct advantage over an unrepresented one. They are able to draw—that is, extract—a greater degree of value from the system than they would have had they dealt with a represented opponent. This asymmetry of representation has an extractive effect all on its own. It also undermines the functioning of the adversarial system itself.

What is more, just as at the turn of the nineteenth to the twentieth century, there is a rule-of-law concern when it comes to the access-to-justice crisis. Then, the elites of the bar feared that new immigrant and lower-income communities, if they were denied competent legal representation, would not turn to the legal system to resolve their disputes. Those disputes might go unresolved, and the affected party might have to suffer through a denial of their rights. Worse still, those who did not see the legal system as open and accessible to them, did not feel they would receive fair treatment once inside it, and feared they would not enjoy a degree of parity in terms of the resources to navigate the system as their adversaries, if they sought to resolve their disputes at all, were likely to turn to extrajudicial—that is, lawless and violent—means to do so.

While we may not face the same sort of lawlessness today that the leaders of the bar perceived as a threat at the beginning of the twentieth century, the fact remains that too many Americans face their legal problems without a lawyer and do not trust the legal system to treat them fairly if they are not represented by a lawyer. Again, as Hadfield explains, "people who feel as though the rules don't care about them don't care about the rules."[11] Concern over a biased judiciary and a complex, opaque system run by lawyers for lawyers often means that people are choosing not to take their disputes to court. As Rebecca Love Kourlis, founding director of the Institute for the Advancement of the American Legal System, observes: "People do not trust the system because the system is not trustworthy."[12]

One perspective on access to justice is that everyone should have a lawyer at their disposal whenever they have a legal problem. But even in such a world, such full representation would not necessarily address some of the broader problems that face American families when it comes to law and the legal system. I consider the "lawyer-in-every-pot" model (so to speak, of course) like the "thin" version of the rule of law itself: a simplistic, and unrealistic, approach to close the justice gap. This gap is not just a problem of a lack of lawyers. The outsized role that lawyers play in the administration of a complex system has helped to create the justice gap. This situation reflects the rule of lawyers and not necessarily the rule of law.

In contrast, a "thick" version of the rule of law, and access to justice, would ensure some form of access to legal assistance when it is needed and an unbiased and transparent legal system that serves the ends of justice and fairness. There is certainly an access-to-justice crisis in the United States, with at least some of it caused by the high cost of legal services. But it also a result of the complexity of the law and the inaccessibility of the legal system to too many Americans. The thick view on the rule of law provides that it should reflect more than just simple notions of procedural fairness. A legal system that is inaccessible and lacks transparency, where members of the community are unable to utilize it to resolve their disputes—and yet, when they may attempt to do so, they are unable to achieve justice for lack of legal representation—is a system that is failing to realize its institutional role of securing a robust version of the rule of law.

But this systemwide failure has created a market opportunity, and innovation in the delivery of legal services is occurring, fueled by technological change. This innovation holds some promise that we might close the justice gap. It also threatens the legal profession as it currently exists and simultaneously holds out the possibility of a transformation of the market for legal services.

Technological Disruption in the Practice of Law

The high cost and general inaccessibility of legal services, coupled with advances in technology, have led to experimentation with new methods of delivering legal assistance. The emergence of "legal tech" is yet another force challenging the legal profession: the threat that technology may supplant the work of lawyers in significant ways. Technology might help to reduce the justice gap because it makes legal services more efficient and less expensive to deliver. At the same time, it might mean that traditional lawyers and lawyering approaches become obsolete. This potential for obsolescence is another challenge the legal profession faces at present, and it bears some similarities to the fears that gripped bar leaders at the start of the twentieth century: that unskilled, lower-class lawyers might step in to steal clients from established practitioners. The introduction of legal technologies threatens to encroach on the legal profession's traditional client base while extending access to justice, at a lower cost, to many more individuals than are currently being served by the legal profession.

This technology-enhanced form of legal assistance might be seen by some as of lower quality than services provided in a more traditional lawyer-client relationship, where the lawyer provides such services in a way that is customized to the needs of the particular client. When technology-enhanced services are not provided by lawyers, then no formal attorney-client relationship, with all of its ethical protections, is formed between the service provider and the consumer. While some form of legal assistance that is made possible by technological advancements might mean that access to such assistance becomes more widespread, there is a tension between reaching more consumers, ensuring services are of a particular quality, and defending the lawyers' monopoly. Just as the established bar sought to exclude a class of lawyers from the practice at the beginning of the twentieth century, there is great skepticism about and resistance to the introduction of technological advances to the practice of law. But few can doubt that change is coming.

Indeed, technological advances in the delivery of legal services threaten to create what the late Clayton Christensen called the "Innovator's Dilemma": new entrants into a market tend to use technological innovations to target the lower end of the market for a product or service.[13] At first, incumbents ignore these new entrants precisely because they are pursuing customers on that lower end of the market, where incumbents tend to realize lower profit margins. The new entrants are able to iterate and improve their products, slowly gaining market share until the incumbents are priced out of competition by these new players in the market. Much of this phenomenon that Christensen identified occurs in markets that are not working well and where incumbents are offering goods or services that are overpriced and provide more features, at greater expense, than what most customers truly want or need. The new entrants are able to provide the customer more of what they want at a price they can afford, leaving incumbents fighting over a smaller and smaller slice of the market. The legal profession is primed for just this kind of disruption, and if lawyers do not manage the introduction of technological change in a way that provides consumers with the meaningful and effective services they need at an affordable price, then the market monopoly lawyers currently enjoy will soon disappear.

While many lament the influence of technology on our personal and professional lives, the legal profession is no stranger to this debate, and there are both technology evangelists and skeptics: those who believe the legal industry is ripe for "disruption" versus those who are doing their best to try to resist what may be inevitable changes to the practice of law, utilizing the time-tested arguments around unauthorized practice of law and consumer protection when doing so.[14] But these sorts of debates have plagued the profession for over a hundred years, if not from the very outset of the profession. In the late 1800s, lawyers bemoaned the introduction of the telephone and the typewriter into law offices, saying they would interfere with lawyer-client relations and would take the craft out of law practice.[15] At the same time, innovations in law practice management since, say, the 1990s because of technology, which may have been perceived as a threat to professionalism, are now the standard by which we measure competence. When a lawyer could have avoided a problem with the identity or location of an adversary that a "simple Google search" would have resolved, or when reference to an electronic database, accessible with a push of a button, would have alerted the lawyer to the fact that a case on which they relied for their arguments was overturned, the failure of the lawyer to avail themselves of those technologies represents an act of malpractice. It is often the case in the practice of law that technology does not merely displace prior practices; its effective use becomes the standard against which lawyer conduct is measured. Indeed, for the last hundred years, the legal profession has assimilated technology effectively in ways that have advanced the practice of law by making it more efficient and effective.

A simple example of the ways in which technology has totally transformed the practice of law is the method by which lawyers, who must rely on the viability of case precedents they cite in support of their arguments, check whether those cases have not been overturned by higher courts. The service that lawyers tend to use for this purpose is the Shephard's commercial citation service, first created in the last decades of the nineteenth century. This service—which is now a verb—involves *Shephardizing*: determining whether the authorities upon which a lawyer is basing their arguments are still good law, that is, whether they have been reversed or narrowed in some way. For over a century, the Shephard's system involved reams and reams of reports that were constantly updated in all manner of supplements, pocket parts, and loose-leaf versions. The company would churn out the reports, and their loose-leaf advance copies, continuously and for virtually every jurisdiction and every court that issued decisions. The hardest part of researching with the traditional Shephard's citation system was that a lawyer was never really sure whether they had left no stone unturned in conducting their research. Had they checked every pocket part, every newly released loose leaf supplement? Was a law librarian walking around somewhere in the library with a critical new publication from Shephard's on their cart and just had not gotten around to shelving it? Was another lawyer—perhaps their adversary—in the library at this very moment hoarding the newly released Shephard's reports and scouring them for just the information the lawyer needed? The process could take hours, even to track down the results for a single case. Making matters worse, one never really knew, for certain, whether those results were complete and accurate. Today, using electronic databases that have the Shephard's function built into them, typically with the split second it takes to generate a single click on a drop-down menu, a lawyer can get a read on any mention of the case in question. Symbols appearing in the headings of the opinion—which the lawyer checks reflexively with a glance, almost like checking a rearview mirror while driving—indicate whether the case has received negative treatment. This serves as a caution to the lawyer to read on, to explore this case and its progeny, and to refrain from citing it without having done so. This incorporation of the critical Shepard's function into digital technology can save the lawyer hours of work in the library trying to answer a relatively straightforward question. It is now accomplished in seconds, with greater accuracy, and is not dependent on the librarian's reshelving practices.

Much of the technology that the legal profession has incorporated into the practice of law since the broad adoption of desktop computing and the emergence of the internet have made the lawyer's task easier, more efficient, and more rewarding. This is due, in part, to the fact that lawyers can focus on the more important and intellectually stimulating aspects of their practice while allowing automation and innovation to handle at least some of the drudgery—endlessly poring over documents, writing out motions and others pleadings in longhand, and even playing endless games of phone tag with opposing counsel, where an email exchange could resolve a simple issue. Computer-aided research generally has proven radically transformative. It began to take hold in the late 1980s, as services like Westlaw and Lexis completely altered the way in which lawyers conduct legal research by making judicial opinions, statutes, regulations, practice commentaries, and, yes, even the Shephard's service describe above available through digital platforms.

Microsoft founder Bill Gates has said we often overestimate the ways in which technology will change our lives in the next two years and underestimate what it will do in the next ten.[16] The transformation of the practice of law from the late 1980s to the early 2000s was dramatic. But lawyers have been assimilating technology effectively into the practice of law for nearly 150 years. Whether it was the telephone that made long-distance and real-time communication more effective (like the telegraph before it), or machine-learning algorithms that assess and synthesize large volumes of decisions or sort through massive quantities of electronic data, many of the technologies that have been incorporated into law practice over the past century have helped to make the practice of law more efficient and more effective; rarely has it threatened the legal profession's monopoly on the practice of law. Christensen's theory about disruptive innovation would suggest that what has occurred in the relationship between technology and law practice is that these technological innovations have been sustaining rather than disruptive.[17] They helped to make the lawyer's job easier, more competent, and, since lawyers charge by the hour, presumably less expensive when those technologies serve to save the lawyer time in the representation of a client. They have also freed up lawyers to serve more clients. While I will address some of the "B2C" forms of technology-enhanced legal services (those services provided directly to consumers), much of what is happening in the legal tech space is "B2B": companies that are making the lawyer's job easier and more efficient. Such B2B innovations tend to be sustaining rather than disruptive generally, at least for those lawyers who adopt them.

Since the 2010s, though, with the advent of machine learning and artificial intelligence (AI), it is possible that some aspects of these new technologies will, in fact, result in significant disruptions in the practice of law and the displacement of some incumbents as legal assistance, fueled by innovation, begins to reach consumers directly, eliminating the lawyer as intermediary. In the next section, I will discuss the technological change that is occurring with respect to the delivery of legal services. Some of these innovations are more likely to disrupt the profession compared to others. I will both describe the broad categories of innovations that are currently being incorporated into the practice of law and the delivery of legal services and classify them as either sustaining or disruptive innovations. The sustaining innovations I will describe are publicity tech, productivity tech, triage tech, remote tech, and artificial intelligence to assist lawyer decision-making. Innovations that I consider to have potentially disruptive effects are the use of AI to resolve disputes and to provide both information and commoditized services to consumers. While I describe these technologies with a broad brush, and provide a few specific examples of the ways these technologies are being incorporated into the practice of law, I will not attempt to describe the entirety of the growing legal tech industry. I will also try to keep the boosterism that can sometimes accompany the tales of the legal tech sector to a minimum.

What I *will* show, however, is that these innovations tend to serve mostly to sustain contemporary law practice and that fears of a radical disruption to the legal profession are largely overblown with the overwhelming majority of these technological developments. Still, there are ways that at least some of these technologies, when combined, could operate to disrupt the practice of law considerably. What is more, while there are consumer protection concerns with respect to these disruptions, they also offer the promise of promoting a thick version of the rule of law, one that advances the values of true professionalism, access, and inclusion.

Sustaining the Practice of Law and Advancing the Rule of Law

The internet and mobile technologies have transformed nearly every aspect of contemporary life, and the profession of law is not immune from this transformation. What the changes have meant for the profession is considerable. By giving lawyers an easy way to promote their work and their availability through digital tools, the internet has been a boon, helping close the knowledge gap about the availability of legal services and the types of law a particular lawyer might practice. As we know from the previously referenced studies related to the reasons consumers are not securing legal representation to handle their legal problems, many in need of legal services often end up not obtaining such services because they do not know how to find a lawyer. A law firm or legal aid office having a web presence makes consumer search for services a little easier. It is thus hard to see *publicity* tech as anything more than a sustaining technology, as opposed to a disruptive one.

Similarly, new tools are boosting the *productivity* of lawyers. As with digitization of the Shephard's service, so much of law practice is now computerized and digitized, from legal research and file management to electronic discovery, word processing, and electronic filing of pleadings and other court documents. Simple internet searches can also assist lawyers in all aspects of their practice. Jim Sandman, the former president of the Legal Services Corporation, served for decades in the law firm of Arnold & Porter. He explains that, when he left the firm to serve as general counsel to the public school system of the District of Columbia, one of the attorneys working under him came into his office and asked a "FERPA question." Not knowing what FERPA was, Sandman, doing what any good lawyer does in such situations, told the attorney he would get back to her. He quickly turned to Google to understand that FERPA stands for the Federal Educational Rights and Privacy Act, which gave him a head start in researching an answer to the question his colleague had posed to him.[18]

While Google can certainly come in handy for some functions, legal research through electronic databases has become ubiquitous and is a sustaining innovation. Electronic legal research and electronic discovery are both forms of *machine intelligence* but generally does not consist of *machine learning* or true *artificial intelligence*.[19] To the extent that lawyers are using machine intelligence to scan and synthesize large databases of information, it is still machine intelligence and not a version of machine learning. In the legal field, true artificial intelligence—which seeks not just to inform human (that is, lawyer) decision-making and the exercise of professional judgment but also to serve in a predictive capacity—is just beginning to enter the practice of law. With this form of technology, lawyers are using artificial intelligence to scan massive numbers of contracts, to predict judicial outcomes, and to synthesize the outcomes of negotiations to point to the typical range within which certain dollar settlements are reached. The incorporation of AI as a way to augment and inform lawyer decision-making and judgment becomes a sustaining technology if it helps the lawyer do their job better, more efficiently, and more effectively.[20] To the extent that lawyers who are able to incorporate AI into their practice become more skilled at predicting outcomes, make better judgment calls to the benefit of their client, and thereby separate themselves from their adversaries and competitors who do not, clients will tend to flock to such lawyers; thus that technology could become somewhat disruptive, at least when it comes to crowding out the laggards and diminishing their market share. Where AI might become truly disruptive, however, is when it serves to displace lawyers and largely take them out of the delivery of legal services as robot lawyers arrive to eat the lunch of carbon-based ones. I will return to this question shortly.

While technology has certainly transformed the practice of law in recent years, a basic facility with these technologies is essential for the average practitioner, and the ABA amended the commentary related to attorney competence to provide that lawyers are supposed to keep abreast of changes in technology and the ways in which it is impacting the practice of law.[21] Still, I will not spend a lot of time regarding *productivity tech* because there is no question that it has absolutely transformed the practice of law, though, once again, more as a sustaining rather than a disruptive technology. Moreover, in theory, productivity tech should also make the practice of law more affordable, accessible, and inclusive: If technology makes lawyers more efficient, it will cost clients less, perhaps bringing the cost of legal services within the economic reach of more Americans; if technology frees up staff time in nonprofits, it will allow those law offices to serve more clients.

Another technology that has transformed the practice of law since 2020, as explored in chapter 6, is the adoption of *remote technologies* in nearly every aspect of contemporary law practice due to COVID-19 protocols. Moreover, one of the things that the pandemic has taught the profession is that it can not only survive in remote environments but also thrive. Lawyers can live in more affordable places, and have less onerous commutes, while continuing to serve their clients effectively. What is more, for clients who have mobility impairments or who live far from the closest law office, being able to engage in "tele-law" with their legal representative certainly makes accessing services easier. Similarly, many court appearances have become less disruptive to the lives of lawyers and clients alike because of the incorporation of remote tech into judicial processes.

It is certainly possible that law offices will return to the type of approach that dominated law practice prior to the pandemic, limiting the extent to which lawyers work remotely. This is likely to drive legal talent to the offices that are more accommodating to flexible schedules, however. This could certainly have a disruptive effect, particularly if some firms refuse to change with workforce demands. Still, remote tech, like much of the productivity tech described earlier, is here to stay, and it will likely dominate, but not disrupt, the practice of law, mostly because of its widespread adoption and incorporation into the daily work of law offices. As I explained in chapter 6, however, there are certainly challenges that remote tech poses when it comes to improving access to justice because lower-income clients, or those in remote areas, might find it harder to utilize the technology implemented by courts and law offices. But, for now, we can consider this type of technology as also being sustaining, not disrupting.

One more area I will explore and categorize as a sustaining technology is *triage tech*. This technology goes beyond mere publicity about lawyer services. To an extent, publicity tech does get to some of the issues that triage tech addresses, though with much less accuracy. The general practitioner of previous eras, who would take on any case that came their way—from criminal defense to real estate closings and estate matters—is largely disappearing. Today, law firms tend to specialize and can advertise in ways that indicate their areas of expertise. Similarly, nonprofit offices will often post the types of services they offer, and who qualifies for such services, on their websites. A hundred years after the first legal aid offices faced limits on who they could serve, the types of cases they could handle, and the manner in which they could handle them, many nonprofits today face similar challenges. For example, LSC funds are restricted, and grantees cannot serve individuals and families that have incomes 125 percent above the poverty rate. It also prohibits organizations receiving its funding from handling certain class actions, cases over abortion rights, cases involving the rights of prisoners, and those involving undocumented immigrants except in very limited circumstances.[22] For private firms and nonprofits alike, their websites can serve a critical function in ensuring that staff time is dedicated to considering only those prospective clients whose cases are the types of cases the organizations will handle. But publicity through static websites is a blunt instrument, likely creating a lot of "false positives"—that is, clients determining, based on the information they have gathered about the firm or legal aid office, that the lawyers of those entities should be able to represent the client. If poorly designed or unclear, it can create false negatives: clients scanning these sites and determining that the firm cannot help them. As a result of these flawed outcomes, lawyers will either have to still spend time assessing cases, only to determine they are unable to represent the client, or will lose out on potential customers who the lawyer might have been able to secure as a client had the lawyer's website not steered that individual away from the firm. Triage technology can provide a more refined sorting function, helping match clients to the services they need.

In many communities, nonprofit providers have collaborated in the creation of common online portals, like the LawHelp network of websites, through which prospective clients can determine whether they are eligible for nonprofit provider services in their communities. A prospective client can log on to the portal to determine whether there is a nonprofit provider that serves the geographic area where they live, whether they handle the type of case for which the prospective client requires services, and whether they meet the different providers' eligibility criteria. One organization, Briefly, has started to work with nonprofit providers to automate their triage functions, creating systems that ask prospective clients to answer a series of questions to come to the most appropriate outcome for that individual.[23] Such systems can determine whether the person is eligible for the group's services, whether the person presents a problem the group can handle, and even whether the service can identify another provider that might be a more appropriate fit. Briefly built one of these systems for the Houston Volunteer Lawyers group.

Elizabeth Tran, the legal director at Houston Volunteer Lawyers, explains that the idea for creating the legal intake emerged from a realization that the organization could "conserve" its "human resources" by using such a tool and thereby make life easier for those seeking the organization's services, including clients and those who it could not serve.[24] Prior to making the screening tool available to prospective clients, the group held a "physical clinic" that it "would set up on Saturdays and have a 100-plus people stand in line for hours because that was the only process we knew for so long." Tran considered it "archaic" for the organization "to have people stand in line to apply for services" and then to end up turning away 40 or 50 percent of applicants because they presented with a legal problem the group could not help them address or the applicant was ineligible for the group's services (either because their income exceeding the group's limits on who they will serve or the individual was outside the group's geographic catchment area). The group also fielded phone calls and messages from individuals seeking services, which were coming in at roughly a hundred calls each day. At the same time, the group might be able to respond to fifty such calls per day, making it difficult for the organization to respond to these callers in a timely way. Tran felt this system did not "put the client first." But when COVID hit, Tran explains, "it was an opportunity for us to figure out" how to improve the organization's intake through technology, which is when they worked with Briefly to create their screening tool.

In most lawyer triage systems, prospective clients present with different problems; they are asked a series of questions; and, depending on their answer, they are assigned different outcomes: for example, representation by the group, referral to another organization, and/or a conclusion that the prospective client does not qualify for any services that either the organization or the network of entities to which it refers applicants provide.

But here's where the Houston Volunteer Lawyers' intake tool differs from an analog version, and it is deployed with no staff intervention. Once inside the screening tool, the user enters a sort of guided, choose-your-own-adventure exercise. They answer a series of questions and, depending on the answers provided, that consumer is directed to the appropriate outcome for that individual. The screening tool guides the consumer through the process and then identifies the appropriate course of action for that individual. The consumer could receive representation from the organization or referral to another service provider.

They might also learn that they are not eligible for assistance. All of this is done virtually, in minutes, with no visits to an office, lengthy screening interviews, or games of telephone tag.

Tran explained that, prior to the use of the tool, the organization might take three months to get back to an applicant to let them know whether it could provide services to that individual. Now, for those applicants who complete the organization's online screening tool (which takes them about three to four minutes to do), the organization typically is able to cut that response time from three months to three days. More important, though, the screening tool also is able to determine potential eligibility—or ineligibility—for the organization's services or whether an individual should be referred to another organization at an even faster pace. Indeed, for someone to learn they do not qualify for the organization's services, and/or whether there is another organization that might serve them better, takes just three minutes.

The tool is also available in English and Spanish. In addition, individuals who speak other languages can use Google Translate right in the platform so that they can understand the screening questions in their own language. As Marilyn Brown, the organization's director of grants and special projects, explains, in 2022 the organization's two versions of the screening tool (English and Spanish) had more than 50,000 views; roughly 42,000 consumers started their applications on the site; and over 27,000 completed applications, for a greater than 60 percent completion rate across the two sites.[25] Those 27,000 consumers thus had their applications processed through the platform at a cost of relatively little staff time, and they did not have to wait around for months to find out whether they qualified for services from the group.

Such triaging systems, if fine-tuned and smartly designed, can reduce the false positives and false negatives in the search for legal services, saving clients, and lawyers, valuable time and further addressing the knowledge gap, which is a critical component of the access-to-justice crisis itself.

For the most part, the technologies described so far have been largely sustaining innovations, making the practice of law more accessible and more efficient. But there are certainly some technologies that could have a disruptive impact on the practice of law. In many ways, though, as I will explain in the next section, at least some of these disruptive technologies might actually serve to advance the values of professionalism, access, and inclusion. In some ways, then, they may be truly disruptive—but also wholly consistent with what should be the profession's values.

Disruptive Technologies

One area in which AI is currently being deployed in ways that might displace lawyers and disrupt one sector of the legal profession is dispute resolution. One of the core skills that lawyers who handle disputes—from commercial litigation to civil rights and personal injury actions—is their ability to "value" a case: to place a price on what a particular dispute is worth, that is, the award they might be able to secure for their client (or which an adversary might obtain against that client). This skill is an important one for lawyers to possess and drives both lawyer and client decision-making throughout the course of representation: whether the client will retain the lawyer, whether the lawyer will take on the case, whether the case will settle, if the case will be appealed after an adverse ruling, and so on. A lawyer will value a case based on their experience in taking on similar representations, their sense of the strength or novelty of the claims, their knowledge of the judge assigned the case or the viability of claims filed in a particular jurisdiction, the strength of the adversary, or the nature of the harm suffered—the list goes on. An experienced and knowledgeable attorney will have a distinct advantage over one who cannot properly evaluate the case because the attorney less capable of properly pricing a case will generate both false positives and false negatives: that is, they might undervalue a case, thus driving away potential clients unhappy with the assessment, or they might overvalue a case and devote considerable resources to a matter that will end up losing, perhaps costing more in resources to litigate it than the firm might secure through a contingency fee.

While the relative skill of the lawyer in these areas is critical, what if there was an omniscient mind, one that knew the results of every negotiation, the value of every claim, the strength of every argument? What if an algorithm could process all of that information and generate the "true" value of a claim? This omniscient lawyer would be very good at their job. And if they were a judge, they would always generate perfect outcomes. Today, while we cannot say that there is a lawyer or judge out there with this sort of perfect knowledge, automated and online dispute resolution platforms, like Modria, can strive to generate results, relatively quickly and inexpensively, and achieve a modicum of justice, certainly more justice than someone would receive if they chose not to pursue such justice in the first place.[26] If what these sorts of online dispute resolutions systems are doing is vindicating rights that would otherwise go unrealized and unprotected, they represent progress. To the extent participants in such systems are achieving some recourse, where they would get none otherwise, that, too, represents a benefit to the use of such systems. It is not exactly disruptive in terms of the legal profession if the participant would not otherwise retain a lawyer to pursue their claim; it does further the ends of justice, however, because it is advancing the rule of law. When participants who would otherwise hire a lawyer to pursue their claim can access such a system without a lawyer, this type of innovation can be disruptive. At the same time, if participants are channeled into zombie systems that do not provide meaningful recourse for significant violations of rights, then such "innovations" do not represent progress and are merely extractive, providing the appearance of justice while shielding lawlessness from accountability.[27]

Other potentially disruptive technologies that law offices use for the purposes of publicizing their work—like websites and social media—often serve another purpose: to offer information to the public not about their services (which they also do) but about the law itself; they can offer consumers an opportunity to address legal needs without having to pay a lawyer to do so. Lawyers often create and make available through publicly available channels basic know-your-rights informational guides. These sources can provide clients, prospective clients, and the community in general critical guidance about changes in the law; the contours of rights and responsibilities; and the resources that might be available, either through the office creating the guide or other sources. These guides help users navigate important legal issues they might face with minimal interventions by the author of the guides.

For lawyers in private firms, making these resources available, even at no charge, can serve to establish and publicize their expertise in an area of law. In turn, by marketing that expertise, the hope is often that it will lead prospective clients to find the information and then reach out to the firm precisely because of their apparent knowledge in a particular area of law. Some firms will even make information available to already existing clients, perhaps in a password-protected corner of their website, simply to save the client from having to pay the firm for routine advice that the lawyers might prefer not to have to repeat to clients time and again. Clients can appreciate having access to this information, a benefit of being represented by the firm, without having to pay counsel for the time it would otherwise take for the lawyer to explain the issue to the client. Making these resources available becomes a loss leader for these firms, that is, an expenditure of resources to draw in customers who would pay for the firm's other services. Carolyn Elefant has created just these sorts of resources. For roughly twenty years, she has operated a popular blog that explores the challenges that solo practitioners and small firms face in today's legal services market, but she says this has not been the source of many referrals. Instead, several years ago, she created a guide to help explain landowner rights in energy pipeline disputes and shared it at no cost as an ebook.[28] According to Elefant, this book, which has circulated widely, has generated millions of dollars of revenue for her practice from clients who came to her because the guide was shared with them.[29]

In addition, nonprofit law offices—never at a loss for clients—often generate legal information about the types of issues that are the focus of their work and make it publicly available to members of the community, simply because those offices do not have the resources to provide assistance to every member of the community who requires representation. Because of this, the use of these know-your-rights guides serves at least two goals: They provide some guidance to those community members the office would not otherwise be able to serve due to funding constrains; and they enable community members, even without the benefit of formal legal representation, to address and possibly even prevent some relatively minor legal problems from becoming much worse. For nonprofit providers, the provision of this type of service is not new. In fact, for decades, legal aid offices and other public interest organizations have produced analog pamphlets and fact sheets, conducted live community training sessions, and set up tables at courthouses to provide assistance to the community—even where those offices could not provide a particular individual with full and direct representation. What is different now is that these resources have been digitized and made more widely available. For nonprofit providers that make this type of information available to the community, it is not to lure more clients to the office, which is how private practitioners might use this tactic, but rather to try to reduce the number of prospective clients who need the office's services. Whether law offices are using information tech to increase or reduce the number of clients they ultimately represent, in both of these modes the technology is a sustaining innovation, because it helps firms either recruit more clients or bring resources to community members who might not otherwise receive any.

It is certainly possible that, if the information the consumer receives is so complete and comprehensive that it renders the lawyer obsolete, this technology could serve as a disruptive technology. While it is conceivable that these sorts of passive resources might provide sufficient information to the user to navigate a complex legal problem, what is more likely is that this mode of service delivery does not necessarily provide sufficient information and guidance so that the consumer can fully resolve that problem. The limits of information tech are likely a constraint imposed by the technology itself. Outward-facing, passive, and noninteractive resources are less likely to truly assist a consumer deal with a complex legal problem. Such complex issues require more than simple and static resources and more than one form of technology. Such technological capacity might seem like something out of *Star Trek: The Next Generation*, where Captain Jean-Luc Piccard asks the "computer" to evaluate some complex problem. The reality is, some companies and nonprofits are beginning to combine several of these technologies to provide more comprehensive and responsive services, at least to a degree, as I explain below.

The final, and most intriguing, development in legal tech is not really one technology but can be seen in the fact that many of the previous technologies, taken together, are producing a mode of service delivery that does pose the greatest threat to the practice of law: that is, legal assistance, aided by technology, that provides some form of service to consumers in a manner that is highly accessible and offered at a much lower cost than traditional legal services. In this area, providers are offering highly commoditized services to clients that turn the relationship between service and client on its head: they match the service to the client rather than the client to the service. In the traditional mode of legal services delivery, lawyers offer what Richard Susskind calls "bespoke" services: specialized services, like the custom tailors on Saville Row, catered to the needs of each client.[30] Those services are designed based on the needs of a particular client after the lawyer assesses the client's needs and crafts a plan for the representation in light of those needs. In the commoditized model, the product leads. The provider creates the product not with a particular client in mind but with a particular legal need in mind. The product is made available, and it is the customer who is assessed for whether they fit the product and not the other way around. These products function to triage clients, that is, to determine their propriety for the service and not the reverse. As Henry Ford once said, "Any customer can have a car painted any colour that he wants so long as it is black."[31]

The technology that makes this all possible is not just a single technology but a range of the technologies described here: publicity tech, triage tech, productivity tech, and AI (including generative AI), wherein all the tech works together. While there are upfront costs in setting these technologies in motion, once those systems are in place, the service-delivery machine can work to carry out all the functions to generate the results for customers whose needs are met by the technology. Critically, the triage function serves as a sort of gatekeeper: It does not just channel customers into particular services that the provider offers; it also determines whether those services are appropriate for that customer. In other words, the customer does not drive the delivery of services. The services offered dictate who the right customers are for those services. LegalZoom is one of these providers, probably the dominant one at present, that is delivering services in this fashion.[32] The company has determined that there are discrete areas in which its commoditized services are appropriate to deliver to their customers and at a deeply discounted rate when compared to what those services would cost in the open market. LegalZoom customers can create simple business corporations, prepare basic estate planning documents, and even secure rudimentary protections for intellectual property, all through a largely digital interface. The customer provides basic information through the company's website, and, assuming LegalZoom's products meet that customer's needs, the site generates the artifacts necessary to do so, whether those are corporate documents, wills, or something else. Think of a computerized tax service like TurboTax: the customer answers a series of questions and the technology generates a product tailored, to a degree, to the customer's needs. And all of this is done at a fraction of what a traditional legal services provider would charge. When a potential customer's needs are outside the categories of services that LegalZoom offers, or the simple products the company's interface can generate are not appropriate for the nature or complexity of the customer's needs, LegalZoom collaborates with licensed lawyers that the customer can retain to assist them by providing more customized services in a traditional attorney-client relationship and at more customary prices.

If Christensen's theories of disruptive innovation are accurate, the cumulative effect of some of these types of services might be that the livelihoods of some solo practitioners and small firms—those that might operate on the lower end of the legal services market to begin with— might be at the most risk from disruptive innovation. But advances in technology are such that the types of innovations that make service delivery less expensive, and might have threatened the business of small firms and solo practitioners when they first came to the market, are now more readily available even to those lawyers who might not have had the resources just a few years ago to set up their own competing systems. Indeed, as Carolyn Elefant explains, "it would have cost a lawyer several hundred thousand dollars to set up a competing site" to a company like LegalZoom, "and now you could set it up for a few thousand dollars at most, using out-of-the-box software."

This type of innovation is also happening in the nonprofit space. Pro Bono Net has been at the forefront of the delivery of legal information and navigational assistance through technology for nearly thirty years. Mark O'Brien, one of its founders and current executive director, got his start in the law when he took a position at the law firm Davis Polk in the early 1990s. O'Brien, who is not a lawyer, worked as a paralegal in order to support his desire to break into acting.[33] At the time, few of the big firms had attorneys and other staff dedicated exclusively to coordinating their pro bono efforts. After some time, a crisis emerged: the running aground of a ship in New York Harbor, the *Golden Venture*, with hundreds of immigrants who had been illegally trafficked into the United States. O'Brien was frustrated that the firms were not coordinating their efforts, had no mechanisms for taking the provision of pro bono services to scale, and had limited success in supporting nonprofit legal providers in a cross-institutional way. For O'Brien, there was a "complete misalignment of expertise, knowledge, and incentives" and an inability to take training and service delivery to scale. This was reflected as well in the failure to harness technology to improve such service delivery. As O'Brien explains, the loose network of lawyers serving the clients in need of immigration services would circulate "fax chain letters" that could be used in briefs, but they all had to be typed out again and again in every case. There was also no central repository for recruiting lawyers to work on representing the immigrants, many of whom had been relocated by immigration authorities throughout the country to await deportation proceedings.

Partly as a response to the frustration O'Brien felt about the massive gaps in services and the lack of coordination in the field, he and his colleague Michael Hercz, a lawyer at White & Case, created Pro Bono Net, which started by serving as a sort of matchmaker between nonprofit organizations and for-profit firms to connect pro bono services to the needs of low-income clients. Nearly thirty years later, it is now the nation's leading provider of digital legal information, do-it-yourself court forms, and direct services to consumers in need of legal guidance or referrals. These services are often provided through the LawHelp network mentioned previously, a collection of state-specific websites that help individuals find nonprofit legal services in their state as well as information about their rights. It also operates LawHelp Interactive, which enables individuals to create their own legal documents in a range of cases. For O'Brien, the work of Pro Bono Net is not to use technology for technology's sake; it is a means to an end. That end is "legal empowerment," which involves building capacity among and between wide-ranging networks so that organizations and individuals can work toward meaningful change and social justice. Pro Bono Net does this by working with partners to share information, scale up resources and knowledge, and provide a platform through which organizations and individuals can protect and advance their rights, all within a nonprofit, and technology-enabled, framework. And the Pro Bono Net constellation of sites has served millions of consumers in its decades of operation.

Another organization that uses technology to share information with consumers to assist them in vindicating their rights is JustFix. The Just-

Fix website contains information and tools for tenants in New York City to enable them to secure repairs from their landlords. It provides information that lays out the laws concerning housing standards governing residential tenancies in New York City, provides easy-to-use templates that tenants can use to inform their landlords about their legal obligations, and also offers a guide to tenants explaining how they can file actions in the local housing court in the event a landlord is not complying with the law. While taking a landlord to court can be an intimidating and costly process for a low-income or working-poor tenant who would have to miss several days of work to do so, JustFix provides an easy-to-use interface that might help tenants avoid having to take their landlords to court if they are aware of their rights and are able to complain to their landlord about violations of the law directly. By putting knowledge and resources in the hands of tenants, it might end up saving a lawyer time and effort down the road in having to litigate issues over housing repairs. When a landlord's obligations to repair a housing condition is triggered only by the tenant giving notice to the landlord about such a condition, and an informal oral communication to a member of the maintenance staff can be ignored (or denied having been received), having a formal mechanism through which a tenant can relay and document complaints about housing conditions, which Just-Fix provides, is an effective way to protect tenant rights. It also stands a better chance of eliciting a positive response from a landlord who can address the problem when it first arises. Such early intervention in a housing problem, which is also a legal problem, can prevent it from getting worse: today's leaky pipe can be tomorrow's collapsed ceiling. A child in the home might have asthma, and asthma triggers, like a rodent infestation, might exist in the home. If allowed to fester and worsen, they could lead to a medical crisis. Giving tenants the tools to complain to landlords in a fashion that is informed by those tenants' legal rights can help prevent the physical—and the legal—problems from getting worse. As Sateesh Nori, a former eviction defense lawyer who is the executive director of JustFix, explains, the organization's resources provides tenants with "easy answers now before that leak becomes a giant hole in the winter."[34]

For many tenants, they might not even realize that their housing problem is actually a legal problem. But by helping tenants to see it that way, it can empower them and motivate them to take action. For Nori, a tenant might know that something is wrong: "You rented an apartment and there shouldn't be a hole in your ceiling; you know that there shouldn't be a mouse on your baby's crib; you know it shouldn't be 58 degrees in the middle of winter in your bedroom." But the tenant might not know that these conditions constitute violations of the law or that tenants have a means of vindicating their legal rights. For tenants who might be intimidated by going to court once they frame their situation as a legal problem, JustFix helps them assert their rights without having to resort to court. For JustFix, this is seen as a "marketing problem." Tenants know things are not right, but if they can frame their problem as affecting their legal rights, it might motivate them to take action.

JustFix's resources were particularly helpful during the darkest days of the pandemic. Many court functions were shut down; still, the only way to take one's landlord to court was to travel by public transportation and wait in line to file the case in court, so, as Nori explains, a tenant had to "choose between your health and your housing conditions." What is more, since so many court functions were suspended because of the pandemic, tenants had to "get through the gatekeeper literally"—the court officer standing in front of the courts—to convince them to let the tenant in to file their court case. By putting early-intervention resources at the disposal of tenants, JustFix helps to reduce the risk that a relatively minor problem does not turn into a full-blown crisis, requiring the tenant to move out and lose their home if they cannot get their landlord to act to address the conditions in the home in a timely fashion.

Returning to the work of Briefly, another area where that company is excelling is in the creation of informational resources about the law that can help inform nonlawyers about their legal obligations. Unlike with LegalZoom, which is B2C, a great deal of Briefly's services are B2B. It delivers "white label" resources for lawyers to use in their practice. They develop engaging and beautifully designed videos that lawyers can then customize and provide to clients and the community alike as they see fit. These may include a training video that a firm might provide to its clients so that their lower-level managers and salespeople might learn the basics of contracting or employment law, or one that can work as a primer on data privacy or cybersecurity issues. The law firms can provide these services to their clients as a way to offer some basic services, at a very low cost, and then have their clients pay them for more complicated issues. One consortium on nonprofit providers collaborated to create a video that they made available to the public that gave basic information about how housing courts in a broad region of upstate New York were handling residential evictions under COVID-19 protocols and the various eviction moratoria that issued from different government agencies. While every local jurisdiction had slightly different information to provide to the residents of those areas, the majority of the material in the videos Briefly produced was the same. It then trained the legal staff of the different organizations to customize the content of the videos to cater to local conditions.

When a law firm or legal services office creates the algorithms, content, and interfaces necessary to provide these digitized, commoditized services; preserves all client confidences and refrains from engaging in conflicted representation; provides competence services; and is held accountable should those services amount to malpractice, the delivery of commoditized legal services should raise no ethical concerns when it comes to the quality or manner of the service provision. At the same time, this will pose a threat to traditional providers, especially if the firm offers those services at a much lower cost than its competitors, and could, given the nature of the service provision, generate a greater volume of service than traditional providers. Such innovative providers would likely disrupt the legal industry, and there could be little the profession as whole could do to stop them.

The issue with commoditized services is that they are not always provided under the rules governing the legal profession. As some providers in this space will argue, particularly for-profit providers, they are not actually engaged in the practice of law. And if they are not engaged in the formal practice of law, then they are not subject to the rules that govern that practice. If truly outside the practice of law, and threatening to disrupt that practice nonetheless, it is in this space—where a range of new technologies comes together to deliver a product that looks a lot like legal services—that the traditional practice of law faces its greatest threat, and this is why I have included technological innovation as one of the six forces likely to impact the practice of law in the near future and for the long term. Whether or not technology truly disrupts the practice of law is really a less important question than whether these innovations advance some of the larger values for which the profession is supposed to stand, the most important of which in this context is access to justice. The only reason the profession is ripe for this type of disruption is because of the yawning justice gap. The market for legal services is clearly broken. It is certainly possible that technology could address the distortions in the legal services market simply by destroying it. Would such a process do more harm than good? In the following discussion, I will try to engage with some of the questions the technology-enhanced commoditization of legal services raises as a way to scope out the nature of the threat, the benefits that this commoditization may generate for consumers, and the potential downsides of this disruption. I will deploy the values-based framework that I have used throughout this book to determine if the move toward technology-enhanced legal services will help fulfill, or undermine, these values.

Technology, Access to Justice, and the Values-Based Approach

A values-based approach to determining the proper way to address these two forces confronting the American legal profession—the access-to-justice crisis and the ways in which technology might transform the practice of law—begins with questions of institutional fit and institutional purposes. What is more, when we see the access-to-justice and legal technology challenges through the lens of what I have described as the core values of the profession—professionalism, access, and inclusion—a sense of the path forward to address these challenges emerges.

First, resolving the access-to-justice crisis should be a central imperative of the profession. The justice gap raises significant professionalism concerns on several levels. There is a clear need to ensure that all Americans have the capacity to participate in the legal system to the extent necessary to defend their rights. The American system of justice is adversarial in nature, and it requires some equivalency in terms of legal acumen for the parties operating within that system to ensure it works the way it is supposed to—that is, that it provides fair procedures, utilized effectively by the parties, in the pursuit of a just result. This presupposes, as a critical element of that system, that the parties pressing their interests have a basic level of competence to operate within that system. When that competence is not met, the edifice and logic of the adversarial system itself falls. Thus, it is not difficult to connect the institutional characteristic of the legal system—its very adversarial nature—to its institutional value of competence within that system that creates the access-to-justice imperative.

The other core institutional characteristic of this legal system—let alone its version of democracy itself—is the notion of the rule of law that is supposed to be at the heart of American traditions and history. A willingness to resort to the resolution of disputes through the legal system and to accept the outcomes of those disputes, even when unfavorable, is a core element of the rule of law. When an individual sees that the system does not treat them fairly, that the system is corrupt, or that access to that system is not available to the individual, it is then that they either seek redress through extralegal means, in defiance of and disregard for the rule of law, or they simply withdraw from the system, disengaging from the processes that are supposed to resolve disputes and provide meaningful recourse for the resolution of those disputes. When the rule of law is absent, the community takes matters into its own hands. When we deny access to justice, we not only undermine the rule of law; we also undermine faith in the legal system and drive the community toward lawlessness. And a lawless community is a community that does not need lawyers. What is more, if we accept that justice delayed is justice denied, what is justice never pursued?

Turning to the core professional value of inclusion, in the context of addressing the access-to-justice crisis and the expansion of technology in the practice of law, inclusion takes on at least two meanings. The first, which echoes some of the rule-of-law values described above, looks at the notion of meaningful access to the legal system as an imperative to ensure the system does not deny every American the ability to resolve their disputes through it. By ensuring access to justice, the legal profession ensures that the legal system itself is inclusive, that all are treated equally before the law, and that all can trust that system as a source for resolving their disputes in a fair way.

Then there is the second question regarding inclusion, one that assesses the institutional characteristics of the profession using the typology described in chapter 5: Is the profession an extractive or nonextractive institution itself? When viewing the forces of access and technology through this lens, we can see that the profession exploits its monopoly to advance its own ends by taking advantage of the scarcity of representation to drive up its own value at the expense of clients. When it does so, it is operating in an extractive way. When the asymmetry of resources is exploited by the represented against the unrepresented, that may generate short-term gain for that party; it also has potential long-term and catastrophic consequences. That sort of short-term gain, for clients and their lawyers alike, with adverse, long-term consequences is not just unsustainable; it also qualifies such behavior as extractive and exploitative. Extractive systems are those that advantage the haves at the expense of the have-nots. The significant justice gap exists in the United States by virtue of the monopoly the legal profession enjoys means that the profession fails to operate as an inclusive institution.

If one could wave a magic wand and provide full representation for every American in every situation where they have a legal need, then there would be no access-to-justice crisis. That is unlikely to happen anytime soon, nor, do I believe, is it necessary. Professionalism in this context requires that the profession does not operate in a way that undermines the proper functioning of the system by making the goal of full participation in the legal system unattainable. As we know from some of the analysis of the justice gap, it exists within the United States for several reasons, one of the most important of which is the high cost of legal services. The profession will say that the high cost of legal services is at least partly due to the trouble and expense it takes to obtain a law degree: roughly three years of the lawyer's life and nearly $200,000 in tuition for law school alone, not to mention the time and expense necessary to obtain an undergraduate degree. For many lawyers, there are additional costs associated with operating a law office, including hiring support staff and paying for space, overhead, and the like. The monopoly on the ability to provide legal assistance undoubtedly drives the cost of legal services higher. That is how monopolies work. But with the privilege of maintaining that monopoly comes a responsibility to ensure that everyone should have access to the services the profession provides—or at least to the services that serve the ends of the thick version of the rule of law. The fit between the monopoly and the ends that monopoly should serve must outweigh its costs. When the monopoly undermines access to the services itself, it is no more than a cartel. It is possible that this monopoly serves the value of professionalism, or at least a narrow vision of it, by ensuring competent legal services. But to the extent it creates a barrier to all Americans having meaningful access to legal representation to meet their legal needs, it undermines the other values of access and inclusion at the same time.

Certainly, there are instances where there is no substitute for a lawyer to provide full services to a client (for example, when they are facing criminal charges, the loss of a home or custody of a child, or deportation). In some of these settings, particularly in the criminal context, the right to counsel is, for the most part, secured. In others, though, there is no doubt that consumers require legal representation, by a competent lawyer, to protect their rights fully. In these situations, an increase in funding for civil legal assistance for low-income people is an imperative, and we see some campaigns in cities throughout the United States having some success in securing the right to counsel in particular areas of law, most notably in the eviction context; in large cities like New York and Philadelphia, local governments have funded a right to counsel in that setting.[35] There are certainly situations in which full legal services are required—full stop—and the extent to which any American is going without legal assistance in those situations where this type of service is needed means that the legal profession is not playing the role it must play. When millions of Americans face these types of legal problems without a lawyer, there is an unquestioned need to fill that gap, and there may be no other way to do so than to provide adequate funding to legal services to achieve that goal.

Still, at present, only Americans who earn less than 125 percent of the poverty rate qualify for LSC-funded services. While some legal services funding from foundations or alternative government sources might permit grantees to provide services to those making more than this amount, there is still a large percentage of Americans who do not earn so little that they qualify for legal services from nonprofit providers or make so much that they can afford to pay a lawyer. Thus, even with full funding to meet the need of families eligible for nonprofit providers, there will still be millions of American families in the gap between qualifying for such services and being able to afford a lawyer. Some other interventions are needed, then, to close the justice gap for anyone who cannot otherwise afford a lawyer.

But even a thick version of the rule of law—one that guarantees more than formal procedural justice—does not necessarily require that every dispute requires a lawyer to be paid the cost of full representation to resolve it. I will go out on a limb and state that cost is one of the main drivers of the justice gap, if not the main cause. If that is the case, are there ways to lower the cost of ensuring that every American possesses the legal competence necessary to navigate the legal thicket without necessarily providing them with a lawyer whenever they face a common legal problem? I believe that there are a number of ways to accomplish this goal. Once again, the purpose of the American legal profession is to support the thick version of the rule of law within a constitutional, participatory, multiracial democracy where the legal system operates on an adversary model. If we begin with that premise, the imperative of securing access to justice for all Americans should become clear. The best way to do that within existing financial constraints is to reimagine what access to justice means and when appropriate, affordable, effective, and accessible legal interventions, and by whom, can secure such access. Such a reimagining is likely to change the role of lawyers in the delivery of legal services.

Before I describe these strategies, let me provide two important caveats. First, I will mostly identify the ways those committed to achieving full access to justice will utilize some of the technologies described above as disruptive technologies. I take it as a given that, in the right hands, sustaining technologies and capacities can delivery legal services in an efficient and effective way. Classified as such, they can help make the lawyer's efforts go farther and faster, thereby serving more clients and, presumably, serving them better. To the extent they can advance the cause of closing the justice gap (and they can), we should utilize them aggressively. Second, to the extent lawyers are engaged in the provision of all of these different modes of service delivery, questions of professionalism—that is, issues of competence, diligence, and accountability—are answered. When a lawyer provides services through these modes, we should have no concerns that the consumers receiving these services are getting less than is needed and that the lawyer is providing them in a professional manner. The lawyer should also have the wisdom and judgment to know when these less-than-full services are appropriate in any given situation. What follows, then, is a discussion of the extent to which the more disruptive technologies can actually be harnessed to change the legal profession and the delivery of legal services to better attain the ideal of full access to justice. An approach geared toward achieving that end would involve the following measures.

Simplified Legal Problems and Dispute Resolution Mechanisms

One way to promote greater engagement with the legal systems and to ensure many consumers are able to navigate those systems on their own is to simplify laws and procedures to such a degree that most consumers can understand their rights and how to protect them within those systems. To do so will require a commitment on the part of legislatures, courts, and the legal profession to create such systems that are easier to navigate, even if that means there will be less of a need for lawyers to operate within them. There will always be the complex case or problem that requires a more complex solution, but the lack of transparency in legal systems, and the inability of consumers to navigate them on their own, is a significant barrier to achieving meaningful access to such systems without full legal representation. To achieve support for such efforts, one could imagine settings where the parties to contracts or legal relationships accept predesigned agreements that conform to certain simple requirements. When such agreements are adopted, it is easier to unwind them or to enforce them, and their use would offer the parties some degree of protection against more complicated challenges. In the mortgage context, regulators have created what are called "qualified mortgages" that have fewer riskier features and afford all parties to the mortgage a degree of protection from them because such features are omitted.[36] One could see approaches like this expanded into other areas to simplify other legal relationships, to guard against common problems, and to give the parties some comfort that their rights are adequately protected.

Similarly, we could certainly simplify court procedures more generally, but legal systems could also look to alternative dispute resolution mechanisms to fast-track the most common and simplest disputes that might be more easily resolved rather than having the parties endure the cost, expense, and time associated with full judicial resolution. One could imagine the development of more exchanges, like the Modria platform, through which parties could submit their disputes for resolution through something resembling an online bidding process that is automated to achieve a resolution of the dispute. For simple disputes over money, like small-claims matters, the parties could weigh the perceived value of their claim against the cost and expense of resolving the matter through complex and costly judicial processes. At some point, through such online bidding, the parties might find a point of settlement that is acceptable. If not, the matter can always be litigated when that system does not generate a resolution acceptable to both sides. There are certainly cases that should not go through such exchanges given their complexity or what is at stake, but it is possible that we might resolve at least some disputes over simple matters that might come down to straightforward questions of dollars and cents, like claims over lost luggage, canceled flights, damaged goods, or the cost of home repairs, through such online exchanges. While creating exchanges like this might not have been possible a decade ago, the technology exists to create such bidding systems today, which might mean that fewer disputes are resolved through the courts or that consumers choose to pursue claims they might not prosecute if they had to go to court to do so.

Improved Legal Information Delivery Systems

There is no question that technology can bring critical legal resources to those who might otherwise not have access to them, either because such services are easier to secure than a traditional legal services provider or are simply more affordable. When individuals can glean some information from a website or other technology-based system that enables them to protect their rights or resolve disputes they have with others in an effective and efficient way, it promotes the values of access and inclusion. To the extent that the information provided to the individual is accurate and assists the individual in navigating through their legal issue in a competent fashion, the only threat to the legal *profession* is that this service might undermine the lawyer monopoly. If neither the individual nor the community is harmed by the availability of such information, and that individual receives appropriate guidance to manage their legal problem effectively, this use of technology promotes both inclusion and access and does not undermine professionalism itself.

Increase the Delivery of Limited-Scope Services

Another way to streamline the delivery of legal services is through providing targeted and brief services in a timely fashion that can reduce the need for full service representation at a later date because smaller, less complex legal problems are addressed, do not fester, and do not develop into a situation requiring more comprehensive—that is, full-service—representation. A common practice in many of the legal services offices in which I have worked is to assist clients only when their problem becomes one that requires full legal assistance. For example, it is routine in many legal aid offices that handle cases involving public assistance benefits to tell the prospective client to apply on their own and to take the case as far as they can. If they are denied, they can apply for a full hearing to review the denial before an administrative law judge and try to obtain legal assistance at that juncture. This approach makes some sense. It is certainly possible that the prospective client might succeed in their application by attempting to apply on their own, never needing legal assistance for any review of a denial. One could imagine, however, that effective brief advice, at the beginning of the application process, might actually make that consumer's application more likely to succeed or could prevent the applicant from making what might be a damning admission that would doom their application from the outset. This sort of just-in-time/just-enough services—that is, targeted, timely, and effective legal assistance at the right time and in the right amount—might actually help prevent the need for full intervention later in the process.

Utilize More Effective Triage Systems to Identify Individuals Appropriate for Such Service

Finding an ideal response—when is the right time to provide assistance, how much assistance to provide, and to whom to provide it—will require appropriate triaging systems, which, as we see from the example from the Houston pro bono group, technology can help to provide. Through technology, effective triage systems—coupled with timely, effective advice, also delivered through technology-based platforms—can often address problems before they turn into full-blown crises. Prospective clients in these situations have problems that they want to solve, and not every problem requires a lawyer to address it. In business school, it is common to trot out the story, apocryphal as it might be, that the owner of a chain of hardware stores once asked their staff how the company might market a quarter-inch drill. After hearing some ideas and rejecting them, the owner communicated that what the customers wanted was not a quarter-inch drill, per se, but a quarter-inch hole and that the drill was just a means to that end.[37] Here, Clayton Christensen called this the "job to be done" by a particular product or service.[38] For many clients, the job to be done is not "get a lawyer"; it is "resolve my legal problem." Indeed, as ASAP's Swapna Reddy points out, even though the organization supports a network of hundreds of thousands of asylum-seekers, handles inquiries from the members utilizing that network, and lets those members shape the services ASAP provides, she cannot remember a single instance where those members said that what they needed was a lawyer.[39] Many said they wanted help resolving issues with their asylum applications, but not once had anyone said what they really needed was a lawyer.

If the legal profession assumes the job-to-be-done approach, it will embrace strategies that work to resolve the legal needs of the communities they serve and not think that the only way to address those needs is the provision of full representation at every turn. I will admit that it is common for those in the nonprofit legal services community to resist efforts to supply anything less than full-service representation in every case. Even though it is unlikely that the funding to achieve that will ever be forthcoming, there is a fear that attention on anything less than full-service representation will divert resources that might otherwise go to that type of assistance; we cannot let the perfect be the enemy of the good, however, and must accept that there are broader values at stake than achieving the goal of simply securing full-service representation in every case. Those broader goals can be served by viewing the delivery of legal services as existing on a continuum, and they can be achieved through many different modes and tactics. It is also important to recognize that the provision of legal services for a few while many go without such services has extractive qualities in and of itself.

Expand and Strengthen Commoditization

A combination of simpler processes, better information delivery systems, and improved triaging platforms to get the right information to the right person at the right time can also, when combined, lead to greater commoditization of legal services: the delivery of out-of-the-box, one-size-fits-many solutions. For at least some legal needs, basic, straightforward services can meet the standard of competence by the delivery of appropriate services in a timely manner. It is inevitable that, unlike with some of the previously mentioned strategies for addressing legal needs, the delivery of commoditized services will result in allegations that such services, when they are not provided by lawyers, are subject to the charge that the entity providing them is engaged in the unauthorized practice of law.

According to the ABA's Model Rules, it is unethical for a lawyer to practice law in a jurisdiction where they are not admitted to practice.[40] Since the rules of professional ethics apply only to lawyers, they do not apply to nonlawyers: that is, when a nonlawyer holds themselves out as a lawyer, or even provides services that constitute the practice of law, those nonlawyers do not violate the rules of professional ethics because those rules do not apply to them. Instead, when nonlawyers engage in the practice of law, they are often violating the substantive law of the jurisdiction in which they are acting.

The question of whether the provision of some form of "law-like" guidance represents the practice of law will depend on the nature of those services themselves. In one case that emerged prior to the digital era, *New York County Lawyers' Association v. Dacey*,[41] the New York Court of Appeals considered whether the publication of a book authored by a nonlawyer that provided guidance to consumers regarding estate planning constituted the unauthorized practice of law. New York's highest court endorsed the dissenting opinion of the lower appellate court, which concluded that the guidance provided in the book was not specifically tailored to the needs of any particular person; as a result, the defendant was not engaged in the unauthorized practice of law.[42] Decided before the digital age (though one court has recently discussed its holding at some length),[43] the line that the *Dacey* court drew between authorized services and unauthorized ones is still viable: explaining the law to laypeople in general terms to empower them to represent themselves without providing information tailored to the particularized needs of any individual does not constitute the unauthorized practice of law. At the same time, providing specific guidance to assist an individual to navigate through their particular situation does.

When properly licensed lawyers provide commoditized services in any given context, there is no unauthorized practice issue. If such commoditized services are not provided by a lawyer, the key question then becomes: Do they constitute the practice of law? The challenge, then, for those nonlawyers seeking to provide commoditized services is ensuring that they do not cross the line drawn by the court in *Dacey*. In many contexts, a service can offer simple legal strategies to the consumer that enable them to determine, for themselves, whether a particular approach fits their situation. The consumer would obviously need to have some degree of guidance related to the appropriate situation where a particular piece of legal advice can satisfy that individual's legal needs. Here is where the triage platforms described above can be utilized: a consumer could answer a few simple questions to determine whether some guidance is appropriate in their situation. If they do not answer the questions in such a way that suggests that limited guidance is proper for them, they will be informed of that fact through that system. Pro Bono Net operates a highly effective tool for helping immigrants navigate the process for becoming a citizen in the United States. This platform, Citizenshipworks, guides a user through the process, and the program is constantly assessing whether the individual has a case that is more complicated than the platform can handle, or it presents a legal wrinkle that the consumer will need a lawyer to hammer out on their behalf.[44] For many users of Citizenshipworks, however, the platform provides them with enough guidance to enable them to complete the process successfully, without the need for a lawyer.

Commoditized services, on their own, can certainly provide a particular consumer sufficient information for them to address their legal situation where that situation is straightforward and lacks the type of complexity that requires full-service legal representation. When combined with appropriate triage tools, a provider of commoditized services can direct them to those who can resolve their legal problem in an appropriate way, to address the consumer's job to be done.

Expand Experimentation

Local authorities with responsibility for overseeing the operation of the legal profession within their respective jurisdictions are critical to the deployment of these sorts of strategies. They must permit a degree of experimentation that will examine the value of different innovations, and identify the risks that might be associated with them, in real time. Some states have loosened some restrictions on particular types of actors, particularly in housing cases and some family matters, including Arizona, Minnesota, Oregon, and Utah.[45] Washington State permitted some nonlawyers to provide legal services in the housing context but has since suspended the program.[46] But what is more exciting is where states have adopted what are known as regulatory "sandboxes," which are designed to permit innovation and loosen certain restrictions to permit experimentation with different service-delivery models and techniques. This might include allowing advocates without a law license to provide some services or the expanded use of what is sometimes called "unbundled" legal services, where assistance is offered regarding one aspect of a consumer's case, like helping to negotiate a settlement.[47] It does not entail a commitment on the part of the advocate to handle all aspects of the matter and permits intervention at a critical point in the legal services continuum. Both Arizona and Utah have embraced such an approach and are welcoming new business models and tactics for improving access to justice that traditional ethics rules might otherwise prohibit.[48] More experimentation is needed in this area, and more jurisdictions should adopt this approach.

One of the benefits of federalism in the context of regulating the legal profession is that, for the most part, states are the first line of defense in terms of overseeing the legal profession. As a result, they can serve as laboratories for assessing the extent to which new types of service-delivery models and tactics can further advance the goals of professionalism, access, and inclusion. As Deborah Enix-Ross explains, the ABA favors jurisdictions deciding what is right for them: "We know that there is a justice gap, and we know that there needs to be creative ways to help make sure that we don't widen the gap and, in fact, close that gap."[49] Local jurisdictions can "figure that out" while the ABA "can provide resources to show what others are doing, including in immigration cases, and in tenant cases, having trained people who are taught and understand how to handle those matters if that works for those jurisdictions." Enix-Ross adds that it is important to note, however, that when lawyers provide services "we have codes of conduct and codes of ethics, and we have to abide by those." These "provide a layer of protection for the public" and help hold lawyers accountable; "any system where you have nonlawyers performing what traditionally we might think of as legal activity you need to be able to protect the public." In such settings, the ABA has "played a role in saying what are the options and here are some of the elements one ought to consider when putting those kinds of programs in place." For the ABA, professionalism means ensuring consumer protection, which is a laudable goal. Whatever services are provided should not actually do harm to consumers; that is a given. At the same time, I would argue that professionalism in this context also means that lawyers will strive to ensure not that every lawyer has a job but that the legal system is securing every American's legal job to be done. Greater experimentation will help to identify the strategies that can achieve that goal and the barriers that exist in preventing it from being realized.

Enlist Other Professionals

One of the most important ways to improve access to justice, and to solve legal problems in an affordable way, is to deliver some services through nonlawyers. As described above, some states have permitted the provision of limited legal services through nonlawyer professionals.[50] In many law offices, paralegals provide a great deal of services. They prepare real estate closings and handle many family law and estate matters, and they can do so effectively under the supervision of a licensed attorney at a fraction of the cost of a lawyer. In all the legal aid offices in which I have worked over the years, each provided a great deal of advice and guidance to consumers through paralegals and other paraprofessionals under the supervision of a licensed attorney. Paralegals also handle matters in trial-like settings, such as welfare benefits hearings, immigration matters, and veterans benefits appeals. Should court processes and legal matters become less complex generally, states should feel more comfortable granting more latitude to nonlawyers to provide a wider range of services within contexts where a little navigational guidance could supply adequate support to individuals to address their legal problems.

At the same time, as we look to provide more engaging platforms for the delivery of information, and as we design those simpler processes themselves, lawyers and court systems should work with a broader array of professionals, such as graphic artists; experts in communications and marketing; those trained in design; and, of course, computer programmers. The company Briefly has one lawyer on staff; the rest of the individuals who work there are from different professions. Lawyers who wish to enter the field of digital service delivery should utilize the tools of design thinking[51] and business process analysis;[52] employ the tools of data science; engage in testing their products with actual consumers to improve the user experience; and ensure that the information and service systems are engaging and attractive, accessible, and intuitive. Lawyers can do none of this on their own. In many ways, then, to achieve the professionalism in the broadest and best sense of the term, lawyers will actually need to work with other professionals.

Running with the Machines

Many of the innovations described here are already with us. As a result, they may not seem so far-fetched. Still, how could a computer ever replace a lawyer? To return to the Bill Gates adage, we overestimate the changes that will take place in two years but underestimate those that will occur over ten. Indeed, during the summer of 2022, in an area one might consider the unique province of humans, a work of graphic art generated by artificial intelligence won an art competition.[53] And now AI has become a means of generating original content in response to a plain-language inquiry, including as it relates to legal problems.[54] I do not think we are that far off from a world where legal assistance generated through a digital interface will match, or even exceed, the quality of service that a lawyer, on their own, might provide. Such services will also pass what I might call a "Legal Turing test" for artificial intelligence: one would not be able to tell whether one is receiving legal guidance from a bot or a human. If there is no harm here, and the service is appropriate to meet the individual's needs, then the value the profession realizes from denying access to such services that meet those needs appropriately represents nothing more than the preservation of the lawyer's monopoly on the delivery of legal services. The risks in a monopolized market is that the holder of the monopoly can charge whatever they want for their services. The result is that some will pay whatever it costs for those services, and others will go without. We are in that situation with the market for legal services today.

Technology can certainly play an extractive role when it comes to expanding the provision of some form of legal services. When an individual or business seeks out, obtains, and pays for a modicum of legal guidance from a website or an artificial intelligence–fueled source, and that information proves harmful, the entity providing that service is operating in an extractive fashion by drawing profit from the delivery of a substandard product. It is critical, then, to hold the providers of such services to account when their guidance steers the consumer wrong. To date, there is little evidence that the entities that have appeared in this space have engaged in fraud or steered consumers wrong, however. That is certainly possible, and, presumably, authorized practice of law charges, or even simple fraud cases, might rein in such behavior.

Still, the practice of law has been improved immensely by the introduction of technology, so much so that few lawyers still exist who do not utilize some form of technology in their practice. What lawyers are clearly doing already, and need to embrace more, is utilizing the ways in which technology can help the profession better realize the values of professionalism, access, and inclusion. In the late 1990s, the chess world was rocked when IBM's Deep Blue computer defeated chess grandmaster Garry Kasparov. While this is fairly common in chess matches today, what is proving effective in such competitions is teams of humans paired with computer technologies, what are commonly referred to as "centaurs," a reference to the mythical beast with the body of a horse and the torso and head of a human.[55] Erik Brynjolfsson and Andrew McAfee call this type of collaboration racing "with the machines" rather than against them.[56] It is clear that most lawyers operate as legal centaurs: little of what they do is not in some way aided by modern technologies. The advent of technology has opened up a potential avenue through which the legal profession can embrace a more robust vision of the professionalism, which, ironically, might actually diminish the role of lawyers in the delivery of legal services while making legal empowerment more accessible and inclusive. Professionalism does not always require lawyers. It also embodies that notion of disinterestedness, and the legal profession should promote efforts that serve the needs of the community, not just those of the profession. For these reasons, the profession should embrace technological and other innovations for the ways they can further the values of professionalism, access, and inclusion in the broadest sense. Reports of the death of lawyers from generative artificial intelligence, are, at least for now, premature. Evolving technologies are not yet up to the task of replacing lawyers. Still, while we might not see dramatic change in the profession over the next two years, it is over the next ten that the profession could function a lot differently than it ever has before. It must learn to adapt to and prepare for such change with foresight and a commitment to its core institutional values.

9

The Purpose of the Profession

The history of the American legal profession is the history of America. From its early days as a small group of elites who helped establish a new nation based on principles of equality, to its present state, with lawyers striving not just to undermine our democratic institutions but also to save them, this country was founded on the idea that the United States is a nation of laws and not men. As such, the legal profession has played a central role in the history of this nation, serving not just as a reflection of its values and institutions but also as their designer, architect, curator, and guardian—for better and for worse. Lawyers helped to create the union and our lowercase *r* republican structure founded on principles of democracy while protecting slavery and setting the nation on a path toward providing outsized power to political minorities by placing smaller, less populous states on nearly equal political footing with larger ones. They also created an amendment process to the constitutional structure that permitted a radical change in civil rights in the wake of the Civil War and that gave women the right to vote half a century later. They developed and curated the institutional edifice of Jim Crow and advanced and defended against the Red Scare. Lawyers would begin the efforts to dismantle the institutions of segregation and white supremacy, an effort this is ongoing today, and were central actors in the campaign to destroy our democratic institutions in the wake of the 2020 election. When we tell the story of America, lawyers and the legal profession are both heroes and rogues. Some bend the long, moral arc of the narrative toward justice and equality, while others seek not just to preserve the status quo but also to take the story backward to a darker, less just, less equal chapter. While we may not want to believe that lawyers write the American story, no one can deny their centrality to it.

One of the reasons lawyers have played such an important part in the American experience goes back to the principles of the nation's founding. In a nation where, as Thomas Paine would declare, "law is king," there is a need for the legal system to reflect what should be the core American values of democracy, diversity, and equality. In a multiracial, diverse, democratic, complex, geographically large, and economically dynamic nation, the ties that might hold a more homogeneous and smaller community together, or the authoritarian force that might bind it, are less viable, less potent, and less possible in a nation that professes to adhere to the principles of democracy and equality. At the core of these ideas and ideals are the institutions that align with the characteristics, culture, and myths of American democracy. And those institutions are, in turn, not just the product of the legal profession. It is the profession's institutional role to preserve them.

How well the profession has performed in that role is hardly subject to debate: it is a mixed record at best. In chapters 1–4, I tried to show the ways in which the profession served to advance the democratic values yet also undermined them. Indeed, the legal profession has had significant effects on society as a whole, playing a central role in shaping the institutions through which democratic values are both realized and suppressed. They have advanced or stifled democratic norms and built the structures in which those norms are embedded and institutionalized. The profession thus has had significant *impacts on* the institutions of American democracy. It also *functions as* an institution within that democracy, with a certain primacy in that societal role because of the place that law holds in preserving the institutional order—for better and for worse.

The legal profession, over time, has assumed an institutional shape itself, with discrete contours, characteristics, and norms. These institutional aspects of the profession determine the practices of, and expectations for, its members. In many ways, the current shape of the legal profession was molded by elite insiders roughly a hundred years ago. In response to a perceived crisis in the legal profession at that time, the profession that emerged from that crisis, and the one that exists to this day, both bear a distinct resemblance to the institutional form those elites imposed at that time. With its law firms, law schools, codes of ethics, bar associations, barriers to entry, and public interest bar, the institutional components of the legal profession are, in many respects, still the foundation on which the profession rests. In the face of the many crises that have beset the profession in the intervening century, that foundation may have formed cracks, sometimes significant ones, but it never collapsed. If the profession does not make meaningful change to respond to the current challenges, however, are the forces at work that the profession faces today going to shake but not shatter that profession in the coming decades? It is certainly possible. It is more likely, I believe, that if the institutions of the profession—forged in a very different time and that reflected (and still reflect) very different values than the profession should espouse—do not change to meet these challenges, the profession will no longer play a critical role in sustaining a participatory and republican system of government, civil rights, and individual liberty, that is, the institutions of democracy itself. Without such change, the profession, and democracy, may not persist.

How should the profession change in the face of these challenges? What are the values it must espouse? What are the institutional needs of our multiracial democracy? How are the threats the profession faces both symptoms and signals of the greater risks to the continued viability of that democracy? If a viable and robust legal profession is so critical to this democracy, can a weakened, diminished, or ineffective legal profession fulfill its central role in preserving and perpetuating that democracy? Since I believe that the American legal profession plays such an important part in preserving and advancing the values and institutions of our democracy, threats to the profession are, themselves, threats to democracy itself. If the profession does not rise to the challenge of these threats, the profession—and the democratic institutions it is supposed to uphold—will fall. While I have identified and attempted to address five of the six forces that the profession currently faces, a sixth, which is no less pernicious, still looms. What is more, as I will try to argue here, the profession can potentially address those five other forces by grappling with that sixth threat, which is a danger that comes mostly from within the profession. That final threat is *the problem of lawyer disaffection*: the notion that many lawyers are unhappy in their role, in their work, and in the way they function. I will argue that we actually have a potential answer to address this problem, but it will entail a comprehensive approach to all of the six forces, and that answer centers around the three institutional values I have noted previously: *professionalism, access,* and *inclusion.* Before I discuss how those values present a potential response to all six of the forces currently at work that are threatening the legal profession, let me first chart out the elements of the sixth threat: lawyer disaffection.

The Sixth Threat: Disaffection

Like with almost every facet of life in the United States and around the world, the COVID-19 pandemic placed great strains on the practice of law in virtually all aspects of that practice and in all sectors of the profession. Law offices and law schools operated in remote environments, and courtrooms became virtual. Time-honored aspects of the practice—like the office drop-in from a superior and the late-night strategy session— became niceties, not necessities. Still, the profession learned that it could function in ways that were, prior to the pandemic, uncommon: client meetings, supervisory and mentoring sessions, and even court appearances did not need to be attended in person. Flexible work schedules that adjusted to the needs of families and lawyers with mobility impairments were not just possible; they were preferred. And the world kept spinning. The legal profession largely made the jump to hyperspace—to remote operations with few significant problems and with no notable diminishment of its functions or in lawyer competence. This fact accelerated a conversation about lawyer work habits that had been largely suppressed for years but had started to grow in volume even before the pandemic. What the pandemic did, however, was show the profession that a different mode of practice was possible, one that could prove more humane, accessible, and inclusive. But awareness that something was broken about the way the profession operated had begun to emerge before we knew anything about social distancing, transmission rates, and viral loads.

In 2016, an American Bar Association survey of practicing attorneys showed that 20 percent of respondents exhibited signs of alcohol dependence,[1] with roughly one-third of respondents under thirty years old reporting that they engaged in problematic drinking.[2] More than one-quarter of respondents (28 percent) suffered from depression, and nearly 20 percent reported experiencing anxiety.[3] Alarmingly, lawyers are 50 percent more likely to commit suicide than individuals from other professions.[4] As the researchers pointed out, since most of the data around these indicators of poor lawyer well-being is self-reported, it is difficult to know just how far-reaching and pervasive some of these mental health issues are for lawyers.[5] Making matters worse, many attorneys fear exposure of their mental health or substance abuse problems,[6] have expressed concerns that they cannot discuss well-being issues or mental health struggles with their employers,[7] and even resisted seeking treatment because they feared it would not remain confidential.[8]

Still, not all sectors of the profession show similar signs of distress. In a 2015 study, researchers Lawrence S. Krieger and Kennon M. Sheldon showed that service-oriented lawyers—those in roles such as public defender, criminal prosecutor, government agency lawyer, indigent legal services provider, and in-house counsel for nonprofit organizations—reported greater well-being than prestige lawyers, that is, those in private practice in law firm settings of a hundred or more lawyers; plaintiff's tort/malpractice law, corporate, commercial, or transactional law; international business and commercial transactions; securities or partnership law; tax and estate planning; or patent and copyright law.[9] Service lawyers also reported more positive daily moods and equal life satisfaction to those in the prestige positions.[10] A third group that included attorneys in general practice, family law, private criminal defense, and other fields reported the lowest life satisfaction and daily mood. Krieger and Sheldon conclude that their data indicates that "money, grades, and prestige" are not accurate indicators for the well-being of attorneys.[11] According to this data and their study, finding "interesting, engaging, and personally meaningful" work is the most important component of attorney job satisfaction.[12] Autonomy and what the authors call "authenticity" were also significant indicators of attorney well-being.[13] Similarly, legal scholar Melissa Weresh has argued that engaging in public service lawyering may help lawyers struggling with depression or may otherwise improve satisfaction as a legal professional because of the "established relationship between service/altruism/volunteerism and well-being."[14] Weresh suggests that public service orientation should be highly encouraged to combat declining lawyer well-being.[15]

Furthermore, researchers Cheryl Ann Krause and Jane Chong argue that addressing the well-being of lawyers requires going to the root of the psychological components of wellness and that solutions to the well-being crisis should be dual-purpose, "aiming not only to improve life for the individual lawyer but also to reaffirm the integrity of the law as a profession."[16] What is more, for Krause and Chong, declining mental health and high suicide rates are troubling for the legal profession because its members play a fundamental role in protecting clients' interests and in "ensuring and strengthening the rule of law."[17] There is also a correlation between inclusion and well-being.[18] The work of DEI programs has been critical to improving attorney satisfaction, even when so much more needs to be done to improve this feature of the profession.[19]

There are many strategies for promoting attorney well-being, from stress management, clinical treatment, and mindfulness to structural solutions like changing lawyer business models to remove billable hours or immediate psychological stressors.[20] But Krause and Chong argue that a piecemeal approach is not effective. First, they suggest that well-being should be integrated into an attorney's duty of competence, which they argue falls to the judiciary to enforce.[21] This duty of competence includes allowing lawyers with limited experience more courtroom opportunities and interactions with clients in order to enhance their training and accelerate the development of their skills and judgment so that they might master their craft.[22] For Krause and Chong, because newer attorneys "are too often simply assumed to lack the necessary legal experience to take on important roles, when in fact they have unique strengths and interests," those should be "identified and leveraged" in ways that will be beneficial not just to "their clients and employers" but also to their own well-being.[23] Second, Krause and Chong reiterate Krieger and Sheldon's emphasis on encouraging attorney autonomy over how they get their work done and what work they do.[24] When a lawyer is overworked and overwhelmed, and does not have control over their own schedule or the matters they can take on, it will not only inhibit their sense of agency; it could also undermine their sense of purpose, especially if they are denied the opportunity to work on projects—pro bono or otherwise—from which they could derive significant meaning.[25]

What lawyers need, then, is a sense of mastery of professional skills, a degree of autonomy over how they work and on what they work, and a sense of purpose. It turns out that these are three critical components of professional satisfaction, well-being, and even motivation.

Mastery, Autonomy, and Purpose

In his work *Drive: The Surprising Truth About What Motivates Us*,[26] Dan Pink, a former lawyer and speechwriter turned best-selling author, notes that intrinsic motivation, as opposed to extrinsic motivation like financial rewards, is more durable and produces greater job satisfaction. We produce such intrinsic rewards from our work when we obtain what he identifies as the three main "nutrients" of job satisfaction and motivation: *mastery*, *autonomy*, and *purpose*.[27] These three components of professional well-being, when viewed through the prism of professionalism, access, and inclusion, point to the ways in which the legal profession can address lawyer disaffection while also confronting the other forces I have identified throughout this work.

When it comes to professionalism, as Krause and Chong argue, providing newer lawyers with more meaningful opportunities to develop their craft and hone their skills addresses the question of mastery. When we accept that access and inclusion are other values the profession should embrace, we can see how providing members of the profession with greater autonomy (over how they work, when they work, what kind of work they do, etc.) increases professionalism and strengthens the attorney's ability to practice; but doing so also enhances their autonomy, giving them greater freedom in and control over their practice. It also turns out, as I discussed in greater depth in chapter 6, that flexible and accessible work practices that increase a lawyer's autonomy will likely make the practice of law more inclusive as well.

Finally, when speaking of purpose, as Sheldon and Kreiger have shown, those who work in more public service–oriented fields have more job satisfaction than those who work in the private sector. We could certainly leave this issue there and say that only public- and nonprofit-sector lawyers can find purpose in their work and job satisfaction. But I do not think it is true that there is no job satisfaction in the private sector. In fact, many lawyers in that sector still report some degree of job satisfaction and positive well-being. Yet there is something to the fact that public- and nonprofit-sector lawyers may find greater job satisfaction in their work, and the reason for that is something the entire profession can try to replicate.

The likely reason for higher job satisfaction among lawyers in the public and nonprofit sectors is that they, in the theories of psychologist Victor Frankl, are working for a cause larger than themselves. Frankl, an Austrian psychotherapist sent to the Nazi concentration camps, had developed nascent psychological theories prior to his internment. Although several family members were murdered in the camps, he survived and went on to blend his early theories with his experiences in those camps. His remarkable memoir, *Man's Search for Meaning*, explores the centrality of the pursuit of purpose in the human psyche and the importance of serving a cause larger than oneself for human flourishing.[28] The reality is that members of the legal profession, by playing their part in ensuring they fulfill the highest ideals of the profession in everything they do, can end up doing just that: serving a purpose greater than their own personal gain. That returns us to the core question this book attempts to answer though: What is the purpose of the legal profession, specifically the American legal profession, in this moment and for the future?

The American Legal Profession's Purpose

A legal profession under an authoritarian regime can operate to stifle democratic yearnings, ensure control by the regime through the support of unfair and unjust legal and regulatory systems, and manipulate the system of justice to further entrench autocratic power.[29] In a kleptocratic, extractive society (which could also be autocratic and often is), the legal profession creates and sustains the infrastructure within which elites siphon resources from the system for their own gain, while their lawyers benefit from understanding how the system works and extracting their own fees from the profits they garner for their clients.[30] Within either system, disputes are often settled through a legal system that is skewed to preserve authoritarian rule, or they are resolved in the streets and through violence, without regard for the rule of law, or under a rule of law so distorted that the rules, if followed, guarantee an outcome favorable to the elites. In a democratic, multiracial democracy that embeds individual liberty within a constitutional structure designed to advance majority rule while simultaneously respecting minority rights, and that resolves legal conflicts through an adversarial judicial system, the legal profession has a critical role to play not just to create but also to maintain the legal processes that realize those principles. In such democratic societies, and taking an expansive view of institutions as including organizations, systems, norms and practices, the legal profession is not just a source of those institutions or merely a guardian of such institutions; it is a necessary component of those features of democratic society—an institution that makes other institutions possible. Any effort that matches the functions of the legal profession as an institution to the institutional needs of that democratic society will necessarily strive to defend individual liberty, advance democratic systems, protect minority rights, and operate to sustain fair and just adversarial processes for the resolution of disputes. These functions become the purpose of the profession. And it is from this purpose that we derive the profession's institutional values of professionalism, access, and inclusion.

Reform of the Profession's Institutions

It is one thing to say there are values the profession should espouse; it is another to say they should be institutionalized in the way I have been talking about institutions throughout this work. At the turn of the nineteenth to the twentieth century, the profession institutionalized certain values by embedding them in codes of ethics and then operationalizing them through bar associations, law schools, the stiffening of barriers to entry, and the legal system itself. Those institutions still provide structure and shape to the American legal profession. In some ways, the profession was trying to address a range of challenges it faced at the end of the nineteenth century: that is, the social, political, cultural, and technological changes underway at the time. It did so in a particular way: by turning the idea of inclusion on its head. Elites in the profession concluded that, to include growing immigrant, urban, working-class communities in the industrial economy of a moderately participatory democracy (one in which, at the time, women largely did not enjoy the right to vote and African American men were routinely denied the right to vote in the Jim Crow South), what was needed was a legal profession that adhered to a particular set of values and practices and operated in a way that tended to limit access to the profession itself, particularly for members of the very communities elites in the profession most feared. Those elites embraced a narrow vision of professionalism, believed access to justice was a necessary evil (to preserve peace and prevent revolution), and accepted the premise that the *appearance* of inclusion was better than either alternative: a sense that the legal system was unavailable to the working poor, or that it was actually available to them in a meaningful way. Thus, the profession embraced, and operationalized, a cramped version of professionalism, access, and inclusion in its institutions, which from the beginning were formed in this narrow fashion and remain so to this day.

It is no surprise that the legal profession, operating within those institutions, continues to fail to solve some of the very puzzles it was attempting to address in the beginning of the twentieth century. While the profession still faces some of those same challenges, at present there are also new ones, or at least some of the same challenges have emerged in different shape. In order to address these challenges in a more effective way, the profession must start with the institutions that give the profession its form and guide its functions and then assess the ways in which they need reform. This requires a fair degree of introspection; but it also compels one to take a view from the outside in, to bring the concept of institutional fit back into the discussion: that is, the profession must calibrate itself to the needs of the broader community it is designed to serve. Such an effort requires an alignment of the values of professionalism, access, and inclusion to the needs of a multiracial, participatory democracy, one that operates on the adversarial system and advances individual rights, civil rights, human dignity, and the rule of law. Aligning the internal institutions of the profession with the broader institutional needs of the community represents the best chance of securing institutional fit. What follows is a discussion of several ways the profession can bring about such institutional fit by reforming several of the institutions of the profession itself, starting with areas for reform of its codes of ethics but also exploring the role that courts, law schools, the public interest bar, and legal organizations generally must play in realizing the values of professionalism, access, and inclusion for the present and future.

Strengthening Codes of Ethics

As explored in chapter 4, the era of codes of ethics for lawyers began toward the end of the nineteenth century, and the ABA adopted its own set of rules in 1908, which has been revised over the years, with the Model Rules of Professional Conduct operating as its current iteration. Most states follow the principles set forth in those rules, and some track them essentially verbatim. But a comparison of the current rules and the initial Canons of Professional Ethics reveals that the specter of some of the more restrictive elements of the Canons still hover over the Model Rules. While the Supreme Court scaled back some of the restrictions on lawyer advertising in 1977,[31] other aspects of the 1908 Canons, like provisions related to the unauthorized practice of law (UPL), prohibitions on sharing fees with nonlawyers, and limits on financial assistance that a lawyer can provide to a client during the course of representation, still linger and reflect those aspects of the earlier rules that were designed to rein in practices that were perceived as those of lawyers serving lower-income clients. Providing a check on those practices necessarily made it harder to serve such clients and tipped the scales in favor of those lawyers who served the would-be adversaries of those clients, such as employers that might deny them wages or railroad companies that injured them.

The first step in revising the rules of ethics—both at the national level, where they serve as guidance to the states, and at the state level, where they are enforced—is to recognize those areas where the rules still reflect this animus against lawyers serving low-income and working-poor clients. While it would not impact lawyers directly, the restriction that most impacts these communities are rules against the unauthorized practice of law. I say it does not impact lawyers directly because, if we were to loosen the restrictions on UPL, that would mean that more individuals will have the ability to provide services to individuals and families in need of some legal assistance. Tax preparation, some immigration practices, welfare hearings, and cases involving veterans benefits are already undertaken by authorized nonlawyers. States like Washington have experimented with allowing nonlawyers to assist in certain eviction cases. There are areas, like these, where one does not need to spend three years in law school and tens or hundreds of thousands of dollars to provide effective assistance in discrete settings, particularly those settings affecting low- and moderate-income clients and where the relative "value" of the case is so low it is hard to justify paying a lawyer and/or the client cannot afford one. At the same time, although an individual may face a claim of alleged debt that might amount to even as little as a thousand dollars because of an unpaid credit card bill (which they may or may not owe and for which the interest and fees has accumulated for years), that individual may not have several thousand dollars to pay a lawyer, by the hour, to defend them in court.

In such settings (eviction cases, consumer debt cases, etc.), the over-whelming majority of low- and moderate-income defendants face their legal problems without a lawyer. Many lose these cases by default be-cause they simply do not show up to defend themselves. Others show up and are simply unable to mount any serious defense because they do not understand their rights, and their adversaries are not about to explain them to them—nor should they. In fact, current ethics rules prohibit them from doing so, which is probably sound policy.

Loosening UPL rules in those areas where low- and moderate-income individuals largely face their legal problems without the benefit of a lawyer, and where lawyers tend not to serve because of the lack of a viable business model for doing so, would seem to be one way to try to close the justice gap where the lack of representation can cause great hardship and leave rights unprotected. For example, in the mid-2000s, the organization for which I worked studied hundreds of consumer debt cases, out of the hundreds of thousands of such cases filed each year in the New York City courts alone.[32] In those cases we reviewed, we found that not a single defendant was represented by counsel and the major-ity of judgments that the plaintiffs secured in those cases were granted on default, meaning the defendants never even appeared to contest the cases. Yet a review of the case files showed that many of the plaintiffs were what are known as "debt buyers"—they purchased the alleged debt from a credit card company or cellular phone service provider for pen-nies on the dollar and were thus making a windfall on the judgments they secured. Making matters even worse, the "evidence" these debt buyers presented was rarely sufficient to establish that the defendants even owed the debt in the first place. A lawyer—or even anyone with a modicum of legal training in the area—would have identified the de-fects in the plaintiffs' cases and gotten them dismissed. These cases were often so flawed that, whenever my organization would appear on behalf of a defendant, let alone submit an answer in the case contesting the plaintiffs' allegations, the next thing we would find out is that the plain-tiff had withdrawn the case, a tacit admission that there was not only no "there there" but also that those plaintiffs knew our representation would uncover that fact.

Expanding access to some form of effective assistance in these sorts of cases and others where lawyers tend not to tread generally can only advance the rule of law. It is fair to say that one of the impulses animating UPL provisions is consumer protection: we do not want someone who is unable to provide effective assistance to an individual because of the nature of the case or its complexity to fail to protect the client's rights adequately. That is a fair concern and one that should be taken seriously. Regulators, courts, and legal organizations should have the necessary knowledge and experience to assess the contexts and cases that lend themselves to less-than-full legal representation and can identify those consumers who would benefit from some form of legal assistance and those where a lawyer is needed to ensure the consumer's rights are appropriately protected and vindicated.

The argument for consumer protection cuts a number of different ways in the UPL context. The typical case that is made in favor of UPL restrictions is that consumers must be protected from unscrupulous nonlawyers who will not have the wherewithal to protect those consumers' rights yet will take their money. In such settings, and making matters worse, untrained individuals might provide services to consumers that are not just inconsistent with the standard of care expected of a lawyer in a similar situation but also may jeopardize the consumer's rights and threaten their interests. Someone who is trained only in eviction law might not recognize that a tenant is also the victim of racial discrimination and harassment or might have a personal injury claim against their landlord for physical illnesses caused by mold or rodent infestation. Someone with a modicum of knowledge about other areas of law—the type of information a law student gains in law school and must study for a bar exam—would enable that individual to identify those other legal issues and, at a minimum, advise the consumer that they should consult with a lawyer with an expertise in those areas and that they will have to do so quickly because statutes of limitations limit the time after an injury within which an individual must assert a claim. A good lawyer often knows what they do not know. In many instances, a trained lawyer is expected to know and advise a client about a range of claims, even those about which they are not an expert, and even if all they say is "you should consult another lawyer about that."

At the same time, it is ironic to argue in the name of consumer protection that consumers should not receive the protection of some form of legal assistance when the alternative is no assistance whatsoever, which is far more often the case when nonlawyer assistance is not available to the consumer. Here, the perfect is clearly the enemy of the good, especially when the alternative to the perfect is often nothing at all.

The impacts that a thoughtful loosening of UPL of restrictions will have on lawyers, and even the courts, do not offer sufficient reasons to maintain these restrictions as they currently exist. Yes, it might mean some lawyers will lose out on clients. For the most part, by focusing on those areas where lawyers tend not to serve such clients, there is little risk. For the borderline cases, the lawyers who operate in these spaces might have to adapt their business model to serve more clients at a lower fee or move their practice into an operation where they are able to take on nonlawyer practitioners who can operate under loosened restrictions and take the more complex cases or those clients who want, and can afford, more comprehensive representation.

The real impact this will have on the practicing bar is that clients who would otherwise go unrepresented are now going to have some form of assistance. And the lawyers who represent their adversaries may not like that. Too bad. Courts may also feel that having lawyers on both sides of a case might make more work for those courts. Lawyers for, say, defendants in consumer debt cases will now do things like file motions. They might even show up in court and not lose by default judgment, meaning the courts might actually have to adjudicate these disputes. Again, this simply cannot be a reason to deny both sides some form of legal representation, even if it is not a full-dress lawyer.

Another argument is that some lawyers may have to compete with nonlawyers for some of these clients. Trained lawyers generally spend three years of their lives and tens if not hundreds of thousands of dollars to get a law degree. I am not unsympathetic to this position, given that I both went through law school myself and now train future lawyers. If we turn back to Clayton Christensen's theories on disruptive innovation, we should begin to address the justice gap in areas where lawyers tend not to practice and where typically over 90 percent of consumers face their legal problems without the benefit of a lawyer. If we loosen UPL restrictions in such areas to permit advocates to practice within them, and train them to spot the more complex problems that are not appropriate for nonlawyer assistance, we can make great strides toward closing the justice gap in several critical areas where the unrepresented predominate.

If we are to return to the issue of professionalism, it is not hypocritical to promote assistance that is not provided by a lawyer as advancing professionalism when the lack of representation itself creates a professionalism problem. The lawyer's duty to ensure access to justice and to preserve the functioning of our adversarial system requires adversaries that have some rough parity of expertise. No, a nonlawyer will not have the same training and experience as a lawyer. But such training and experience may not be necessary in simple cases where a consumer would otherwise go unrepresented. Since one of the institutional values the legal profession is supposed to uphold is the rule of law as vindicated through an adversarial system, some degree of equality in the ability to navigate legal systems effectively is an essential component of that adversarial system. Anything short of that provides the appearance of the rule of law without fully realizing it.

Another rule-of-law issue that changes to the rules of ethics could address is heightened penalties for actions that directly serve to undermine the rule of law—through, for example, the use of legal process to strike at our democratic institutions, including the peaceful transfer of power. The rules of ethics, and their corollaries in rules of practice, like Rule 11 of the Federal Rules of Civil Procedure, provide that lawyers must have a good-faith basis for the legal claims they interpose and the factual assertions they make. There is no provision in any of these rules, however, that would distinguish between falsifying a medical report to obtain a few thousands dollars for a client in a personal injury case and trying to block the peaceful transition of presidential power. Guidance to courts related to the application of Rule 11 provides that judges can take into account whether particular actions were willful or just negligent or to what extent a penalty is required that will deter future conduct. Once again, none of the rules, or any guidance related to them, suggest that assertions of frivolous claims and facts should be treated differently from any others on substance. I would assert that the rules and the guidance related to them should make it clear that heightened penalties are appropriate for actions that are directed squarely at undermining the rule of law, as we have seen in the events following the outcome of the 2020 presidential election.

Finally, while loosening restrictions on UPL rules and enhancing penalties for rule-of-law violations will certainly inure to the benefit of the community, in order to align lawyer practices with community well-being even further, another area where this can be addressed is in the rules related to those circumstances in which lawyers can share confidential information when doing so might prevent death or serious bodily harm to members of the community. While one might think of this situation as involving a client threatening a witness or an adversary, it can also occur in settings where a company may be engaged in harmful environmental practices or their products are affirmatively harming consumers. While the companies perpetrating these harms should enjoy legal defense and receive punishment that comports with the requirements of due process, there are times when lawyers can actually prevent some of this harm from occurring in the community in the first place, and the rules certainly make some accommodation for them to do so. Indeed, the rules currently provide that a lawyer "may" reveal confidential information when doing so will prevent such harm from occurring.[33] This could be a situation where a client threatens to harm an adversary or a witness who might hurt the client. It can also occur in a situation where a company is responsible for releasing toxins into the water supply, or an entrepreneur is hocking some medical technology that does not accomplish what they say it will accomplish, and customers are harmed as a result. The existing structure certainly permits lawyers to reveal confidential information in such situations. Perhaps we do not think this goes far enough and that lawyers should be required to share such information as appropriate. All that is well and good, and some states go that far in their own versions of the applicable rules in certain circumstances. Still, a deeper analysis of the permission structure inherent in the rules is that it errs on the side of protecting the lawyer and not the community.

The commentary to the rules provides that a lawyer's decision to refrain from sharing confidential information is not subject to review by disciplinary authorities after the fact, where, for example, a client does in fact murder their adversary and the lawyer had information that, if revealed, could have prevented the crime.[34] Indeed, a lawyer can watch as a client loads a firearm and prepares to hunt down their adversary and do nothing to prevent the action. The lawyer's decision to *not* alert the authorities or the adversary of the imminent danger is not subject to review by disciplinary authorities. At the same time, the rules do not offer the same get-out-of-jail-free card for the lawyer who *does* report an imminent threat. If the decision to withhold information is one that is not subject to review, but the same is not true of the decision to report, it is clear that the incentive structure created by the rules is one that likely encourages nondisclosure rather than disclosure. Thus, a lawyer can be subject to discipline if they make the wrong call by reporting a client for creating risk in the community—that is, if their assessment of the situation is not reasonable and no one was truly at risk. At the same time, if the lawyer does not report—even if the client kills someone or kills a lot of people—and the lawyer had information that could have prevented those harms from occurring, there are no ethical consequences for the lawyer for having taken no action. Ethical rules that are designed to protect the lawyer at almost any cost, over the interests of the community, require reassessment if we are to align the ethical rules with the desire for community well-being.

Once again, this ability to balance the concept of zealous advocacy with the bounds of the law is the essence of lawyer professionalism. It is what makes lawyers professionals in the first place. As a lawyer, one must advance the client's interests, using all the legal tools available to do so, while recognizing that there are sometimes good reasons why the community's interests might outweigh those of the individual or where the rules of the game are such that the client has no legal recourse to pursue their ends. One can advocate for a change in the rules, but one cannot break the rules to advance a client's goals.

It is through such zealous—and lawful—advocacy that change can happen in a democracy. The recent campaign for marriage equality is just one example of such an effort. Advocates for marriage equality moved within existing constraints to build a movement that started in the states, seeking legislative reform, victories in state courts, and ballot referenda in numerous jurisdictions. In 2004, conservative advocacy groups put voter referenda outlawing same-sex marriages on the ballot to boost turnout of conservative voters. By 2012, through the painstaking advocacy of marriage equality advocates, referenda in three states advancing the issue passed and one outlawing it failed.[35] By 2015, the Supreme Court ruled that laws outlawing same-sex marriage violated the U.S. Constitution.[36] When the composition of the Supreme Court changed such that it placed the Court's precedents around marriage equality in jeopardy, advocates mustered enough support in Congress to pass legislation, with bipartisan support, that protected marriage equality.[37] All of this advocacy occurred within a "legal" framework—that is, it represented the use of existing tools creatively, zealously, and with passion to bring about a change in the law. It also represented the epitome of lawyer professionalism.

At the same time, zealous advocacy has its limits, and lawyers and clients alike may wish to go beyond those limits. While we might want lawyers to feel empowered to advocate for their clients aggressively while simultaneously taking into account the impacts that their actions will have on the community and serving as a check on both clients and their colleagues who might want to go beyond the bounds of the law, the rules generally leave little room for lawyers who wish to do so in the face of opposition from their colleagues and their clients. Indeed, although lawyers are generally obligated to report another lawyer when their behavior "raises a substantial question as to that lawyer's honestly, trustworthiness, or fitness" to practice law, this is rarely enforced.[38] Moreover, when lawyers do report such conduct, the rules afford them no protection from colleagues and clients when they do. Should a lawyer refuse to take action that a client insists on taking, the client can terminate the relationship. If a lawyer reports a coworker, that lawyer can generally lose their job or miss out on a promotion or bonus. While there is some precedent for a lawyer finding some protections when they formally report misconduct,[39] just speaking out inside a meeting or to their superiors about a planned course of action is not protected conduct under the rules. While a lawyer may have a retaliation claim under another set of laws—say, for example, if they were to report racial or gender discrimination within an office and face some adverse employment consequences as a result—such protections come from outside the rules of ethics. Lawyers should have greater protections when they raise concerns that a planned course of action is improper or constitutes advocacy beyond the bounds of the law. The "self-regulatory" system that the legal profession prefers offers hollow hope to those who might wish to operationalize it. While we may not want lawyers to have to constantly look over their shoulder out of fear a colleague might report them for misconduct, when a lawyer does engage in clear misconduct, the lawyer who reports such misconduct should not face recrimination or retaliation for their efforts to uphold lawyer professionalism and the rule of law.

The Role of Law Schools

Since the 1930s, law schools have become the main entryway to the profession and serve as the starting point for the inculcation of law students in the values and norms of the profession. As the history recounted in chapter 4 shows, when law schools first came to prominence in the 1920s, and admission to them became more difficult, more expensive, and more time consuming, these developments had the cumulative effect of making them places of privilege. They were also places of exclusion, where, for most law schools, women and people of color were largely excluded until laws made such discrimination illegal. Still, today, while the gender makeup of most law schools' student bodies reflects that of the larger community, when it comes to race, class, and sexual orientation and identity law schools still have more work to do to ensure that the makeup of their students reflects the diversity of the nation. They also have much more work to do in diversifying the faculty, administration, and staff working in law schools and in creating a culture of inclusion, equity, and belonging within legal education.

Since law schools are places where the values of the profession are often the first place where students will learn them, law school programming and curricula should offer ample opportunities for students to engage in public service work and to learn, through such work, the importance of realizing the purpose of the profession and the ethics at the heart of a purpose-driven, professional career. But law schools should also take greater care in meeting students where they are and sustaining the reasons they went to law school in the first place. For many aspiring lawyers, they want to become lawyers because they are idealistic and want to have a positive impact on the world. For too many, law school drains them of their idealism. At the same time, law schools have started to place greater focus on the formation of professional identity in which one's individual values are considered in light of the values of the profession. Students should find where those values align with the profession and determine where, as practitioners, those aspiring lawyers will fit within the practice of law. As my colleagues Mary Walsh Fitzpatrick and Rosemary Queenan have written, law schools, instead of trying to force students into a particular way of practicing or a particular type of practice, should encourage students to identify their own individual values and then reconcile them, as appropriate, with those of the profession. This will allow aspiring lawyers "to make self-directed decisions about ethical and other conflicts and how they represent their clients and contribute to the legal community as lawyers, leaders, and professionals. Aligning individual and professional values also fosters greater autonomy, leading to increased career satisfaction."[40]

That professional identity should also advance and embrace the professional values of professionalism, access, and inclusion as they are described here. Since lawyers can advance the purpose of the profession regardless of the sector in which they work, law schools should ensure that, no matter what a student's desired career path within the law, they understand the connection between fulfilling their professional role within that path. A student who wishes to practice business law should understand the role they play in guiding their clients to adhere to the law just as much as one who wishes to serve as a public defender or prosecutor. They also should choose a path within the law that best meshes with their own personal identity and values so that the personal is in harmony with the professional.

Every law student should also understand the role they play in ensuring access to justice for all Americans, including recognizing the ways that they can contribute to closing the justice gap, whether that is through donating their time to assist the unrepresented through pro bono efforts, advocating for greater funding for nonprofit legal services, or donating funds to promote access to justice. Their entrance into the profession and the extent to which they benefit from the monopoly on the provision of legal services comes with a societal price, and law students should understand that, with that monopoly power, they have a responsibility to ensure that it serves an inclusive, and not an extractive, function.

Another way to advance the principles of access and inclusion would be for law schools to embrace and offer more career opportunities in the law and to support the loosening of restrictions on UPL rules. Law schools can advocate for changes to the rules to allow for more opportunities for nonlawyers to provide legal assistance, which might, at first blush, appear as being against their interests. But it does not have to be that way. Law schools can offer a range of degree and training opportunities, along a continuum, that would make legal assistance more available to those who need it and offer more students the chance to develop legal expertise and serve their communities. It is not everyone who can step away from the working world for three years, at considerable cost, to earn a law degree. Those who can are fortunate, but many simply cannot afford to do so. In health care, the provision of services is provided by many different professionals, with different types of training, along the continuum of care; we could look at the delivery of legal services in the same way.

If we view the provision of legal assistance as a continuum, and those who provide such assistance as needing varying degrees of expertise and training to operate within different spaces along the continuum, we can bring greater professional diversity and likely invite individuals with different backgrounds and experiences into the profession. What is more, alternative degree programs would not be subject to the same restrictions on distance learning, described below, that the ABA imposes; as a result, law schools can offer them through a blend of online and in-person programming, which will make them more accessible and less expensive to offer, and those cost savings can be passed along to prospective students.

In addition, under ABA rules, a student who matriculates must complete their degree in seven years.[41] This undoubtedly has the effect of discouraging students who must earn a living while attending law school or who have significant family commitments from attending law school in the first place. Moreover, other ABA rules provide that a student earning a degree other than a juris doctor (JD), like a master's degree in law, cannot apply the coursework they complete for that other degree toward subsequent completion of the JD, even if they are the exact same classes required of both.[42] If a student could earn a master's, or even a certificate or other degree prior to earning the master's, accumulate credits over the course of study, and then could return to law school later in life to cap off their studies and obtain their law degree, it could open the door to more individuals entering the profession at an earlier stage, serving their community, attending to their family or other obligations, and then achieving the status of attorney later in their career. Or they could choose not to and decide they wish simply to serve their community according to the level of training they have already received. At present, the rules favor the law degree, and that has a way of further entrenching privilege.[43]

Law school hierarchies also have a tendency to entrench hierarchy and privilege in more ways than one, and one of the main drivers of that force is the rankings of law schools by the media outlet *U.S. News & World Report*. Since those rankings began in 1990, law schools, law students, and law firms alike have used the rankings as a way of making a whole range of decisions that bear little relationship to those individuals' and entities' respective needs. For law schools, the rankings have led them to channel resources to bulk up on the types of things that improve their standing within the rankings, and they privilege such things as admissions exam scores and undergraduate grade point averages for prospective students. Those rankings also penalize law schools where students take on more relative educational debt. For law students, they often choose a higher-ranked school over one that might be a better fit for them in terms of geographical preference or the type of law they want to practice after graduation, where one law school that is ranked lower generally might excel in the prospective student's planned field of study. Law firms look to the rankings when making employment decisions, even where the things that the rankings certainly do not capture— like the grit, life experience, or resilience of a particular student—might be more important to an employer than how a candidate fared on a standardized test taken four years earlier. Indeed, a student who comes from an impoverished background, who faced considerable hardship to get to law school, and had to earn money while supporting a family during law school probably knows how to work and will not take their position within a firm for granted. That student might not have scored as well on the law school admission test as someone who was groomed for law school from a very young age, who had tutors and training on the test, discussed the law and legal careers over dinner with their lawyer parents, had an Ivy League undergraduate education (just like those parents), and submitted letters of recommendation from alumni of the law school who have made considerable contributions to the school's endowment. If I were an employer, I would probably prefer the former student to the latter as one I would want working alongside me, but that is typically not how the profession works at present. And the rankings certainly do not operate in that way.

Still, as this book goes to press in 2023, thanks to the growing opposition to the rankings from law schools themselves, particularly the more highly ranked ones, it is possible that *U.S. News* ranking system will have become less relevant, carrying far less clout and impact on legal education than in the past. Nevertheless, law schools have played a considerable role in shaping the profession for over a hundred years. It is high time for law schools, as a prime institutional actor within the profession, to take their role in advancing the institutional values of professionalism, access, and inclusion more seriously.

Other Barriers to Entry

In addition to requiring aspiring lawyers to attend law school at considerable cost, entry to the legal profession often requires that a prospective lawyer take a bar examination. Most states have moved to the Uniform Bar Exam, which makes it easier for prospective lawyers to "grade into" a range of states by getting a passing score on that exam. Still, that exam, and others like it in the states that still administer their own exams, hardly test what is required of a prospective lawyer to practice law. It tests one's ability to memorize a range of topics that one might never come across in the actual practice of law. First, while many lawyers commit certain issues to memory that they come across in their practice, and may need to refer to the rules of evidence while on their feet in a courtroom, the practice of law, like life itself, is an open-book test. And lawyers should, and often do, research and refer to the relevant law, regulations, court cases, and so on as they emerge in their practice. One colleague with whom I had the privilege of working was a forty-year veteran of housing court litigation. For nearly every tenant he represented, and he probably handled thousands of their cases over his career, he would consult the relevant statute governing landlord-tenant eviction proceedings to see if there was some new way of looking at the law that he had never contemplated that might assist the client's case. He would do this even though he helped to draft the statute as a young attorney at the beginning of his career!

The truth is, the best lawyers are constantly reviewing the legal materials relevant to their practice to ensure they are providing competent and effective service to their clients. Law practice has become more and more specialized over the years, and while lawyers must have a breadth of knowledge in a few areas of law, they need to master an area or two of law by developing deep expertise, which comes with experience and doing their homework over and over again. The rote memorization of doctrine in a wide range of subject matter areas, as bar exams require, represents literally the opposite of what most lawyers do in their practice.

It seems, however, that bar examiners and state courts are beginning to recognize that the bar exam itself is hardly a test of one's potential aptitude for the competent practice of law. A movement is underway to create a next-generation bar exam.[44] This is welcome news. The hope is that such an effort will align what bar examinations test with what competence in the practice of law requires.

Another barrier to entry is the so-called character and fitness portion of bar admission review that is conducted by state officials tasked with managing that admission. This process will try to identify individuals who, those officials assess, cannot be entrusted with the responsibility and fiduciary obligations that come with having a law license. While every year some applicants may find themselves facing significant hurdles to admission, most applicants can work their way through this process. Still, certain aspects of this process are troublesome and can have a disproportionate effect on those from minoritized populations or those with a mental disability. For years, many states had questions that asked whether an individual had ever been treated for mental illness. For a young person expecting to seek bar admission, this would make it less likely that they seek such treatment if they knew they had to disclose it when applying to the bar.[45] Others ask whether a candidate for admission had ever been *charged* with a crime (let alone convicted). These applications also typically ask the applicant to disclose if they were charged as a youthful offender, the record of which would be sealed when the individual charged reached the age of majority. Given the overpolicing and overcriminalization of youth of color, these types of questions are likely to make it more difficult for candidates from such communities to make it through the character and fitness portion of the admission process as easily as those who did not face similar experiences. What is more, law schools inquire of applicants whether they have any of these types of issues in their past before they consider them for admission so that they can determine whether the applicant will face any barriers to bar admission after graduation. This is a reasonable step that schools take to try to prevent a student from matriculating only to have them face significant hurdles to actual admission to the bar after graduation from law school.

There may be legitimate character and fitness concerns as they relate to some applicants. In order to improve inclusion as it relates to those candidates for admission (to both law school and the bar) who may face such hurdles, bar admission officials should review their requirements for bias and for the risk that they might not serve any legitimate consumer protection purpose. They can also partner with law schools to assist prospective students at the law school admission stage to provide a sense of what type of questions the bar admissions officials might have of a particular candidate. Some of the things that the character and fitness process screens for—an experience with the criminal justice system, for example—might actually be the types of things we may look for in an attorney because that experience might make them more empathetic toward those facing the prospect of entering that system as well. To the extent that these requirements chill applicants with certain backgrounds that might be beneficial for the profession, or that might have a disproportionate effect on certain communities, they should be jettisoned in the effort to promote access and inclusion.

The Role of Courts

Courts and court systems have a significant role to play in addressing the forces affecting the legal profession. From being the main gatekeepers around bar admission requirements in many states and maintaining the disciplinary machinery that can lead to suspension and disbarment of attorneys, to enforcing court rules around attorney misconduct, courts serve as a critical institution within the legal system. As such, their action, or inaction, can play a pivotal role in any effort at reform.

That pivotal role begins even before lawyers join the profession. State courts typically control who can enter the profession within any particular state. While the ABA may accredit law schools and sets the standards for those schools, state courts often have the final say over who can apply to take the bar exam in their jurisdiction. State courts can certainly require that only graduates of accredited law schools can apply to take the bar exam, but they can also impose additional requirements, ones that the ABA does not demand. For example, as this book goes to print, the New York Court of Appeals, the state's highest court, which sets admission standards for the bar in the state, does not accept some of the recent changes the ABA adopted around distance learning. The ABA allows students to earn roughly a third of their total credits toward the bar exam through distance-learning courses, while New York permits roughly half that amount. Similarly, while the ABA has approved "hybrid" JDs in a few schools, where students earn the bulk of their credits through distance-learning education, New York has not formally accepted graduates through those programs, even though one school that offers such a program, Syracuse University, is located in the state. While the ABA accreditation standards have a way of making admission more exclusive, when state courts and other authorities go beyond the ABA's requirements, they make it even harder for students who might benefit from the more flexible arrangements that even the ABA permits. At the same time, New York has also created the innovative Pro Bono Scholars program, which allows students to take the bar examination a semester early, provided they commit to offering volunteer services to the community for several months after sitting for the bar and while they await their bar results. State courts should review their own requirements for bar admission to ensure that they are, at a minimum, as flexible as ABA requirements; but they can do better by pushing the ABA to make some of the changes suggested above, like allowing for students to earn credits in the pursuit of a range of degrees and over longer periods of time. They can also explore adopting programs similar to New York's innovative Pro Bono Scholars program.

State courts are also the primary gatekeepers when it comes to UPL rules. They not only tend to define the practice of law in caselaw; they also police its boundaries and can work with state legislatures to authorize nonlawyer assistance in a range of legal settings. Such arrangements can make courts function better, where pro se litigants could obtain guidance that can help them understand their rights, assert their claims effectively, and focus on issues relevant to the matter before the court. This can actually save courts time, so it is in the interests of the court systems to advocate for the authority of nonlawyer advocates to assist in those cases where they can serve the litigants and the court system effectively.

At the same time, courts should also work with legislatures, advocates, and the "customers" of the court system (that is, litigants) to streamline court proceedings and practices to make them more user-friendly. Remarkable work is being done by groups like the Legal Design Lab at Stanford Law School to help court systems design court systems so they are less daunting and confusing. In the nineteenth century, lawyers worked to make court systems more complex and byzantine in order to justify the lawyer's existence, solidify their role, and make those systems difficult for the layperson to navigate. We are long past a time when court systems should be fair, straightforward, and accessible. Such efforts will take the commitment of the courts to invite input from more than just the lawyers who stand to benefit from complexity. To understand the experience and improve it from an end user's perspective, those who maintain court systems should certainly listen to consumers and advocates who have to navigate those systems. They should also invite technologists to help them design user-friendly websites that provide guidance to litigants on court practices and procedures and offer easy-to-complete form pleadings and other documents. They should also utilize remote appearances wherever possible and to schedule those appearances in such a way that will take into account the fact that it is extremely difficult for the working poor to simply take a day off to attend court when they might speak to the judge for a few minutes, if they do at all. Courts can also schedule simple matters that can be handled remotely in five- or ten-minute increments so that litigants can join the court's session at a specific time rather than sit in court for most of the day for something that can be handled remotely. This will take some planning and effort, but it will make the courts more accessible and effective. Of course, such innovations will have to account for the digital divide that might make it more difficult for all consumers to access websites and remote access technologies, so courts should coordinate with legal services offices and locations like libraries to provide computer kiosks and other means of accessing court functions.

Courts are also the primary entity responsible for policing misconduct in the courts. When it comes to the lawsuits challenging the results of the 2020 election, they did an admirable job. Since most of the cases in which candidates, advocacy groups, and even individual voters tried to overturn the results of the 2020 election were filed in federal court, the rules governing federal litigation, specifically Rule 11 of the Federal Rules of Civil Procedure, apply to such cases, and courts have not shied away from penalizing lawyers for frivolous claims brought to advance that effort.

As discussed in chapter 7, however, Rule 11 makes no explicit reference to heightened punishment when lawyers take direct action to undermine the rule of law, although courts reviewing the Big Lie litigation certainly considered the nature of the action when considering what type of punishment to pass down for conduct related to those cases. As the court found in *King v. Whitmer*, sanctions were required in that case "to deter the filing of future frivolous lawsuits designed primarily to spread the narrative that our election processes are rigged and our democratic institutions cannot be trusted."[46] The court found it notable that "many people have latched on to this narrative, citing as proof counsel's submissions in this case." It did not matter that this narrative was one that "may have originated or been repeated by Former President Trump and it may be one that," as the plaintiffs' alleged, "'many Americans' share";[47] the court concluded that, although that may be the case, "neither renders [the narrative] true nor justifies counsel's exploitation of the courts to further spread it."[48]

The Advisory Committee on Civil Rules, the body appointed by the federal courts that helps to draft the Federal Rules of Civil Procedure, has highlighted a range of sanctions that courts can impose, from striking a frivolous complaint or claim to recommending disciplinary action against the lawyers who interposed baseless claims and assertions.[49] The punishments the court dispensed in *King v. Whitmer* reflect this range. Finding that the lawsuit "should never have been filed" and the defendants "should never have had to defend it,"[50] it ordered the plaintiffs' attorneys to reimburse the defendants for the attorney's fees incurred in defending the action, because, if such a penalty were not imposed, "counsel will not be deterred from continuing to abuse the judicial system to publicize their narrative."[51] The court explicitly referenced the advisory committee's recognition that in "unusual circumstance[s]" such an award is appropriate. Furthermore, because of the claimed "violations of Michigan election law without a thorough understanding of what the law requires, and the number of failed election-challenge lawsuits that Plaintiffs' attorneys have filed," the court also mandated "continuing legal education in the subjects of pleading standards and election law."[52] Finally, the court found that the lawyers' practices "call[ed] into question their fitness to practice law," which warranted "a referral for investigation and possible suspension or disbarment to the appropriate disciplinary authority for every state bar and federal court in which each attorney is admitted."[53]

However, as explored in chapter 7, Rule 11, and such corollaries as 28 U.S.C. §1927, which prohibits litigants from "multipl[ying] the proceedings in any case unreasonably and vexatiously," make no explicit reference to any particular type of case or whether heightened punishment is appropriate in cases where litigants are directly attacking the rule of law or seeking to undermine the courts and democracy itself. While it is recommended "under unusual circumstances" that courts can award attorney's fees to the prevailing party in a frivolous action, nowhere does it say what those unusual circumstances are. At the same time, courts, when attaching a penalty to misconduct, can consider what type of penalty is "needed to deter" someone from repeating the conduct "given the financial resources of the responsible person." What size penalty is sufficient to deter such future conduct when legal campaigns might have virtually unlimited funds to advance these and similar efforts in the future? When presidential campaigns currently cost billions of dollars to run, what deterrent effect will a fine of a few hundred thousand dollars have? It might be seen as nothing more than the cost of doing business, no matter how sordid that business might be. Courts should feel empowered not only to match the size of the penalty to the gravity of the offense but also to take into account the financial wherewithal of the litigants and assess a penalty that will truly deter similar future conduct. Courts could even consider punitive damages, but that would be beyond the scope of penalties permitted under Rule 11. But that does not mean courts are powerless to impose them, which brings us to the next tool in the judicial toolbox.

While Rule 11 and related statutes seem like somewhat blunt, limited tools for reining in conduct that undermines the rule of law, courts have one more avenue for checking such behavior, and we are already seeing courts begin to do so in certain Big Lie litigation. Courts, through what are known as their inherent powers, have the authority to punish attorney misconduct that falls outside the scope of Rule 11 and other explicit rules. As the Supreme Court affirmed in the early 1990s, the creation of federal courts as a pillar of our constitutional structure endowed such courts with certain powers simply by virtue of being courts, such as the power to punish misconduct by the litigants before them.[54] Whether those inherent powers have been relegated to filling in the gaps regarding such misconduct where rules or statutes have displaced those powers, or those powers stand on their own regardless of the existence of such rules, are questions that are not necessary to resolve for our purposes here. Those inherent powers are useful in several ways when it comes to rule of law–threating behavior.

First, although the advisory committee on Rule 11 has stated that heightened punishment is appropriate in "unusual circumstances," courts have determined that they have the inherent power to punish behavior that undermines their authority, which, I would argue, includes behavior that threatens the rule of law.

Second, even behavior that is a blatant violation of Rule 11 can escape punishment because of what has come to be known as Rule 11's "safe harbor." As part of amendments to Rule 11 adopted in 1993, there now exists in the rule a provision where a party enjoys a twenty-one-day window in which to withdraw any pleading or other document if there is a threat that filing will draw a request for sanctions from an adversary under Rule 11.[55] A party that wishes to seek sanctions under Rule 11 generally must serve on their adversary the motion that seeks such sanctions but not file it for twenty-one days. During that twenty-one-day window, the party against whom the sanctions are sought can withdraw whatever claim it is alleged is frivolous. Once a claim is withdrawn, that party cannot be sanctioned for having filed it in the first place under Rule 11. The purpose of this safe harbor was to permit courts to avoid resolving Rule 11 motions if a party were to recognize there was some chance that the court might sanction them. Still, a lot of mischief can occur in twenty-one days before the party withdraws the allegedly frivolous claims, especially in a situation like the aftermath of an election, when various deadlines emerge that practically set in stone dates by which election officials, and, in turn, courts, must take certain actions. We saw the Supreme Court respond to one such deadline in the litigation that ensued in the wake of the contested election of 2000, the so-called safe harbor for states to certify their own election results following a national election.[56] The January 6 insurrection was also based on an explicit date set forth in the Electoral Count Act, which sets forth not just the date but also the specific time when Congress should certify the results of the election (1:00 p.m.).[57]

In election-law litigation, there is a compressed time frame within which legislators, election officials, and even the courts must act to ensure the proper certification of the results of an election. Because of that, even frivolous claims may enter the political bloodstream and incite extralegal and violent actions that undermine democracy and the rule of law before a court can punish frivolous behavior under Rule 11. Indeed, a speedy time frame for litigation does not square neatly with Rule 11's twenty-one-day safe harbor provision. This means that courts should take immediate action when appropriate and punish, through their inherent authority, the filing of legal claims that might cause harm during the twenty-one day window or those that might otherwise slither out of the grasp of Rule 11 because they were withdrawn prior to the expiration of that time frame. Similarly, a case could be dismissed before the defending party even gets the chance to file a Rule 11 motion. In such situations litigants, and the courts, are not impotent.

At least one court, in *O'Rourke v. Dominion Voting Systems*,[58] dealt with a situation where the plaintiffs' claims were voluntary dismissed before several of the defendants had a chance to trigger the twenty-one-day notice requirement, which would have set the stage for a subsequent motion for sanctions.[59] The court nevertheless entertained, and granted, a motion for sanctions under the court's inherent authority, as well as under 28 U.S.C. §1927, which has no safe harbor provision. That ruling was recently upheld on appeal.[60]

Third, using their inherent authority, courts could also look to more meaningful financial penalties for well-heeled and well-funded litigants for whom an award requiring them to pay a few hundred thousands dollars of their adversary's attorney's fees will have no deterrent effect. Courts could consider more serious financial penalties utilizing inherent powers, penalties that will truly deter, even if they may come across as punitive in nature. To put things in perspective, the litigants in the *O'Rourke* case sought $160 *billion* in damages in their frivolous case over Dominion Voting Systems's supposed hijacking of the 2020 election.[61] Such a claim is certainly outlandish. Nevertheless, does it seem so outlandish to raise the cost of deterrence when a party and its lawyers feel free to make such a claim?

Once again, whether we think the inherent powers are there only to fill in gaps in existing rules and statutes, like Rule 11 or 28 U.S.C. §1927, or stand on their own regardless of what those other provisions offer, the inherent authority can be exercised to heighten punishment where these other provisions make no explicit mention (as in rule of law–undermining actions) or where Rule 11's safe harbor might actually insulate frivolous conduct when it has caused harm during the safe harbor period.

Relatedly, one aspect of a court's inherent authority is its ability to manage its own docket and schedule cases, motions, and hearings according to a schedule it controls.[62] In such high-profile, pressure-cooker cases that operate on a swift timeline, like election cases, courts should accelerate their substantive determination of actions that, by virtue of their being filed in the first place, threaten to create a whiff of illegitimacy that could taint elections or other legal proceedings. In such situations, courts can fast-track hearings on those cases and dispose of them as appropriate. In probably the most significant of the cases filed in the wake of the 2020 election, that filed by the state of Texas and other states where conservative attorneys general attempted to bring a case directly before the Supreme Court to challenge the certification of electors in several other states, the Supreme Court disposed of the case in just four days,[63] a time frame that likely gave even the most seasoned of Supreme Court practitioners whiplash. Courts facing similar rule of law–threatening litigation should take the Supreme Court's lead and exercise their inherent authority to rule on those proceedings with dispatch and speed—consistent with due process, of course.

At the same time, courts should refrain from exercising any of this authority, either that which is given to them explicitly in the rules or as part of their inherent authority, in ways that undermine the rule of law and the evolutionary nature of our laws and democratic institutions by wielding such powers to stifle and chill legitimate zealous advocacy. As described in chapter 7, when Rule 11 was amended in the early 1980s to give it more bite, advocates argued—and the evidence, though mixed, seemed to bear this out—that it was being used disproportionately to punish civil rights litigants; it was amended again a decade later to

232 THE PURPOSE OF THE PROFESSION

try to minimize any adverse impact on legitimate forms of advocacy. Courts should ensure that they apply existing rules, any new rules that might emerge, or the courts' inherent authority to punish rule of law–undermining behavior in such a way that they do not chill legitimate advocacy. By refraining from doing so, they will honor the adversarial and evolutionary nature of our system as it strives to protect individual rights, civil rights, and human dignity.

Similarly, in advancing such rights, and the principles of access to the profession and inclusion, judges can exercise their authority to manage the conduct of those who practice before them.[64] After a report of the New York State Bar Association showed that only 25 percent of lead lawyers in litigation in court were women (it is the lead lawyer who tends to have the most prominent role in a case and actually speaks and advocates in court the most), Judge Jack Weinstein of the federal district court for the Eastern District of New York adopted a rule for his courtroom that encouraged junior lawyers to take a more active role in litigation before him: arguing motions, questioning witnesses, presenting evidence, and so on. While the rule did not explicitly say that women and people of color should take a larger role in speaking in court, his intention when adopting a rule to accommodate a larger role for "junior lawyers" was designed to do just that, recognizing that, in a slowly diversifying legal profession, such junior lawyers tended to be more diverse than the upper ranks of firms, which are more white and male.[65] Just as clients can press for greater diversity in their legal teams, as I argue below, so, too, can the courts at least try to make space for newer lawyers, hopefully from different backgrounds than their lead-lawyer colleagues, to gain experience and advance in their careers and in the profession through courtroom opportunity and success.

Similarly, courts have adapted to remote functions, some more than others, and as courts continue to expand their in-person operations, they should be mindful of using remote technologies when feasible to make it easier on litigants and lawyers when doing so makes sense. Little is gained by requiring lawyers to travel across the country for a ten-minute court appearance in which the parties will discuss scheduling matters with the court. Clients also gain when they do not have to compensate their lawyers for all of that travel time. While it is certainly difficult for trial courts to perform critical tasks that are best performed in person, like gauging witness credibility, at least some of what judges do in the courtroom could be easily carried out using remote technologies. At the same time, during the pandemic, and before in immigration or parole hearings, courts have taken testimony by video and have had to assess the credibility of the witnesses through that medium.[66] With advances in technology, court systems should do what makes the most sense, what can make adjudication accessible and fair, and what can accommodate the needs of the litigants before them. Indeed, transferring those functions that make sense to remote settings will also make litigation more accommodating to lawyers and clients with mobility impairments that might make court appearances arduous and taxing. Similarly, for working-poor clients or those for whom making it to court is a costly endeavor, being able to log in to a court appearance at a designated time will enable them to participate and engage in the legal process in a more meaningful way and not have to make a choice between putting food on the table for their family and trying to vindicate their rights. Thus, to the extent that remote functions can make the court system more accessible, they will also promote not only access to justice but also inclusion.

Bringing Clients into the Reform Effort

Clients can play a significant role in shaping lawyer behavior by setting expectations for their lawyers to advance the institutional goals described here. Indeed, they have shaped such behavior in the past and will continue to do so in the future. In earlier times, some clients had no problem telling their lawyers that they were not comfortable with a nonwhite lawyer, a Jewish lawyer, or a female lawyer. They could express their interest today in having multiracial and diverse teams representing them. As Deborah Enix-Ross explains: "[L]aw firms tend to react to what clients want." What is more, clients should want this type of diversity because research consistently shows that diverse teams perform better and clients should expect their teams to reflect that diversity with an eye toward better performance from their lawyers. Similarly, they should recognize that they might get better performance from their lawyers if their lawyers worked on schedules that accommodated those lawyers' needs and made time and space for them to do their most creative work. While at least one client made waves among the elite firms in 2021 when it announced that it wanted its lawyers in their offices,[67] for the most part law firms have still held to flexible work schedules. Clients want their lawyers doing their best work, and that best work likely includes operating under a humane return-to-work policy and flexible hours. They will want their lawyers available to them, for sure, but at least some have expressed a willingness to communicate with their lawyers through remote technologies, whether simply by phone or via video link. When we consider the concept of professionalism described in chapter 5, it certainly includes the notion that lawyers should act in a way that engenders their clients' trust, especially the trust that their lawyers are behaving in such a way that furthers the clients' best interests. To the extent the legal profession shows that it is supporting efforts that make representation more effective and efficient, thereby saving their clients money, that will help generate that trust. In other words, lawyers can use the opportunities available to them through remote technologies to show that they can operate in an inclusive rather than extractive fashion. And clients should demand that of them.

Clients can also mobilize to demand the broader adoption of these innovations as well as simplification of court procedures and filings, an increase in the number of settings where nonlawyers can serve consumers, and a streamlining of simple legal functions that can enable consumers to protect their rights effectively without resort to legal representation. As discussed in chapter 8, in the banking context, regulators have approved mortgages with consumer protection features such as qualified mortgages. A consumer seeking to enter into a mortgage can inquire as to whether the mortgage is a recognized qualified mortgage and thus will know that it will not contain certain risky features, like balloon payments or excessive fees. Consumer advocates should work with regulators and legislators to look for opportunities to simplify legal practices to reduce the number of situations in which a lawyer is necessary to vindicate one's rights. That may not be in the legal profession's pecuniary interests, but, again, making the law more accessible and inclusive, and reducing the number of situations in which legal representation is necessary, advances the goal of inclusion and reduces the extent to which our laws have extractive qualities.

Finally, consumers, as a class, should advocate for greater access to justice through funding for nonprofit legal services for those who cannot afford a lawyer. Once again, through a combination of simplification of legal processes and making more matters subject to nonlawyer professionals, we can reduce the overall justice gap in meaningful ways, but there will always be a need for full-service representation. If we reduce the number of situations in which such full-service representation is necessary, and the legal profession is willing to make concessions in such areas with the goal of protecting consumers, even if it might seem like it is not in their best interest to do so, there might be greater support for broader funding for legal services, and the legal profession will not appear like it is simply protecting its monopoly.

The Role of Law Firms and Public Interest Organizations

Lawyers are obviously the most important stakeholders when it comes to making the institutional changes described throughout this work. Will they choose to advance inclusive rather than extractive practices? The legal profession must come to terms with its own history of exclusion. It must recognize not only the ways in which generations of lawyers have been trained in practices that kept prospective lawyers who were not cisgender white males out of the practice of law but also the extent to which the profession adopted habits, norms, and rules that served to institutionalize discrimination in many forms. While the profession has made some strides in weeding out some of those habits and beliefs, it still has a long way to go. And as one surveys the upper echelons of the profession—its bar leaders, the judiciary, senior partners at law firms, and senior faculty and administrators at law schools—we know that the profession has more work to do to ensure the demographic makeup of the profession matches the characteristics of the communities and nation that the American legal profession is supposed to serve. It should also recognize the value of diversity in the teams it puts together and embrace inclusive remote-work practices to the extent they can advance the goal of achieving greater diversity, equity, inclusion, and belonging in the profession.

Lawyers must also resist continuing efforts to preserve the legal profession's monopoly on the practice of law when to do so perpetuates almost exclusively extractive features. There are many areas in which that monopoly serves no purpose other than to deny access to justice to tens of millions of Americans. Where we can simplify the law and legal processes such that laypeople can protect their rights, or can do so with a modicum of legal assistance, we should make those changes, in terms of simplifying the law and easing UPL restrictions. What is more, nonprofit legal services providers are sometimes the fiercest opponents of efforts to make nonlawyer services available in certain settings out of fear that this will reduce the demand for, as well as support for funding, such nonprofit organizations. Such resistance undermines the goal of access to justice and makes even nonprofit providers appear as if they are functioning as extractive institutions. A clear-eyed assessment of those situations in which full legal representation is necessary, and a willingness to concede that certain disputes can be resolved without full representation, might reduce the need for those organizations' services, to be sure, but it also might make the justice gap more manageable and portray nonprofit providers as capable of filling that gap. Reducing and even eliminating the justice gap should be the ultimate goal. If we increase the use of nonlawyer professionals, there will still be plenty of work to go around.

Realizing the Purpose: Professionalism, Access, and Inclusion

In a multiracial democracy that is designed to preserve the rule of law and protect minority rights and individual liberty, that does so by utilizing an adversarial and jurisgenerative approach (through which law is made through interest group advocacy), and that has adopted a dispute-resolution model where interests are advanced through an adversarial process, the legal profession plays a central role in all aspects of the functioning and realization of that system. Whether it is serving in an advisory capacity in the drafting of legislation that provides the structure for that system, assisting interest groups in their campaigns to shape those laws, or promoting individual liberty and protect minority rights within the judicial system, the democratic institutions and values upon which that society relies are realized through processes in which members of the legal profession are central players. From this role, tailored to the needs of the institutions and communities in which it arises, we can discern what *professionalism* means in this context—the American context.

In this setting, professionalism for the legal profession requires that its members not only defend and advance individual liberty and minority rights but also restrain that advocacy within a rule-of-law framework. In other words, lawyers must engage in zealous advocacy within the bounds of the law. The American democratic ideal is supposed to reflect fair, participatory, and inclusive processes, including that all participants have an equal opportunity to engage in the rulemaking process itself. An effective process will, in turn, generate acceptance of the outcomes of that process, regardless of the outcome. The same is true for a system of justice that is supposed to resolve disputes in accordance with the rule of law, including disputes around lawmaking processes themselves. Both of these processes—lawmaking and dispute resolution—are adversarial in nature and operate under the assumption that the optimal outcome of these processes is achieved when advocates press their claims in a fair competition for their respective desired results. This description, of course, identifies the ideal, and it is rarely realized in practice. Nevertheless, the adversarial nature of these processes requires that the parties press their interests and do so despite what may seem to be the prevailing wisdom or outsized or misplaced notions of the general interests of the community.

Indeed, zealous advocacy that promotes the interests of clients, even in the face of community opposition, helps to realize the democratic values of individual liberty and minority rights. The legal profession plays a critical role in ensuring the protection of these values because of the position it holds within lawmaking and conflict resolution processes. When a member of the legal profession assumes the mantle of advocacy for individual and/or minority rights, they must strive to press for the client's interests within the democratic system, must be willing to put their client's interests before their own, and must try to assume their client's perspective on the problem to the greatest extent possible. That is one aspect of the republican virtue of disinterestedness discussed in chapter 2: lawyers must put aside their own interests to advance the interests of their clients. Yet, all too often, members of the legal profession have, since colonial times, been seen as protecting their own interests rather than those of their clients or the community, serving in a status quo–defending role, and engaging in extractive rather than productive practices. Professionalism in the American democratic system today, however, requires a form of advocacy—even zeal—in the face of community opposition to protect and advance individual liberty and minority rights, not the interests of the profession.

At the same time, advocacy must be balanced against the need to respect the democratically generated norms and rules governing dispute resolution. One cannot undermine one value—democratically chosen structures and systems—in the interest of another—individual rights. There are rules governing disputes and rules for changing the rules. Professionalism in a democratic system requires that members of the legal profession follow the rules of the adversarial system and even the rules for changing the rules. This is another facet of disinterestedness: the ability to place community interests, when appropriate, ahead of the parochial interests of an individual client or cause. This approach also has core rule of law–preserving functions as well. Thus, the essence of lawyer professionalism is balancing these potentially competing values: validating the notion that the lawyer must engage in zealous advocacy, but doing so within the bounds of the law. By abiding by the bounds of the law, the lawyers reaffirms the democratic nature of the rules of the game: they are a product of those democratic, inclusive processes. Of course, I am speaking in theory and about an ideal.

This multifaceted approach to professionalism in the context of American democracy has implications for the other values the profession is supposed to espouse: access and inclusion. First, an adversarial system requires that there is a degree of equality of representation within that system. Access to justice, access to law, and access to the profession are all elements of this value. In order for adversarial systems to function the way they are supposed to function within democratic institutions to yield the sort of just outcomes that those institutions are supposed to generate, the adversaries must have a degree of parity in their ability to operate within that system. To ensure access to jurisgenerative processes and to, in turn, have a meaningful impact on those processes, the law itself must be accessible and lawyers must serve interests from across the range of political, social, and economic perspectives to ensure the processes work in the manner in which they are supposed to work.

Second, in order to advance greater access to justice, and access to the profession itself, the profession must embrace the value of inclusion. It must ensure that the profession is open and accessible to anyone who wishes to join the profession and can serve the community competently. Part of that competence involves having an ability to engage in the disinterestedness describe above, to see the world through the eyes of the client. Inclusive—yet adversarial—political and judicial processes require that type of engagement. And the more the profession is open to individuals of different backgrounds, perspectives, and experiences, the more likely it is that varied community interests will receive their fair share of representation in adversarial settings.

Institutional Values, Democracy's Future, and the Future of the Profession

The purpose of this book has been to identify the six forces currently at work that are likely to shape the legal profession for the coming decades. These forces include a global pandemic that has challenged assumptions about the ways that lawyers work and an insurrection that called into question the nature of lawyering and the rule of law, placing democracy itself at risk. They also involve the historically exclusive nature of law practice, the access-to-justice crisis facing most Americans, the rise of technology that is likely to transform the practice of law, and the fact that many lawyers are experiencing a considerable lack of job satisfaction. There is no question that the practice of law is changing and will change in the face of these forces. Whether it will survive in its current form, with a range of institutions created more than a century ago, remains to be seen. What the profession needs is better institutions, created not for the profession that exists or even for a profession designed merely to serve the ends of the profession. Rather, institutions are needed that will match the needs of the American ideal to the functions, practices, norms, and values of the American legal profession. That ideal is something to strive for, but it is also something that a legal profession designed to serve that ideal stands a better chance of realizing. In order to manifest that ideal, the legal profession must adopt and advance values that will help to make that ideal a reality. I have argued that those values are: a particular kind of professionalism, one that is fine-tuned to protect and advance a multiracial democracy, preserve the rule of law, and protect individual and minority rights while promoting community well-being; a commitment to access—to justice, to law, and to the profession; and an ethos of inclusion, which advances equality before the law, civil rights, minority rights, and participatory democracy.

How the legal profession achieves these values while sustaining its members requires it to recognize the important role that mastery, autonomy, and purpose play in ensuring that the profession can realize these ideals. As described earlier in this chapter, these characteristics serve a critical role in advancing well-being, but, when realized, they help to invigorate and channel professional conduct. I would go further and say that they can make achieving the values more likely and, thus, there is a symbiotic relationship between the values of professionalism, access, and inclusion and the practices of mastery, autonomy, and purpose. And it is this alignment of values with practices that might provide the best opportunity for the American legal profession to continue to play its critical role in preserving and sustaining American democracy.

The purpose of the profession is realized in fulfilling this role itself. Members of the legal profession must understand that by advancing the values of professionalism, access, and inclusion they are, indeed, advancing a cause larger than themselves by working to sustain democratic institutions and norms. This does not require every lawyer to work in a nonprofit or for greater social justice generally. But whether a lawyer practices in a private firm, is engaged in criminal defense work or prosecution, works in the counsel's office of a corporation, or serves within a government office, they can and should work, regardless of their place within the profession, to strengthen and advance democratic principles, community well-being, individual liberty, and civil rights.

When it comes to autonomy, lawyers, as professionals, tend to enjoy a degree of autonomy in carrying out their work, as all professionals must, which is why they are professionals in the first place. But when we talk about professional autonomy in this way, we typically think of autonomy from actors outside the profession. We recognize that the legal profession, as a profession, needs to function with a degree of independence from oversight by those who are not lawyers. And they also need this independence when they are advocating for those whose interests run contrary to majority will.

What autonomy-enhancing practices might look like from *within* the profession are those that we have seen instituted in the face of a global pandemic: greater freedom for lawyers to choose how and where they work. It might also entail providing lawyers with greater flexibility as to the type of work and the nature of the cases they take on. In turn, such autonomy might also lead to greater mastery. The type of mastery described here is not just proficiency in a particular area of law; it is also mastery over professionalism itself: the lawyer's ability to practice disinterestedness, to advance individual liberty while respecting democratic values and principles, and to protect minority rights while respecting community values when it is in the long-term interests of the community that the lawyer do so.

Returning once again to the symbol of Janus, who not only looks in two directions at once but also has two sides, the lawyer must also master the two sides of professional disinterestedness—that is, the notion of being a zealous advocate within the bounds of the law. When coupled with advancing access to justice and promoting an inclusive democratic system, the proper role for the profession—both as a response to the forces described here that are currently mustered against it and those that will inevitably arise in the future—represent the values that are most likely to sustain the profession and democracy to the greatest extent possible. It is these values, and these institutions, that will help chart a course forward for the American legal profession, one that is calibrated to the needs of the nation and its aspirations.

ACKNOWLEDGMENTS

Many hands make the load lighter. This work would not have come about without the work of many hands. First, I am grateful for the support of colleagues who provided helpful advice and guidance on prior drafts, including Ava Ayers, Ted De Barbieri, Keith Hirokawa, Rosemary Queenan, Sarah Rogerson, and Jonathan Rosenbloom. Benjamin Barton, Paul Finkelman, and Michael Wishnie provided incredibly useful comments on earlier drafts. Friends also supplied moral support, including Graham Boyd, Adam Bramwell, Dana Carstarphen, Charles Chesnut, Rodger Citron, Chris Coons, Beth Garrity-Rokous, Gates Garrity-Rokous, Brandt Goldstein, Mark Napier, Kurt Petersen, Richard Pinner, Paul Sonn, and Nicole Theodosiou. I also had incredible research assistants, including Polly Boyle, Sarah Dixon-Morgan, Nicholas Erly, Stephanie Fattorusso, Miller Fina, Paige Gottorff, E. Conor Graham, Eunice Lee, Daniella Oh, and Taylor Yensan, who provided support at various points in writing and production. In addition, since the very beginning of this project and right to its end, another student, Alice Broussard, provided tireless and excellent research and editorial assistance. I am also grateful for the wisdom shared by those I interviewed for this work, including Mark Alexander, Marilyn Brown, Deborah Enix-Ross, Danielle M. Conway, Carolyn Elefant, Ali Frick, William Malley, Lillian Moy, Sateesh Nori, Mark O'Brien, Swapna Reddy, James Sandman, Adam Stofsky, and Elizabeth Tran. I also wish to thank leaders at Albany Law School, including former President and Dean Alicia Ouellette and former Associate Dean Connie Mayer, who approved the sabbatical leave that enabled me to complete this work. Similarly, the amazing team at the law school's library, including David Walker and Pegeen Lorusso, gave me unwavering research support throughout the project, as did the remarkable staff who supported me throughout, including Sherri Meyer, Katie Palmieri, Julie Pierce, and Laurie Stevens. I also am in deep debt to Clara Platter and the team at New York University Press for supporting and guiding me throughout this process. Most important, though, I wish to thank family. My sister, Jean Marie Brescia, and brother-in-law, Richard Marsico, who represent the best values of the profession, were extremely helpful as I first conceptualized this work.

My spouse, Amy Barasch, and son, Leo Brescia, have given me the greatest support of all throughout this process, for which I am forever grateful.

The book is dedicated to my parents, Raymond and Kathleen Brescia. They taught me the importance of values, hard work, and decency. My father passed away in the winter of 2021 after a heroic, twenty-five-year fight with cancer and did not live to see this book in print. Nevertheless, his spirit still animates this work.

NOTES

CHAPTER 1. A JANUS-FACED PROFESSION

1 Theodore Roosevelt, *The Harvard Spirit*, Address at Harvard University Commencement, June 28, 1905, in 4 PRESIDENTIAL ADDRESSES AND STATE PAPERS 419–20 (1905).

2 Louis D. Brandeis, *The Opportunity in the Law*, 39 AM. L. REV. 555, 559–60 (1905).

3 *Id.* at 562.

4 ROSCOE POUND, A HUNDRED YEARS OF AMERICAN LAW 8 (1937).

5 STEVEN J. DINER, A VERY DIFFERENT AGE: AMERICANS OF THE PROGRESSIVE ERA 14–29 (1998).

6 John A. Matzko, *"The Best Men of the Bar": The Founding of the American Bar Association*, in THE NEW HIGH PRIESTS: LAWYERS IN THE POST-CIVIL WAR ERA 75, 76 (Gerard W. Gawalt ed., 1984); ERWIN N. GRISWOLD, LAW AND LAWYERS IN THE UNITED STATES 15–20 (1965).

7 RICHARD ABEL, AMERICAN LAWYERS 87–108 (1989).

8 *Id.*

9 JEROLD S. AUERBACH, UNEQUAL JUSTICE: LAWYERS AND SOCIAL CHANGE IN MODERN AMERICA 50 (1976).

10 Alan W. Houseman, *Political Lessons: Legal Services for the Poor—A Commentary*, 83 GEO. L.J. 1669, 1671–72 (1995); MARTHA DAVIS, BRUTAL NEED: LAWYERS AND THE WELFARE RIGHTS MOVEMENT, 1960–1973, at 10–18 (1993).

11 Lincoln Sav. & Loan Ass'n v. Wall, 743 F. Supp. 901, 920 (D.D.C. 1990).

12 JAMES MOLITERNO, THE AMERICAN LEGAL PROFESSION IN CRISIS: RESISTANCE AND RESPONSES TO CHANGE 101–03 (2013).

13 Andrew A. Lundgren, *Sarbanes-Oxley, Then Disney: The Post-Scandal Corporate-Governance Plot Thickens*, 8 DEL. L. REV. 195, 197–204 (2006).

14 This work borrows the concept of institutional fit from environmental scholar Oran Young, whose work I will explore in greater depth in chapter 5. ORAN R. YOUNG, THE INSTITUTIONAL DIMENSION OF ENVIRONMENTAL CHANGE: FIT, INTERPLAY, AND SCALE 56–82 (2002).

15 DARON ACEMOGLU & JAMES A. ROBINSON, WHY NATIONS FAIL: THE ORIGINS OF POWER, PROSPERITY, AND POVERTY 74–79 (2012).

16 EDITH HAMILTON, MYTHOLOGY 46 (Warner Books 1999) (1942).

CHAPTER 2. AN INDEX TO THE CHARACTER OF THE PEOPLE

1 JONATHAN JACKSON, THOUGHTS UPON THE POLITICAL SITUATION OF THE UNITED STATES OF AMERICA 117 (1788).

2 Anton-Hermann Chroust, *The Legal Profession in Colonial America*, 33 NOTRE DAME L. REV. 51, 68 (1957).

3 LAWRENCE M. FRIEDMAN, A HISTORY OF AMERICAN LAW 63–64 (Oxford Univ. Press 4th ed. 2019) (1973).

4 DAVID THOMAS KONIG, LAW AND SOCIETY IN PURITAN MASSACHU-SETTS ESSEX COUNTY, 1629–1692, 31 (1979).

5 SAMUEL HABER, THE QUEST FOR AUTHORITY AND HONOR IN THE AMERICAN PROFESSIONS, 1750–1900, at 69 (1991).

6 Chroust, *Legal Profession*, *supra* note 2, at 67.

7 *Id.* at 53–55.

8 KONIG, *supra* note 4, at 26–63.

9 *Id.* at 70.

10 FRIEDMAN, A HISTORY OF AMERICAN LAW, *supra* note 3, at 63; Chroust, *Legal Profession*, *supra* note 2, at 59.

11 Chroust, *Legal Profession*, *supra* note 2, at 55–56.

12 *Id.* at 93–94.

13 *Id.* at 90; CHARLES WARREN, 1 HISTORY OF THE HARVARD LAW SCHOOL AND OF EARLY LEGAL CONDITIONS IN AMERICA 21 (1908).

14 FRIEDMAN, A HISTORY OF AMERICAN LAW, *supra* note 3, at 63.

15 HABER, QUEST FOR AUTHORITY, *supra* note, 5, at 73.

16 A. G. ROEBER, FAITHFUL MAGISTRATES AND REPUBLICAN LAWYERS: CREATORS OF VIRGINIA LEGAL CULTURE, 1680–1810, at 68 (1981).

17 HABER, QUEST FOR AUTHORITY, *supra* note 5, at 67–76.

18 *Id.* at 69–71.

19 *Id.*

20 FRIEDMAN, A HISTORY OF AMERICAN LAW, *supra* note 3, at 65.

21 *Id.* at 300.

22 HABER, QUEST FOR AUTHORITY, *supra* note 5, at 71.

23 JAMES WILLARD HURST, GROWTH OF AMERICAN LAWYERS: THE LAW MAKERS 251 (1950).

24 ROEBER, *supra* note 16, at 156 (citation omitted).

25 FRIEDMAN, A HISTORY OF AMERICAN LAW, *supra* note 3, at 66–67.

26 *Id.* at 67–68.

27 *Id.* at 66.

28 William Ewald, *James Wilson and the Drafting of the Constitution*, 10 U. PA. J. CONST. L. 901 (2008).

29 FRIEDMAN, A HISTORY OF AMERICAN LAW, *supra* note 3, at 65–69.

30 Robert G. Natelson, *The Constitutional Contributions of John Dickinson*, 108 PENN. ST. L. REV. 415 (2003).

31 JAMES WILLARD HURST, GROWTH OF AMERICAN LAWYERS: THE LAW MAKERS 252–53 (1950).

32 FRIEDMAN, A HISTORY OF AMERICAN LAW, *supra* note 3, at 70.

33 Erwin C. Surrency, *The Lawyer and the Revolution*, 8 AM. J. LEGAL HIST. 125, 126 (1964).

34 RON CHERNOW, ALEXANDER HAMILTON 135–36 (2004).

35 HURST, GROWTH OF AMERICAN LAWYERS, *supra* note 31, at 254.

36 FRIEDMAN, A HISTORY OF AMERICAN LAW, *supra* note 3, at 290.

37 2 THE WORKS OF JOHN ADAMS 58 (Charles Francis Adams ed., 1850).

38 Chroust, *Legal Profession, supra* note 2, at 79–80.

39 HURST, GROWTH OF AMERICAN LAWYERS, *supra* note 31, at 253.

40 *Id.*; FRIEDMAN, A HISTORY OF AMERICAN LAW, *supra* note 3, at 70. Paul Finkelman, *Alexander Hamilton, Esq.: Founding Father as Lawyer*, 1984 AM. BAR. FOUND. RES. J. 229, 235 (1984).

41 Robert F. Boden, *The Colonial Bar and the American Revolution*, 60 MARQ. L. REV. 1, 3 (1976) (citations omitted).

42 M. H. SMITH, THE WRITS OF ASSISTANCE CASE 17–40 (1978).

43 EDMUND S. MORGAN & HELEN MORGAN, THE STAMP ACT CRISIS: PROLOGUE TO REVOLUTION 219 (3rd ed. 1995).

44 WILLIAM CUDDIHY, THE FOURTH AMENDMENT: ORIGINS AND ORIGINAL MEANING 380–81 (2009).

45 James M. Farrell, *The Writs of Assistance and Public Memory: John Adams and the Legacy of James Otis*, 79 NEW ENG. QUART. 533, 536 (2006).

46 Letter from John Adams to William Tudor (Mar. 29, 1817), in 10 THE WORKS OF JOHN ADAMS 247–48 (Charles Francis Adams ed., 1854).

47 MORGAN & MORGAN, THE STAMP ACT CRISIS, *supra* note 43, at 72.

48 *Id.*

49 *Id.*

50 Surrency, *supra* note 33, at 127.

51 Anton-Hermann Chroust, *The Lawyers of New Jersey and the Stamp Act*, 6 AM. J. LEGAL HIST. 286, 290–91 (1962); Surrency, *supra* note 33, at 128.

52 Surrency, *supra* note 33, at 128–31.

53 *Id.*

54 Boden, *The Colonial Bar, supra* note 41, at 3. Pound puts the number of lawyers who signed the Declaration at twenty-five. ROSCOE POUND, THE LAWYER FROM ANTIQUITY TO MODERN TIMES 173–74 (1953).

55 Bennett Capers & Bruce A. Green, *Colloquium: Subversive Lawyering, Foreword*, 90 FORDHAM L. REV. 1945, 1946–47 (2022) (citations omitted).

56 Boden, *The Colonial Bar, supra* note 41, at 7–9.

57 *Id.* at 7.

58 Speech of Edmund Burke, Esq., on Moving His Resolutions for Conciliation with the Colonies (Mar. 22, 1775), *reprinted in* 1 BURKE, SELECT WORKS 182 (E. J. Payne ed., The Lawbook Exch. 2005).

59 *Id.*

60 *Id.* at 183.

61 1 THE CORRESPONDENCE OF GENERAL THOMAS GAGE WITH THE SEC-RETARIES OF STATE, 1763–1775, at 79 (Clarence E. Carter ed., 1931).

62 THOMAS PAINE, COLLECTED WRITINGS 34 (Libr. of Am. 1995) (emphasis in original).

63 JACKSON, THOUGHTS, *supra* note 1, at 117.

64 *Id.*

65 Boden, *The Colonial Bar, supra* note 41, at 21.

66 GORDON S. WOOD, THE RADICALISM OF THE AMERICAN REVOLUTION 5 (1991).

67 *Id.* at 8.

68 *Id.* at 11.

69 MASS. CONST. pt. 1.

70 Boden, *The Colonial Bar, supra* note 41, at 26–27.

71 THOMAS PAINE, DISSERTATIONS ON GOVERNMENT, THE AFFAIRS OF THE BANK, AND PAPER-MONEY 5 (1786).

72 David Ramsay, *Oration on the Advantages of American Independence,* in PRINCIPLES AND ACTS OF THE REVOLUTION IN AMERICA 67 (H. Niles ed., 1822).

73 WOOD, RADICALISM, *supra* note 66, at 6.

74 *Id.* at 98–100.

75 *Id.* at 96.

76 *Id.* at 102.

77 *Id.* at 229.

78 *Id.*

79 CHERNOW, ALEXANDER HAMILTON, *supra* note 34, at 30–31.

80 FRIEDMAN, A HISTORY OF AMERICAN LAW, *supra* note 3, at 300.

81 Surrency places the number at 100. Surrency, *supra* note 33, at 134. Friedman estimates that this number is closer to 200. FRIEDMAN, A HISTORY OF AMERICAN LAW, *supra* note 3, at 289.

82 Roscoe Pound, *David Dudley Field: An Appraisal,* in DAVID DUDLEY FIELD, CENTENARY ESSAYS: CELEBRATING ONE HUNDRED YEARS OF LEGAL REFORM 8 (Alison Reppy ed., 1949).

83 CHERNOW, ALEXANDER HAMILTON, *supra* note 34, at 163–66.

84 *Id.* at 79–81.

85 *Id.*

86 *Id.* at 85–86.

87 *Id.* at 167–70.

88 Finkelman, *Alexander Hamilton, Esq., supra* note 40, at 233.

89 *Id.* at 234.

90 *Id.*

91 HABER, QUEST FOR AUTHORITY, *supra* note 5, at 75.

92 *Id.*

93 *Id.* at 75–76.

94 *Id.*

95 ORIGINAL BROADWAY CAST OF HAMILTON, NON-STOP (Atlantic Records 2015).

96 Finkelman, *Alexander Hamilton, Esq., supra* note 40, at 234–35.

97 *Id.* at 236.

98 CHERNOW, ALEXANDER HAMILTON, *supra* note 34, at 168–69.

99 WOOD, RADICALISM, *supra* note 66, at 229.

100 Letter from Thomas Jefferson to John Adams (Oct. 28, 1813), in 6 THE PAPERS OF THOMAS JEFFERSON, RETIREMENT SERIES 562, 563 (J. Jefferson Looney ed., 2009).

101 *Id.*

102 *Id.*

103 I will use the term "federalist" here to identify those who advocated for the adoption of a new constitution in the 1780s, which is different from the Federalist political party that emerged after the adoption of that constitution.

104 NEIL IRVIN PAINTER, CREATING BLACK AMERICANS: AFRICAN-AMERICAN HISTORY AND ITS MEANINGS, 1619 TO THE PRESENT 70–72 (2006).

105 Gordon S. Wood, *Interests and Disinterestedness in the Making of the Constitution*, in BEYOND CONFEDERATION: ORIGINS OF THE CONSTITUTION AND AMERICAN NATIONAL IDENTITY 78–79 (Richard Beeman, Stephen Botein & Edward C. Carter II eds., 1986).

106 Claire Priest, *Creating an American Property Law: Alienability and Its Limits in American History*, 120 HARV. L. R. 385, 447–48 (2006).

107 WOOD, RADICALISM, *supra* note 66, at 251.

108 Wood, *Disinterestedness, supra* note 105, at 81.

109 ELIZABETH GASPAR BROWN, BRITISH STATUTES IN AMERICAN LAW, 1776–1836, at 23–45 (1964).

110 JEFFERSON ON JEFFERSON 39–43 (Paul M. Zall ed., 2002).

111 17 THE WRITINGS OF THOMAS JEFFERSON 418 (Andrew Adgate Lipscomb & Albert Ellery Bergh eds., 2010).

112 James Madison, *Vices of the Political System of the United States, reprinted in* 9 The Papers of James Madison 345, 353 (Robert A. Rutland & William M. E. Rachal eds., 1975) (1787).

113 *Id.* at 353–54.

114 Thomas Jefferson, Autobiography Draft Fragment, January 6 through July 27 (1821), http://hdl.loc.gov/loc.mss/mtj.mtjbib024000.

115 GORDON S. WOOD, THE CREATION OF THE AMERICAN REPUBLIC, 1776–1781, at 300 (1969) (hereinafter WOOD, CREATION).

116 JACKSON, THOUGHTS, *supra* note 1, at 116.

117 *Id.* at 116–17.

118 *Id.* at 117.

119 WOOD, CREATION, *supra* note 115, at 52–65.

120 Letter from James Madison to George Washington (Apr. 16, 1787), National Archives, Founders Online, https://founders.archives.gov/documents/Madison/01-09-02-0208#:~:text=This%20was%20a%20letter%20drawn,by%20Congress%20on%2021%20Mar.

121 EDWARD S. CORWIN, THE CONSTITUTION AND WHAT IT MEANS TODAY 412 (3rd ed. 1975).

122 THE FEDERALIST NO. 57, at 375 (James Madison) (The Belknap Press of Harv. Univ. Press 2009 ed.).

123 Wood, *Disinterestedness, supra* note 105, at 85.

124 THE FEDERALIST NO. 57, *supra* note 122, at 379 (James Madison).

125 Wood, CREATION, *supra* note 115, at 512–13.

126 Letter from Jefferson to Adams, *supra* note 100, at 563–64.

127 JACKSON, THOUGHTS, *supra* note 1, at 66.

128 *Id.*

129 *Id.* at 79.

130 Letter from Samuel Adams to John Adams (Dec. 8, 1777), in 3 THE WRITINGS OF SAMUEL ADAMS 416 (Harry Alonzo Cushing ed., Octagon Books 1968).

131 THE FEDERALIST NO. 35, *supra* note 122, at 66 (Alexander Hamilton).

132 *Id.* (emphasis added).

133 ROEBER, *supra* note 16, 166. The third author, Madison, had little formal legal training.

134 HABER, QUEST FOR AUTHORITY, *supra* note 5, at 75.

135 THE FEDERALIST NO. 78, *supra* note 122, at 516–17 (Alexander Hamilton).

136 Finkelman, *Alexander Hamilton, Esq., supra* note 40, at 233–34.

137 *Id.* at 245–50.

138 *Id.* at 247.

139 CHERNOW, ALEXANDER HAMILTON, *supra* note 34, at 606–10.

140 *Id.* at 169.

141 On Burr's recognition as a hero of the Revolutionary War, *see* NANCY ISENBERG, FALLEN FOUNDER: THE LIFE OF AARON BURR 210–12 (2007). On the Burr conspiracy, see BUCKNER F. MELTON, JR., AARON BURR: CONSPIRACY TO TREASON 55–80 (2002). On Burr's apparent lack of the civic republican spirit, see GORDON WOOD, REVOLUTIONARY CHARACTERS: WHAT MADE THE FOUNDERS DIFFERENT 229–39 (2006).

142 PAUL FINKELMAN, SUPREME INJUSTICE: SLAVERY IN THE NATION'S HIGHEST COURT 44–49 (2018).

143 Paul Finkelman, *Master John Marshall and the Problem of Slavery*, 2020 U. OF CHI. L. REV. ONLINE 1, 12 (2020).

CHAPTER 3. AN INDEPENDENT BAR AND AN HONEST JUDICIARY

1 ALEXIS DE TOCQUEVILLE, DEMOCRACY IN AMERICA 23 (Henry Reeve trans. 2013).

2 *See, e.g., Id.* at 392–404.

3 *Id.* at 324–34.

4 *Id.* at 325–26.

5 *Id.* at 332.

6 *Id.* at 329.

7 *Id.*

8 *Id.*

9 *Id.* at 326.

10 *Id.* at 330.

11 *Id.*

12 *Id.*

13 *Id.*

14 *Id.* at 326.

15 *Id.* at 333.

16 *Id.*

17 *Id.*

18 *Id.*

19 Michael Ariens, *Lost and Found: David Hoffman and the History of American Legal Ethics*, 67 ARK. L. REV. 571, 597 (2014).

20 ANTHONY GRUMBLER, MISCELLANEOUS THOUGHTS ON MEN, MANNERS, AND THINGS 233–34 (1837).

21 MORTON J. HORWITZ, THE TRANSFORMATION OF AMERICAN LAW, 1780–1860, at 147–51 (1977).

22 *Id.* at 141–45.

23 LAWRENCE M. FRIEDMAN, A HISTORY OF AMERICAN LAW 302–03 (Oxford Univ. Press 4th ed. 2019) (1973).

24 *Id.*

25 Davison M. Douglas, *The Jeffersonian Vision of Legal Education*, 51 J. LEGAL EDUC. 185, 189–90 (2001).

26 Carol M. Langford, *Barbarians at the Bar: Regulation of the Legal Profession Through the Admissions Process*, 36 HOFSTRA L. REV. 1193, 1202 (2008) (citations omitted).

27 RICHARD L. ABEL, AMERICAN LAWYERS 4–6 (1989).

28 DOUGLAS T. MILLER, JACKSONIAN DEMOCRACY: CLASS AND DEMOCRACY IN NEW YORK, 1830–1860, at 25 (1967).

29 2 ANTON-HERMANN CHROUST, THE RISE OF THE LEGAL PROFESSION IN AMERICA 165–66 (1965).

30 FRIEDMAN, A HISTORY OF AMERICAN LAW, *supra* note 23, at 147–70.

31 ROBERT H. WIEBE, THE SEARCH FOR ORDER, 1877–1920, at 116 (1967).

32 Langford, *Barbarians at the Bar, supra* note 26, at 1200.. *See also* Indiana Constitution, Art. 2, §2 (guaranteeing right to vote to white men) and Art. 7, §21 (tying bar admission requirement to right to vote) (1851).

33 FRIEDMAN, A HISTORY OF AMERICAN LAW, *supra* note 23, at 303.

34 MILLER, JACKSONIAN DEMOCRACY, *supra* note 28, at 23.

35 SAMUEL ROBERTS WELLS & DANIEL HARRISON JACQUES, HOW TO BE-
HAVE: A POCKET MANUAL OF REPUBLICAN ETIQUETTE 124 (1856).

36 FREDERICK ROBINSON, LETTER OF JUNE 25, 1831, TO THE HON. RUFUS
CHOATE, CONTAINING A BRIEF EXPOSURE OF LAW CRAFT, AND SOME
OF THE ENCROACHMENTS OF THE BAR UPON THE RIGHTS AND LIBER-
TIES OF THE PEOPLE 4 (reprinted 1832).

37 Id.

38 Id. at 4–5.

39 Id. at 10.

40 Id.

41 Id.

42 Id. at 11.

43 Id. at 13.

44 Marbury v. Madison, 5 U.S. 137, 177 (1803).

45 FRIEDMAN, A HISTORY OF AMERICAN LAW, supra note 23, at 307–18.

46 DAVID DUDLEY FIELD, WHAT SHALL BE DONE WITH THE PRACTICE
OF THE COURTS, SHALL IT BE WHOLLY REFORMED? QUESTIONS AD-
DRESSED TO LAWYERS 12 (1847).

47 Id.

48 Id. at 7.

49 CHARLES M. COOK, THE AMERICAN CODIFICATION MOVEMENT: A
STUDY OF ANTEBELLUM LEGAL REFORM 159–60 (1981).

50 FIELD, WHAT SHALL BE DONE, supra note 46, at 14.

51 Id.

52 COOK, THE AMERICAN CODIFICATION MOVEMENT, supra note 49, at 106–
07.

53 PERRY MILLER, THE LIFE OF THE MIND IN AMERICA: FROM THE
REVOLUTION TO THE CIVIL WAR 246–49 (1965).

54 COOK, THE AMERICAN CODIFICATION MOVEMENT, supra note 49, at 57.

55 MAXWELL BLOOMFIELD, AMERICAN LAWYERS IN A CHANGING SOCI-
ETY, 1776–1876, at 84–88 (1976).

56 CHARLES W. MCCURDY, THE ANTI-RENT ERA IN NEW YORK LAW AND
POLITICS, 1839–1865 (2001).

57 GEORGE MARTIN, CAUSES AND CONFLICTS: THE CENTENNIAL HIS-
TORY OF THE ASSOCIATION OF THE BAR OF THE CITY OF NEW YORK,
1870–1970, at 32–34 (1970).

58 Id. at 89–90.

59 Id.

60 COOK, THE AMERICAN CODIFICATION MOVEMENT, supra note 49, at 72–
75.

61 Roscoe Pound, David Dudley Field: An Appraisal, in DAVID DUDLEY FIELD,
CENTENARY ESSAYS: CELEBRATING ONE HUNDRED YEARS OF LEGAL
REFORM 8 (Alison Reppy ed., 1949).

62 David Dudley Field, *Magnitude and Importance of Legal Science*, in 1 SPEECHES, ARGUMENTS, AND MISCELLANEOUS PAPERS OF DAVID DUDLEY FIELD 517, 523–24 (A. P. Sprague ed., 1884).

63 *Id.* at 530.

64 *Id.*

65 *Id.* at 529.

66 *Id.* at 530.

67 David Dudley Field, *The Law and the Legal Profession*, in 1 SPEECHES, ARGUMENTS, AND MISCELLANEOUS PAPERS OF DAVID DUDLEY FIELD 539, 539 (A. P. Sprague ed., 1884).

68 Field, *Magnitude and Importance, supra* note 62, at 531.

69 *Id.*

70 Field, *Law and the Legal Profession, supra* note 67, at 540.

71 *Id.* at 542.

72 David Dudley Field, *A Short Response to a Long Discourse*, ALB. L. J. 127, 129 (1884).

73 FIELD, WHAT SHALL BE DONE, *supra* note 46, at 7.

74 COOK, THE AMERICAN CODIFICATION MOVEMENT, *supra* note 49, at 188.

75 *Id.* at 191.

76 FIELD, WHAT SHALL BE DONE, *supra* note 46, at 6.

77 *Id.* at 7.

78 *Id.* at 6.

79 *Id.*

80 *Id.*

81 *Id.* at 7.

82 RICHARD L. MARCUS ET AL., CIVIL PROCEDURE: A MODERN APPROACH 118 (5th ed. 2009).

83 MARTIN, CAUSES AND CONFLICTS, *supra* note 57, at 144–47.

84 Pound, *David Dudley Field: An Appraisal, supra* note 61, at 9.

85 *Id.* at 13.

86 Clyde Eagleton, *International Organization for Peace and Law*, in CENTENARY ESSAYS, *supra* note 61, 289–96.

87 Norman W. Spaulding, *The Discourse of Law in Time of War: Politics and Professionalism During the Civil War and Reconstruction*, 46 WM. & MARY L. REV. 2001 (2005).

88 PAUL FINKELMAN, AN IMPERFECT UNION: SLAVERY, FEDERALISM, AND COMITY 157–78 (1981).

89 Quincy Adams and Baldwin both advocated for the freedom of the captives on the ship *The Amistad*. Michael Daly Hawkins, *John Quincy Adams and the Antebellum Maritime Slave Trade: The Politics of Slavery and the Slavery of Politics*, 25 OKLA. CITY U. L. REV. 1 (2000). For an example of one effort to resist the return of an escaped slave from Boston, see Paul Finkelman, *Legal Ethics and Fugitive Slaves: The Anthony Burns Case, Judge Loring, and Abolitionist Attorneys*, 17 CARD. L. REV. 1793 (1996).

90 Taney's opinion in *Dred Scott v. Sanford*, 60 U.S. 393 (1857), could not be clearer about his views on the intent of the creation of the system of laws in the United States that rendered "inferior" enslaved persons and their descendants. According to that opinion, at the time of the adoption of the U.S. Constitution, such individuals were "considered as a subordinate and inferior class of beings, who had been subjugated by the dominant race, and, whether emancipated or not, yet remained subject to their authority, and had no rights or privileges but such as those who held the power and the Government might choose to grant them." *Id.* at 404–05. According to Taney, the "duty of the court is, to interpret the [Constitution] . . . with the best lights we can obtain on the subject, and to administer it as we find it, according to its true intent and meaning when it was adopted." *Id.* at 405.

91 In the words of historian Paul Finkelman, "[o]n the bench Marshall always supported slavery, even when statutes and precedent were on the side of freedom." Paul Finkelman, *Master John Marshall and the Problem of Slavery*, 2020 U. OF CHI. L. REV. ONLINE 1, 12 (2020).

92 WILLIAM M. WIECEK, THE SOURCES OF ANTISLAVERY CONSTITUTIONALISM IN AMERICA, 1760–1848 (1977).

93 BENJAMIN BUTLER, BUTLER'S BOOK: AUTOBIOGRAPHY AND PERSONAL REMINISCENCES OF MAJOR-GENERAL BENJAMIN BUTLER 129 (2014).

94 *Id.*

95 *Id.*

96 *Id.* at 96.

97 ERIC FONER, THE FIERY TRIAL: ABRAHAM LINCOLN AND AMERICAN SLAVERY 170–71 (2010).

98 BUTLER, *supra* note 93, at 257.

99 JOHN FABIAN WITT, LINCOLN'S CODE: THE LAWS OF WAR IN AMERICAN HISTORY 202–03 (2012).

100 Edward L. Pierce, *The Contrabands at Fort Monroe*, ATLANTIC MONTHLY (Nov. 1861).

101 WITT, LINCOLN'S CODE, *supra* note 99, at 198.

102 Paul Finkelman, *Lincoln, Emancipation, and the Limits of Constitutional Change*, 2008 SUP. CT. REV. 349, 369 (2008).

103 *Id.* at 372–75.

104 DAVID W. BLIGHT, FREDERICK DOUGLASS: PROPHET OF FREEDOM 503–09 (2018).

105 DAVID HERBERT DONALD, LINCOLN 373–76 (1995).

106 JAMES M. MCPHERSON, BATTLE CRY OF FREEDOM: THE CIVIL WAR ERA 502–05 (1988).

107 FONER, *supra* note 97, at 171.

108 *See, e.g.*, *The Prize Cases*, 67 U.S. (2 Black) 635 (1863); STUART L. BERNATH, SQUALL ACROSS THE ATLANTIC: AMERICAN CIVIL WAR PRIZE CASES AND DIPLOMACY 18–33 (1970).

109 Mark E. Neely, Jr., The Fate of Liberty: Abraham Lincoln and Civil Liberties 120–24 (1991); John Fabian Witt, *A Lost Theory of American Emergency Constitutionalism*, 36(3) L. & Hist. Rev. 551, 561–71 (August 2018).

110 Cynthia Nicoletti, *Writing the Social History of Legal Doctrine*, 64 Buff. L. Rev. 121, 131–35 (2016).

111 The period has been referred to as the second founding by W. E. B. Du Bois, Thurgood Marshall, and Eric Foner, among others. *See* Burt Neuborne, *Federalism and the "Second Founding": Constitutional Structure as a "Double Security" for "Discrete and Insular" Minorities*, 77 N.Y. U. Ann. Surv. Am. L. 59, 67 n. 28 (2022). *See also* Eric Foner, Reconstruction: America's Unfinished Revolution, 1863–1877 (2014 ed.); Eric Foner, The Second Founding: How the Civil War and Reconstruction Remade the Constitution (2019).

112 Foner, The Second Founding, *supra* note 111, at 66–86.

113 Lou Falkner Williams, The Great South Carolina Ku Klux Klan Trials, 1871–1872, 146–47 (1996).

114 Gary Peller & Mark Tushnet, *State Action and a New Birth of Freedom*, 92 Geo. L. J. 779, 801–04 (2004).

115 Foner, Reconstruction, *supra* note 111, at 807 (footnote omitted).

116 Paul Finkelman, *Not Only the Judges' Robes Were Black: African-American Lawyers as Social Engineers*, 47 Stan. L. Rev. 161, 190 (1994).

117 For a description of the litigation that led to the decision in *Plessy v. Ferguson*, 163 U.S. 537 (1896), referenced again in the next chapter, with lawyers on both sides of the dispute, see Charles A. Lofgren, The *Plessy* Case: A Legal Historical Interpretation 28–60 (1988). Although Lofgren argues that Justice Brown's majority opinion merely reflected the dominant views of the time, *Id.* at 199, the decision has also been described as being relatively unideological. Richard Kluger, Simple Justice: The History of *Brown v. Board of Education* and Black America's Struggle for Equality 74 (1976).

118 Friedman, A History of American Law, *supra* note 23, at 303.

119 Martin, Causes and Conflicts, *supra* note 57, at 4–8.

120 *Id.* at 5.

121 *Id.* at 12–16.

122 Editorial, *A Lawyers' Mutual Protective Association*, N.Y. Times (June 20, 1869).

123 Editorial, *The Degradation of the Judiciary and the Responsibility of the Bar*, N.Y. Times, (December 16, 1869).

124 Martin, Causes and Conflicts, *supra* note 57, at 10.

125 *See* Invitation, *reprinted in* Martin, Causes and Conflicts, *supra* note 57, at 15.

126 Martin, Causes and Conflicts, *supra* note 57, at 19.

127 *Id.*

128 *Id.*

129 *Id.* at 37.

130 *Id.* at 37–38 (citation omitted).

131 *Id.* at 46.

132 *Id.* at 48.

133 Editorial, *The Bar Association of New York*, 3 ALB. L.J. 228, 228 (1871).

134 *Id.*

135 *Id.* at 229.

136 MARTIN, CAUSES AND CONFLICTS, *supra* note 57, at 76. *See also* Andrew L. Kaufman, *The First Judge Cardozo: Albert, Father of Benjamin*, 11 J. OF LAW & RELIGION 271 (1994).

137 3 Documents of the Assembly of the State of New York, 1872, no. 40, 1.

138 *Id.*

139 *Id.*

140 MARTIN, CAUSES AND CONFLICTS, *supra* note 57, at 63.

141 *Id.* at 66–67.

142 *Id.* at 115–17.

143 *Id.* at 109–13.

144 *Id.* at 113.

145 *Id.* at 113–14 (citations omitted).

146 *Id.*

147 *Id.* at 183.

148 HORWITZ, TRANSFORMATION OF AMERICAN LAW, *supra* note 21, at 119.

149 JAMES COOLIDGE CARTER, THE PROPOSED CODIFICATION OF OUR COMMON LAW 84 (1884).

150 *Id.* at 6–7.

151 MILLER, LIFE OF THE MIND, *supra* note 53, at 107.

152 MARTIN, CAUSES AND CONFLICTS, *supra* note 57, at 173–75.

153 *Bradwell v. The State*, 83 U.S. 130 (1872).

154 ABEL, AMERICAN LAWYERS, *supra* note 27, at 90. For accounts of the early struggles of women to gain admission to the bars of various states, see VIRGINIA DRACHMAN, SISTERS IN LAW: WOMEN LAWYERS IN MODERN AMERICAN HISTORY 9–117 (1998).

155 Lelia J. Robinson, *Women Lawyers in the United States*, 2 GREEN BAG 10, 10 (1890).

156 ABEL, AMERICAN LAWYERS, *supra* note 27, at 99.

157 Eli Wald, *The Rise and Fall of the WASP and Jewish Law Firms*, 60 STAN. L. REV. 1803, 1810–27 (2008).

158 ROBERT T. SWAINE, 1 THE CRAVATH FIRM AND ITS PREDECESSORS 450–51 (1946).

159 On the formation of the American Bar Association, see John A Matzko, *"The Best Men of the Bar": The Founding of the American Bar Association*, in THE NEW HIGH PRIESTS: LAWYERS IN THE POST–CIVIL WAR ERA 75–124 (Gerard W. Gawalt ed., 1984); on the creation of the American Association of Law Schools, see ALBERT J. HARNO, LEGAL EDUCATION IN THE UNITED STATES 89 (1953).

160 Majorie L. Girth, *UB's Women in Law: Overcoming Barriers During Their First Hundred Years*, 9 BUFF. WOMEN'S L.J. 51, 71 (2000/2001).

161 J. Noble Hayes, *New York County Lawyers' Association and Its Objects*, 20 GREEN BAG (No. 8) 411 (August 1908).

162 MARTIN, CAUSES AND CONFLICTS, *supra* note 57, at 183–86.

163 Hayes, *supra* note 161, at 411.

CHAPTER 4. THE PROFESSION IN CRISIS AND THE
INSTITUTIONAL RESPONSE

1   2 REFORMING AMERICAN: THEMATIC ENCYCLOPEDIA AND DOCUMENT COLLECTION OF THE PROGRESSIVE ERA 511–12 (Jeffrey A. Johnson ed., 2017).

2   JOHN WHITECLAY CHAMBERS, THE TYRANNY OF CHANGE: AMERICA IN THE PROGRESSIVE ERA, 1890–1920, at 20 (1992).

3   *Id.* at 17.

4   STEVEN J. DINER, A VERY DIFFERENT AGE: AMERICANS OF THE PROGRESSIVE ERA 19 (1998).

5   THEDA SKOCPOL, DIMINISHED DEMOCRACY: FROM MEMBERSHIP TO MANAGEMENT IN AMERICAN CIVIC LIFE 59–74 (2003).

6   ROBERT H. WIEBE, THE SEARCH FOR ORDER 1877–1920, at 164–95 (1967).

7   WILLARD HURST, LAW AND SOCIAL ORDER IN THE UNITED STATES 145–46 (1977); Price Fishback, *The Progressive Era*, in GOVERNMENT AND THE AMERICAN ECONOMY: A NEW HISTORY 288–322 (2007).

8   CHAIM M. ROSENBERG, AMERICA AT THE FAIR: CHICAGO'S 1893 WORLD'S COLUMBIAN EXPOSITION 63–81 (2008). On professionalism and professionalization, see BURTON BLEDSTEIN, THE CULTURE OF PROFESSIONALISM (1976).

9   RICHARD A. HOFSTADTER, THE AGE OF REFORM: FROM BRYAN TO F.D.R. 156–57 (1955).

10 For example, one of Louis Brandeis's opponents in *Muller v. Oregon*, 208 U.S. 412 (1908), which related to maximum hour laws for female workers, was William D. Fenton, a prominent railroad attorney in Oregon who, in that case, defended the freedom of contract to ignore maximum hour laws, and in others to relieve railroads of rate regulation. Southern Pac. Co. v. Campbell, 230 U.S. 537 (1913). For a description of some of Louis Brandeis's work on behalf of workers, see Robert F. Cochran, Jr., *Louis D. Brandeis and the Lawyer Advocacy System*, 40 PEPP. L. REV. 351, 357–58 (2013).

11 C. VANN WOODWARD, *The strange career of Jim Crow* 116 (3rd rev. ed. 1966).

12 GEORGE MARTIN, CAUSES AND CONFLICTS: THE CENTENNIAL HISTORY OF THE ASSOCIATION OF THE BAR OF THE CITY OF NEW YORK, 1870–1970, at 191–92 (1970).

13 *Report of the Committee on Code of Professional Ethics*, 29 ANN. REP. A.B.A. 600, 601 (1906).

14 Justice David J. Brewer, *Address at Commencement of Albany Law School* 16 (June 1, 1904).

15 George F. Shelton, *Law as a Business*, 10 YALE L.J. 275, 275 (1900).

16 *Id.* at 278.

17 *Id. at 275.*

18 Champ S. Andrews, *Law a Business or a Profession*, 17 YALE L.J. 602, 605 (1907–1908).

19 *Id.* at 606.

20 *Id.*

21 29 ANN. REP. A.B.A., *supra* note 13, at 601–03.

22 *Report of the Committee on Legal Education and Admissions to the Bar*, 26 ANN. REP. A.B.A. 395, 419 (1903).

23 *Id.*

24 *Id.*

25 29 ANN. REP. A.B.A., *supra* note 13, at 601.

26 *Id.*

27 *Id.* at 602–03.

28 George P. Costigan, Jr., *The Proposed American Code of Legal Ethics*, 20 GREEN BAG 57, 57 (1908).

29 *Id.*

30 Everett V. Abbot, *Some Actual Problems of Professional Ethics*, 15 HARV. L. REV. 714, 724 (1902).

31 *Id.* (emphasis in original).

32 2 THE WORKS OF JOHN ADAMS 58 (Charles Francis Adams ed., 1850).

33 RICHARD L. ABEL, AMERICAN LAWYERS 109 (1989).

34 Lawrence Maxwell, Jr., *Chairman's Address*, 28 ANN. REP. A.B.A. 582 (1905).

35 *Id.* at 585.

36 *Proceedings of the Section of Legal Education and Admission to the Bar*, 52 ANN. REP. A.B.A. 605, 622 (1929).

37 *Id.* at 623.

38 *Id.*

39 *Id.* at 622.

40 *Id.* at 624.

41 *Id.* at 623.

42 A. B. A., SPECIAL SESSION ON LEGAL EDUCATION OF THE CONFERENCE OF BAR ASSOCIATION DELEGATES 20 (1922).

43 *Id.*

44 *Id.*

45 *Id.* at 19–20.

46 *Id.* at 20.

47 *Id.* at 21–22.

48 *Id.* at 22.

49 President Theodore Roosevelt, *The Harvard Spirit, Address at Harvard University,* June 28, 1905, in 4 PRESIDENTIAL ADDRESSES & STATE PAPERS, 1905, at 419–20; Louis D. Brandeis, *The Opportunity in the Law,* 39 AM. L. REV. 555, 559–60 (1905).

50 Shelton, *supra.* note 15, at 282.

51 LAWRENCE M. FRIEDMAN, A HISTORY OF AMERICAN LAW 296 (Oxford Univ. Press 4th ed. 2019) (1973).

52 ROBERT T. SWAINE, 1 THE CRAVATH FIRM AND ITS PREDECESSORS, 1819–1848, at 614–15 (1946).

53 *See generally id.*

54 MILTON C. REGAN, JR., EAT WHAT YOU KILL: THE FALL OF A WALL STREET LAWYER 20–21 (2001).

55 On the efficiencies associated with the organizational form, see *generally* R. H. Coase, *The Nature of the Firm,* 4 (16) ECONOMICA 386 (1937).

56 MARTIN, CAUSES AND CONFLICTS, *supra* note 12, at 191–95.

57 *Id.*

58 *Id.*

59 John A. Matzko, *"The Best Men of the Bar": The Founding of the American Bar Association,* in THE NEW HIGH PRIESTS: LAWYERS IN THE POST-CIVIL WAR ERA 75–124 (Gerard W. Gawalt ed., 1984).

60 HURST, LAW AND SOCIAL ORDER, *supra* note 7, at 203; CHAMBERS, THE TYRANNY OF CHANGE, *supra* note 2, at 159.

61 DAVID C. HOFFMAN, FIFTY RESOLUTIONS IN REGARD TO PROFESSIONAL DEVELOPMENT (1836).

62 On Hoffman's background and his rejection of Jacksonian democracy, see Michael Ariens, *Lost and Found: David Hoffman and the History of American Legal Ethics,* 67 ARK. L. REV. 571 (2014).

63 HOFFMAN, FIFTY RESOLUTIONS, *supra* note 61, at Resol. 5.

64 *Id.* at Resol. 12.

65 *Id.* at Resol. 28.

66 *Id.* at Resol. 50.

67 Allison Marston, *Guiding the Profession: The 1887 Code of Ethics of the Alabama State Bar Association,* 49 ALA. L. REV. 471, 498–99 (1998).

68 GEORGE SHARSWOOD, AN ESSAY ON PROFESSIONAL ETHICS (5th ed. 1884).

69 *Id.* at 9.

70 *Id.*

71 *Id.* at 26.

72 *Id.* at 53–54.

73 *Id.* at 56.

74 *Id.* at 168.

75 *Id.* at 170.

76 *Id.* at 64.
77 *Id.* at 61.
78 *Id.* at 74.
79 *Id.*
80 *Id.* at 119.
81 *Id.* at 123.
82 *Id.* at 124.
83 *Id.*
84 *Id.* at 132.
85 *Id.* at 133.
86 *Id.* at 66.
87 *Id.* at 79–80.
88 *Id.* at 99.
89 *Id.* at 142.
90 *Id.* at 147–48.
91 Marston, *Guiding the Profession, supra* note 67, at 494–95.
92 *Report of the Committee on Code of Professional Ethics*, 30 Ann. Rep. A.B.A. 676, 676–78 (1907).
93 The Louisiana Bar Association's Code of Ethics, *reprinted in* 30 Ann. Rep. A.B.A. 714 (1907).
94 *Transactions of the Twenty-Eighth Annual Meeting of the American Bar Association in Narragansett Pier, Rhode Island, August 23, 24, and 25, 1904*, 28 Ann. Rep. ABA 3, 132 (1905).
95 29 Ann. Rep. A.B.A, *supra* note 13, at 600.
96 *Id.*
97 *Id.* at 600–01.
98 *Id.* at 601.
99 30 Ann. Rep. A.B.A, *supra* note 92, at 678.
100 *Id.*
101 Charles A. Boston, *A Code of Legal Ethics*, 20 Green Bag 224, 226 (1908).
102 Marston, *Guiding the Profession, supra* note 67, at 478–81 (1998) (citations omitted). The law school of Faulkner University in Montgomery, Alabama, still bears his name.
103 A. B. A., Memorandum for Use of American Bar Association's Committee to Draft Canons of Professional Ethics 2 (1908).
104 Jerold S. Auerbach, Unequal Justice: Lawyers and Social Change in Modern America 45–54 (1977).
105 *Id.* at 50.
106 Moorefield Storey, Reform of Legal Procedure 54 (1911).
107 Reginald Haber Smith, Justice and the Poor: A Study of the Present Denial of Justice to the Poor and of the Agencies Making More Equal Their Position before the Law with Particular Reference to Legal Aid Work in the United States 5 (1919).

108 *Id.* at 86.

109 *Id.* at 228.

110 A. B. A., *The Canons of Professional Ethics*, in Final Report of the Committee on Code of Professional Ethics, 31 Ann. Rep. A.B.A. 567 (1908).

111 ALA. CODE § 49, *reprinted in* 30 ANN. REP. A.B.A. 676, *supra* note 92, at 709. Roughly half of the existing codes at the time had adopted this provision. *Id.*

112 ALA. CODE § 49, *reprinted in* 30 ANN. REP. A.B.A. 676, *supra* note 92, at 710. Most other existing codes adopted this provision, except for Maryland's. *Id.*

113 Obituary Record of Graduates of Yale University Deceased from June 1910 to July 1915 84–86 (1915).

114 A.B.A. MEMORANDUM FOR USE, *supra* note 103, at 71.

115 N.Y. State Bar Ass'n, *Report of the Special Committee on Contingent Fees* (1908), *reprinted in* A.B.A. MEMORANDUM FOR USE, *supra* note 103, at 73.

116 *Id.*

117 *Id.*

118 *Id.*

119 *Id.*

120 *Id.* at 74.

121 *Comments of the Bar Association of the City of Boston* (March 11, 1908), *reprinted in* ABA MEMORANDUM FOR USE, *supra* note 103, at 72.

122 *Id.*

123 Anonymous submission of "Judge A.B.C.," *reprinted in* A.B.A., MEMORANDUM FOR USE, *supra* note 103, at 77.

124 *Id.* at 79.

125 *Id.*

126 A.B.A. CANONS OF PROFESSIONAL ETHICS, *supra* note 110, at 579.

127 FRIEDMAN, A HISTORY OF AMERICAN LAW, *supra* note 51, at 706–07.

128 ALA. CODE § 18, *reprinted in* 30 ANN REP A.B.A. 696.

129 *Grievance Committee of Erie County, reprinted in* A.B.A., MEMORANDUM FOR USE, *supra* note 103, at 36.

130 *Id.*

131 A.B.A. CANONS OF PROFESSIONAL ETHICS, *supra* note 110, at Canon 27.

132 ALA. CODE § 18, *reprinted in* 30 ANN. REP. A.B.A. 696 (emphasis added).

133 A.B.A. MEMORANDUM FOR USE, *supra* note 103, at 43–44.

134 *Id.* at 45.

135 *Id.*

136 A.B.A. CANONS OF PROFESSIONAL ETHICS, *supra* note 110, at Canon 27.

137 *Id.* at Canon 28 (1908).

138 *Id.*

139 *Id.*

140 James M. Altman, *Considering the A.B.A.'s 1908 Canons of Ethics*, 71 FORDHAM L. REV. 2395, 2493–96 (2003).

141 Lewis F. Powell, Jr., *Evaluation of Ethical Standards*, Address at the A.B.A. House of Delegates (Aug. 12, 1969).

142 *Id.* at 6.

143 That is not to say that, even with stronger enforcement mechanisms, the profession, its regulators, and the courts have accomplished effective control over lawyer misconduct. Lax enforcement, a lack of resources for such enforcement, the inability to punish violation of vague principles, and the fact that professional breaches are rarely reported and any punishment that is meted out is often undisclosed all contribute to an environment where attorney misconduct is inadequately policed and rarely punished. *See, e.g.,* Fred C. Zacharias, *What Lawyers Do When Nobody's Watching: Legal Advertising as a Case Study of the Impact of Underenforced Professional Rules,* 87 IOWA L. REV. 971, 1003–12 (2002).

144 *See, e.g.,* Susan D. Carle, *How Should We Theorize Class Interests in Thinking About Professional Regulation?: The Early NAACP as a Case Example,* 12 CORNELL J. L. & PUB. POL'Y 571 (2003).

145 29 ANN. REP. A.B.A., *supra* note 13, at 601.

146 *Id.*

147 ABEL, AMERICAN LAWYERS, *supra* note 33, at 85.

148 ALFRED ZANTZINGER REED, TRAINING FOR THE PUBLIC PROFESSION OF THE LAW 82–85 (1921).

149 FRIEDMAN, A HISTORY OF AMERICAN LAW, *supra* note 51, at 305.

150 Paul D. Carrington, *The Revolutionary Idea of University Legal Education,* 31 WM. & MARY L. REV. 527, 532–33 (1990); on Wythe's guidance of American legal luminaries, see ALONZO THOMAS DILL, GEORGE WYTHE: TEACHER OF LIBERTY 1–2 (1979).

151 FRIEDMAN, A HISTORY OF AMERICAN LAW, *supra* note 51, at 303–04.

152 *Id.* at 304–05.

153 Maxwell, *Chairman's Address, supra* note 34, at 592–604.

154 *Id.* at 585.

155 *Id.*

156 *Id.* at 586.

157 *Id.* at 587.

158 *Id.*

159 *Id.*

160 *Id.* at 583.

161 *Id.*

162 *Id.*

163 *Id.* at 584.

164 *Id.*

165 *Id.*

166 American Bar Association, *Proceedings of the Section of Legal Education,* 28 ANN. REP. A.B.A. 531, 555 (1905).

167 *Id.* at 554.

168 Maxwell, *Chairman's Address, supra* note 34, at 593.
169 *Id.*
170 *Id.*
171 28 Ann. Rep. A.B.A., *supra* note 166, at 574.
172 *Id.*
173 *Id.*
174 *Id.*
175 For a review of some of this evolution, see Friedman, A History of American Law, *supra* note 51, at 594–604. For the movement that privileged the elite law schools, see Benjamin H. Barton, Glass Half Full: The Decline and Rebirth of the Legal Profession 134–37 (2015).
176 28 Ann. Rep. A.B.A., *supra* note 166, at 544.
177 *Id.* at 542.
178 Maxwell, *Chairman's Address, supra* note 34, at 592.
179 Abel, American Lawyers, *supra* note 33, at 42–43.
180 Friedman, A History of American Law, *supra* note 51, at 623.
181 *Id.*
182 *Id.* at 623–24.
183 Katheryn D. Katz, *Kate Stoneman: A Pioneer for Equality*, in Pioneering Women Lawyers: From Kate Stoneman to the Present 1, 2–6 (Patricia E. Salkin ed., 2008).
184 *Id.* at 6.
185 Gerard W. Gawalt, *The Impact of Industrialization on the Legal Profession in Massachusetts*, in The New High Priests, *supra* note 59, at 97, 98–105 (citations omitted).
186 Paul Finkelman, *Not Only the Judges' Robes Were Black: African-American Lawyers as Social Engineers*, 7 Stan. L. Rev. 161, 200–01 (1994).
187 Abel, American Lawyers, *supra* note 33, at 99.
188 *Id.* at 99–100.
189 *Id.* at 90 (citation omitted).
190 James Willard Hurst, The Growth of American Lawyers: The Law Makers 272–73 (1950).
191 *Id.* at 273.
192 *Id.* at 274.
193 *Report of the Special Committee to the Section of Legal Education and Admission to the Bar of the American Bar Association 681–84 (1920), reprinted in* 44 Ann. Rep. A.B.A. 656 (1921).
194 Paul Starr, The Social Transformation of American Medicine 116–23 (1982).
195 *Id.* at 120–21.
196 Abel, American Lawyers, *supra* note 33, at 46–48.
197 44 Ann. Rep. A.B.A. *supra* note 193, at 667.
198 *Id.* at 683–86 (describing proposed requirements).

199 *Id.* at 662.

200 *Id.*

201 *Id.* at 666.

202 *Id.* at 668.

203 *Id.*

204 *Id.*

205 *Id.* at 671.

206 *Id.* at 681.

207 *Id.* at 687–88.

208 A.B.A., 1922 Special Session on Legal Education, *supra* note 42, at 15–16.

209 *Id.* at 22.

210 52 ANN. REP. A.B.A., *supra* note 36, at 624.

211 A.B.A., 1922 Special Session on Legal Education, *supra* note 42, at 22.

212 *Id.* at 70.

213 *Id.* at 71.

214 ABEL, AMERICAN LAWYERS, *supra* note 33, at 85.

215 *Id.*

216 For an overview of these changes, see *id.* at 40–72.

217 *Id.* at 109–11.

218 MARTHA DAVIS, BRUTAL NEED: LAWYERS AND THE WELFARE RIGHTS MOVEMENT, 1960–1973, at 11–12 (1993).

219 *Id.* at 12–13.

220 CHARLES A. LOFGREN, THE PLESSY CASE: A LEGAL HISTORICAL INTERPRETATION 28–60 (1988).

221 On challenges to the Chinese Exclusion laws, see Kevin R. Johnson, *Systemic Racism in the U.S. Immigration Laws*, 97 IND. L. J. 1455, 1469–77 (2022).

222 Scott L. Cummings, *Movement Lawyering*, 2017 U. ILL. L. REV. 1645, 1663–65 (2017).

223 JOHN MACARTHUR MAGUIRE, THE LANCE OF JUSTICE: A SEMI-CENTENNIAL HISTORY OF THE LEGAL AID SOCIETY, 1876–1926, at 193 (1928); AUERBACH, UNEQUAL JUSTICE, *supra* note 104, at 211–12; JACK KATZ, POOR PEOPLE'S LAWYERS IN TRANSITION 46 (1982); Robert W. Gordon, *Lawyers, the Legal Profession & Access to Justice in the United States*, 148 DAEDALUS 177, 181–82 (2019).

224 SMITH, *supra* note 107, at 5.

225 *Id.*

226 Elihu Root, *Foreword*, in SMITH, *supra* note 107, at ix.

227 *Id.*

228 SMITH, *supra* note 107, at 10.

229 *Id.*

230 Lyman Abbott, *Speech at the Twenty-Fifth Anniversary Dinner of the New York Legal Aid Society*, REP. OF SPEECHES 32 (1901).

231 SMITH, *supra* note 107, at 12.

232   *Id.* at 217.

233   Katz, Poor People's Lawyers, *supra* note 223, at 7.

234   Alan W. Houseman, *Political Lessons: Legal Services for the Poor—A Commentary*, 83 Geo. L.J. 1669, 1671–72 (1995).

235   Davis, *supra* note 218, at 16.

CHAPTER 5. THE LEGAL PROFESSION AS AN INSTITUTION

 1   *See, e.g.*, Richard Abel, American Lawyers 13–19 (1989).

 2   Clay Shirky, Here Comes Everybody: The Power of Organizing Without Organization 58 (2008).

 3   Roscoe Pound, The Lawyer from Antiquity to Modern Times 5 (1953).

 4   ABA Commission on Professionalism, ". . . *In the Spirit of Public Service*": *A Blueprint for the Rekindling of Lawyer Professionalism*, reprinted in 112 F.R.D. 243, 248 (1986).

 5   *Id.* at 261–62 (citing Freidson's work done in collaboration with the Commission).

 6   Merriam Webster, "Institution," www.merriam-webster.com/dictionary/institution.

 7   Douglass C. North, Institutions, Institutional Change and Economic Performance 3 (1990).

 8   Geoffrey M. Hodgson, *What Are Institutions?* 40(1) J. Econ. Issues 1, 8 (Mar. 2006).

 9   Roger Friedland & Robert R. Alford, *Bringing Society Back In: Symbols, Practices, and Institutional Contradictions*, in The New Institutionalism in Organizational Analysis 232, 249 (Walter W. Powell & Paul J. DiMaggio eds., 1991).

10   North, Institutions, *supra* note 7, at 7.

11   *Id.* at 73.

12   Richard Flatham, *Liberalism and the Suspect Enterprise of Political Institutionalization: The Case of the Rule of Law*, in NOMOS XXXVI: The Rule of Law (Ian Shapiro ed., 1994) at 297, 297.

13   Eliot Freidson, Professionalism: The Third Logic 12 (2001).

14   *Id.* at 99–100 (2001).

15   Eliot Freidson, *Professionalism as Model and Ideology*, in Lawyers' Ideals/Lawyers' Practices: Transformations in the American Legal Profession 215, 219 (Robert L. Nelson et al. eds., 1992).

16   *Id.* (emphasis in original).

17   *Id.* at 220.

18   Freidson, Professionalism, *supra* note 13, at 105.

19   *Id.* at 131.

20   *Id.*

21   Daron Acemoglu & James A. Robinson, Why Nations Fail: The Origins of Power, Prosperity, and Poverty 74–79 (2012).

22   *Id.* at 74.

23 *Id.* at 74–75.

24 *Id.* at 75.

25 *Id.* at 76.

26 Douglass C. North, *Five Propositions About Institutional Change*, in EXPLORING SOCIAL INSTITUTIONS (Jack Knight & Itai Sened eds., 1995); ACEMOGLU & ROBINSON, WHY NATIONS FAIL, *supra* note 21, at 428–37.

27 North, *Five Propositions, supra* note 26.

28 ACEMOGLU & ROBINSON, WHY NATIONS FAIL, *supra* note 21, at 79–83.

29 Joanna Shepherd, *An Empirical Survey of No-Injury Class Actions* (Emory Legal Studies Research Paper No. 16-402) (February 1, 2016).

30 *See, e.g.,* DAHLIA LITHWICK, LADY JUSTICE: WOMEN, THE LAW, AND THE BATTLE TO SAVE AMERICA (2022); JUAN WILLIAMS, THURGOOD MARSHALL: AMERICAN REVOLUTIONARY (1998).

31 ORAN R. YOUNG, THE INSTITUTIONAL DIMENSION OF ENVIRONMENTAL CHANGE: FIT, INTERPLAY, AND SCALE 55 (2002).

32 *Id.*

33 *See, e.g.,* DAVID WALDSTREICHER, SLAVERY'S CONSTITUTION: FROM REVOLUTION TO RATIFICATION (2009).

34 On informal norms as effective restraints in homogenous communities, see, *e.g.,* ROBERT ELLICKSON, ORDER WITHOUT LAW: HOW NEIGHBORS SETTLE DISPUTES (1991); Ann E. Carlson, *Recycling Norms* 89 CALIF. LAW REV. 1231, 1233–34 (2001).

35 For the argument that the American legal system "embodies our last remaining vestige of a sense of 'community'—of shared values and expectations," which makes the role of law, the rule of law, and the legal profession, so important in American culture, see Timothy P. Terrell & James H. Wildman, *Rethinking "Professionalism,"* 41 EMORY L. J. 403, at 422–23 (1992).

36 ABEL, AMERICAN LAWYERS, *supra* note 1, at 55–75.

37 *Id.* at 64–65 (citations omitted).

38 *Id.* at 55–57 (citation omitted).

39 Aristotle, The Politics and the Constitution of Athens 88 (Stephen Everson ed., 1996).

40 RONALD A. CASS, THE RULE OF LAW IN AMERICA 4 (2001).

41 PAUL GOWDER, THE RULE OF LAW IN THE REAL WORLD 7 (2016). *See also* A.V. DICEY, INTRODUCTION TO THE STUDY OF THE LAW OF THE CONSTITUTION 202–03 (10th ed. 1960).

42 U.N. Secretary-General, *The Rule of Law and Transitional Justice in Conflict and Post-Conflict Societies,* ¶ 6, U.N. DOC. S/2004/616 (Aug. 23, 2004).

43 BRIAN Z. TAMANAHA, ON THE RULE OF LAW: HISTORY, POLITICS, THEORY 91–113 (2004); *see also* C. Edwin Baker, *Counting Preferences in Collective Choice Situations,* 25 U.C.L.A. L. REV. 381, 414 (1978).

44 Philip Pettit, *Democracy, Electoral and Contestatory,* in DESIGNING DEMOCRATIC INSTITUTIONS 105, 106 (Ian Shapiro & Stephen Maedo eds., 2000);

John Ferejohn, *Instituting Deliberative Democracy*, in DESIGNING DEMO-
CRATIC INSTITUTIONS 75, 76 (Ian Shapiro & Stephen Maedo eds., 2000).

45 Daniel Philpott, *Self-Determination in Practice*, in NATIONAL SELF-
DETERMINATION AND SECESSION 81 (Margaret Moore ed., 1998).

46 MICHAEL J. SANDEL, DEMOCRACY'S DISCONTENT: AMERICA IN
SEARCH OF A PUBLIC PHILOSOPHY 26 (1996).

47 TOM R. TYLER, WHY PEOPLE OBEY THE LAW 163 (1990).

48 ROBERT A. DAHL, ON DEMOCRACY 54 (1998).

49 ELINOR OSTROM, GOVERNING THE COMMONS: THE EVOLUTION OF
INSTITUTIONS FOR COLLECTIVE ACTION 83 (1990); TYLER, WHY PEOPLE
OBEY THE LAW, *supra* note 47, at 163.

50 Jane Mansbridge, *Conflict and Self-Interest in Deliberation*, in DELIBERATIVE
DEMOCRACY AND ITS DISCONTENTS 124 (Samantha Besson & José Luis
Martí eds., 2006).

51 DAVID LUBAN, LEGAL ETHICS AND HUMAN DIGNITY 19–64 (2007).

52 On the relationship between the adversarial system and democratic legitimacy,
see DANIEL MARKOVITS, A MODERN LEGAL ETHICS: ADVERSARY AD-
VOCACY IN A DEMOCRATIC AGE 184–99 (2008).

53 Deborah Rhode, *Access to Justice*, 69 FORDHAM L. REV. 1785, 1785–86 (2001).

54 PAUL H. ROBINSON & SARAH M. ROBINSON, SHADOW VIGILANTES:
HOW DISTRUST IN THE JUSTICE SYSTEM BREEDS A NEW KIND OF LAW-
LESSNESS (2018).

55 On cycles of constitutional change, and the institutional arrangements that drive
them and are driven by them, see JACK M. BALKIN, THE CYCLES OF CON-
STITUTIONAL TIME 14–15 (2020).

56 *Id.*

57 Monroe H. Freedman, *Professionalism in the American Adversary System*, 41
EMORY L. J. 467, 469 (1992). On the use of legal advocacy to advance differing
perspectives on civil rights, from both the left and the right, see Karen O'Connor
& Lee Epstein, *Rebalancing the Scales of Justice: Assessment of Public Interest Law*,
7 HARV. J.L. & PUB. POL'Y 483 (1984).

58 GOWDER, RULE OF LAW IN THE REAL WORLD, *supra* note 41, at 142–55.

59 *Id.* at 175–76.

60 Robert W. Gordon, *The Ethical Worlds of Large-Firm Litigators: Preliminary Observations*, 67 FORDHAM L. REV. 709, 727–30 (1998).

61 DAVID LUBAN, LAWYERS AND JUSTICE: AN ETHICAL STUDY 264 (1988).

62 Freedman, *supra* note 57, at 469–71.

63 For a discussion of the tension between rule-of-law principles as ends and means,
see Rachel Kleinfeld, *Competing Definitions of the Rule of Law: Implications for
Practitioners*, CARNEGIE ENDOWMENT FOR INTERNATIONAL PEACE 55
Carnegie Papers (January 2005).

64 For a discussion of the interplay between these concepts, see, *e.g.*, LUBAN, LE-
GAL ETHICS, *supra* note 51, at 24–28.

65 Frank I. Michelman, *Law's Republic*, 97 YALE L.J. 1493, 1501 (1988).

66 1 PHILIP C. JESSUP, ELIHU ROOT 133 (1964).

67 For a reflection on the tension the fictional Atticus Finch experienced in weighing community values and his own integrity in *To Kill a Mockingbird*, see Ava Ayers, *The Half-Virtuous Integrity of Atticus Finch*, 86 MISS. L.J. 33, 49–50 (2017).

68 Richard Wasserstrom, *Roles and Morality, in* THE GOOD LAWYER: LAWYERS' ROLE AND LAWYERS' ETHICS 25 (David Luban ed., 1983).

69 F. Scott Fitzgerald, *The Crack-Up: A Desolately Frank Document From One for Whom the Salt of Life Has Lost Its Savor*, ESQUIRE (Feb. 1936).

70 Legal Scholar Daniel Markovits criticizes this form of professional detachment as leading to a lack of accountability, see MARKOVITS, A MODERN LEGAL ETHICS, *supra* note 52, at 83–90; I believe it is a necessary approach for the lawyer both to restrain themselves from engaging innot just overzealous but also "*under-zealous*" advocacy.

71 THOMAS E. RICKS, FIRST PRINCIPLES: WHAT AMERICA'S FOUNDERS LEARNED FROM THE GREEKS AND ROMANS AND HOW THAT SHAPED OUR COUNTRY 5 (2020).

72 GORDON S. WOOD, THE RADICALISM OF THE AMERICAN REVOLUTION 104–6 (1991).

73 Deborah L. Rhode, *Access to Justice: An Agenda for Legal Education and Research*, 62 J. LEGAL EDUC. 531, 531 (2013).

74 On the intersection of law, political economy, and inequality, see Jedediah Britton-Purdy et al., *Building a Law-and-Political-Economy Framework: Beyond the Twentieth-Century Synthesis*, 129 YALE L.J. 1784 (2020).

75 Gillian K. Hadfield, *The Price of Law: How the Market for Lawyers Distorts the Justice System*, 98 MICH. LAW REV. 953, 955–56 (2000).

76 Charles H. Houston, *The Need for Negro Lawyers*, 4(1) J. NEGRO ED. 49, 49 (1935).

CHAPTER 6. A PUBLIC HEALTH CRISIS AND THE INSTITUTIONS OF EXCLUSION

1 Michelle Foster, *The Effects of the Pandemic on the Legal Industry*, FORBES (Nov. 8, 2021), www.forbes.com/sites/forbesbusinesscouncil/2021/11/08/the-effects-of-the-pandemic-on-the-legal-industry/?sh=fd6616d7f77a.

2 Mark A. Cohen, *Covid-19 Is Transforming the Legal Industry: Macro and Micro Evidence*, FORBES (Sept. 15, 2020, 6:18 AM), www.forbes.com/sites/markcohen1/2020/09/15/covid-19-is-transforming-the-legal-industry-macro-and-micro-evidence/?sh=43b3242a3269.

3 Patrick Smith & Dan Roe, *Remote or "Hybrid Light" in the Office? The Differences Matter to Attorneys and Should to Law Firms*, LAW.COM (May 2, 2022), www.law.com/americanlawyer/2022/05/02/remote-or-hybrid-light-the-differences-matter-to-attorneys-and-should-to-firms/?slreturn=20220821083335.

4   Christine Simmons & Dylan Jackson, *From Big Law to Boutiques, George Floyd's Death Prompts Outrage, Some Action from Law Firm Leaders*, LAW.COM. (June 1, 2020), www.law.com/americanlawyer/2020/06/01/from-big-law-to-boutiques-floyds-death-prompts-outrage-some-action-from-law-firm-leaders.

5   Dobbs v. Jackson Women's Health Org., 142 S. Ct. 2228 (2022).

6   Yvonne Wingett Sanchez, Patrick Marley & Matthew Brown, *Trust in the Supreme Court Falters After Roe Decision*, WASH. POST (July 3, 2022).

7   One pre-pandemic analysis showed that just 4 percent of lawyers worked remotely. Leonard Bierman & Michael A. Hitt, *Globalization of Legal Practice in the Internet Age*, 14 IND. J. GLOB. LEGAL STUD. 29, 30–31 (2007).

8   On the importance of effective supervision generally to ensure effective and ethical representation, see SECTION ON LEGAL EDUC. AND ADMISSIONS TO THE BAR, AMERICAN BAR ASS'N, LEGAL EDUCATION AND PROFESSIONAL DEVELOPMENT—AN EDUCATIONAL CONTINUUM 203–7 (Report of the Task Force on Law Schools and the Profession: Narrowing the Gap, 1992).

9   MODEL RULES OF PRO. CONDUCT r. 1.1 (A. B. A. 2020).

10 *Id.* at rr. 5.1 and 5.2.

11 *Id.* at r. 5.1.

12 CLIO, LEGAL TRENDS REPORT 23–24, 49–59 (2020), www.clio.com/wp-content/uploads/2020/08/2020-Legal-Trends-Report.pdf.

13 Martin Cogburn, *[Survey Results] How Law Firms Are Responding to COVID-19—Remote Work*, MYCASEBLOG, www.mycase.com/blog/2020/04/survey-results-how-law-firms-are-responding-to-covid-19-remote-work.

14 Author Interview with William Malley (August 10, 2022). Information related to Perkins Coie's practices and Malley's experiences are drawn from this interview.

15 Author Interview with Allison Frick (August 26, 2022). Information related to Frick's experiences are drawn from this interview.

16 Lyle Moran, *Will the COVID-19 Pandemic Fundamentally Remake the Legal Industry?*, ABA J. (Aug. 1, 2020), www.abajournal.com/magazine/article/will-the-covid-19-pandemic-fundamentally-remake-the-legal-industry.

17 THOMPSON REUTERS, THE IMPACTS OF THE COVID-19 PANDEMIC ON STATE & LOCAL COURTS STUDY 2021: A LOOK AT REMOTE HEARINGS, LEGAL TECHNOLOGY, CASE BACKLOGS, AND ACCESS TO JUSTICE (2021), https://legal.thomsonreuters.com/content/dam/ewp-m/documents/legal/en/pdf/white-papers/covid-court-report_final.pdf.

18 Author Interview with Carolyn Elefant (January 12, 2023). Information related to Elefant's experiences are drawn from this interview.

19 The Young Law. Ed. Bd., *The New Abnormal: How Firms and Lawyers Can Adapt to the Pandemic-Altered Present*, LAW.COM (Sept. 28, 2020, 3:36 PM), www.law.com/americanlawyer/2020/09/28/the-new-abnormal-how-firms-and-lawyers-can-adapt-to-the-pandemic-altered-present.

20 Author Interview with Sateesh Nori (August 12, 2022).

21 THE NEW YORK CITY FAMILY COURT COVID WORK GROUP: A JOINT
    PROJECT OF THE NEW YORK CITY BAR ASSOCIATION AND THE FUND
    FOR MODERN COURTS, THE IMPACT OF COVID-19 ON THE NEW YORK
    CITY FAMILY COURT: RECOMMENDATIONS ON IMPROVING ACCESS TO
    JUSTICE FOR ALL LITIGANTS (January 2022), http://moderncourts.org/wp-
    content/uploads/2022/02/NY-Family-Court-Report-1-22-2022.pdf.
22 Jeff John Roberts, *'Best Three Months of My Life': Overworked Lawyers Are Actu-
    ally Loving Lockdown*, FORBES (May 30, 2020), https://fortune.com/2020/05/30/
    lawyers-coronavirus-lockdown-work-from-home-law-firms-covid-19.
23 The Young Law. Ed. Bd., *supra* note 19.
24 Danielle Braff, *Thanks to the COVID-19 Pandemic, Law Firms Are Starting to
    Embrace Virtual Offices—but Will It Last?*, ABA J. (Feb. 1, 2021, 1:10 AM), www.
    americanbar.org/groups/journal/articles/2021/-thanks-to-the-covid-19-pandemic-
    -law-firms-are-starting-to-embr.
25 Michelle F. Davis & Jeff Green, *Three Hours Longer, the Pandemic Workday Has
    Obliterated Work-Life Balance, Bloomberg* (Apr. 23, 2020, 7:00 AM), www.bloom-
    berg.com/news/articles/2020-04-23/working-from-home-in-covid-era-means-
    three-more-hours-on-the-job.
26 NALP FOUNDATION FOR RESEARCH & EDUCATION, BEYOND THE
    BIDDING WARS: A SURVEY OF ASSOCIATION ATTRITION, DEPARTURE
    DESTINATIONS & WORKPLACE INCENTIVES 62 (2000).
27 Deborah L. Rhode, *From Platitudes to Priorities: Diversity and Gender Equity in
    Law Firms*, 24 GEO. J. LEGAL ETHICS 1041, 1048 (2011); Judith S. Kaye, *Women
    Lawyers in Big Firms: A Study in Progress Toward Gender Equality*, 57 FORDHAM
    L. REV. 111, 120–21 (1988).
28 Calandra McCool, *How Working Remotely Builds the Case for Accessibility*,
    A.B.A.: L. PRAC. TODAY (Aug. 14, 2020), www.lawpracticetoday.org/article/
    working-remotely-builds-case-accessibility.
29 Kate Beioley, *Coronavirus Forces Lawyers to Face Their Digital Future*, FIN.
    TIMES (Sept. 23, 2020), www.ft.com/content/4b5ad372-050a-4ab3-b2b9-
    4ac032cf8725.
30 Patrick Smith, *Law Firm Personnel Don't Want to Work in the Office. They Want
    to Meet and Socialize*, LAW.COM (Feb. 9, 2022), www.law.com/americanlaw-
    yer/2022/02/09/law-firm-personnel-dont-want-to-work-in-the-office-they-want-
    to-meet-and-socialize; Loeb Leadership, *The Legal Industry's Handling of the
    Disruption Caused by Covid-19 The Findings Report* 2 (2020).
31 Jim Sandman, *Addressing the Justice Gap after COVID*, ADDRESS TO THE MIN-
    NESOTA JUDICIAL BRANCH 13 (December 6, 2021).
32 *Id.* at 14.
33 *Id.*
34 Daniel Victor, *"I'm Not a Cat," Says Lawyer Having Zoom Difficulties*, N.Y. TIMES
    (Feb. 9, 2021), www.nytimes.com/2021/02/09/style/cat-lawyer-zoom.html.

35 Unopposed Plaintiffs' Motion to File Responsive Brief Late at 1–2, Gohmert v. Pence, No. 6:20-CV-660, 2021 WL 17141 (E.D. Tex. Jan. 1, 2021), *aff'd*, 832 F. App'x 349 (5th Cir. 2021).

36 Sandman, *supra* note 31, at 17.

37 *Id.* at 19.

38 *Id.* at 16–18.

39 Author Interview with Deborah Enix-Ross (December 13, 2022). References to comments made by Enix-Ross are drawn from this interview.

40 Author Interview with Swapna Reddy (August 18, 2022). Information related to ASAP, unless otherwise specified, is drawn from this interview.

41 Asylum Seeker Advocacy Project, Best Practices for Providing Legal Aid and Working Remotely (2021), https://asylumadvocacy. org/wp-content/uploads/2020/03/2021.01.22-ASAP-Best-Practices-for-Providing-Legal-Aid-and-Working-Remotely.pdf.

42 *Id.* at 2.

43 *Id.*

44 *Id.*

45 *Id.*

46 *Id.*

47 *Id.* at 3.

48 *Id.*

49 *Id.*

50 *Id.* at 4.

51 Marjorie M. Shultz & Sheldon Zedeck, Identification, Development, and Validation of Predictors for Successful Lawyering 24–27 (2008), http://papers.ssrn.com/sol3/papers.cfm?abstract_id=1442118.

52 Jennifer Gerarda Brown, *Creativity and Problem-Solving*, 87 Marq. L. Rev. 697, 698–99 (2004).

53 Cal Newport, Deep Work: Rules for Focused Success in a Distracted World (2016).

54 Matthew Syed, Rebel Ideas: The Power Of Diverse Thinking 23–25 (2019).

55 Michele Gelfand, Rule Makers, Rule Breakers: How Tight and Loose Cultures Wire Our World, 46 (2018); Eric F. Rietzschel, *What Are We Talking About, When We Talk About Creativity? Group Creativity as a Multifaceted, Multistage Phenomenon*, in Creativity in Groups, 15–18 (Elizabeth A. Mannix et al. eds., 2009).

56 Genna Rae McNeil, Groundwork: Charles Hamilton Houston and the Struggle for Civil Rights 6 (1983).

57 A. B.A., ABA National Lawyer Population Survey (2020). Any references to percentages here have been rounded up or down to the nearest whole number.

58 *Id.*
59 Nat'l Ass'n of Women Laws., 2019 Survey Report on the Promotion and Retention of Women in Law Firms 3–5 (2019).
60 *Id.* at 2, 5.
61 *Id.* at 5.
62 *Id.*
63 A. B. A., ABA Disability Statistics Report 1 (2011) www.americanbar.org/content/dam/aba/administrative/market_research/20110314_aba_disability_statistics_report.pdf.
64 *Id.*
65 A.B.A. Population Survey, *supra* note 57.
66 *Id.*
67 Danielle Root et al., *Building a More Inclusive Federal Judiciary*, Ctr. for Am. Progress (Oct. 3, 2019, 8:15 AM), www.americanprogress.org/issues/courts/reports/2019/10/03/475359/building-inclusive-federal-judiciary.
68 *Id.*
69 A. B. A., 2020 1L Enrollment by Gender & Race/Ethnicity (Aggregate) (2020), www.americanbar.org/groups/legal_education/resources/statistics.
70 *Id.*
71 *Id.*
72 *Id.*
73 *Id.*
74 Nat'l Ass'n for L. Placement, 2019 Report on Diversity in U.S. Law Firms 8 (2019).
75 James Lindgren, *Measuring Diversity: Law Faculties in 1997 and 2013*, 39 Harv. J. L. & Pub. Pol'y 89, 146 (2015).
76 *Id.* at 143.
77 Author Interview with Mark Alexander (September 23, 2022). References to comments made by Alexander are drawn from this interview.
78 American Association of Law Schools, Law deans Antiracism Clearinghouse Project, www.aals.org/about/publications/antiracist-clearinghouse.
79 Author Interview with Danielle Conway (December 12, 2022). References to comments made by Conway are drawn from this interview.
80 *See* Jeh Charles Johnson, Report from the Special Adviser on Equal Justice in the New York State Courts 2 (2020), www.nycourts.gov/whatsnew/pdf/SpecialAdviserEqualJusticeReport.pdf.
81 *Id.* at 54.
82 *Id.* at 31.
83 *Id.* at 61–62.
84 *Id.* at 63.
85 *Id.*
86 *Id.* at 66.

87 *Id.* at 80.

88 Author Interview with Lillian Moy (August 12, 2022). References to comments made by Moy are drawn from this interview.

89 Tsedale M. Melaku, *Why Women and People of Color in Law Still Hear "You Don't Look Like a Lawyer,"* HARV. BUS. REV. (Aug. 7, 2019), https://hbr.org/2019/08/why-women-and-people-of-color-in-law-still-hear-you-dont-look-like-a-lawyer.

90 Vernellia R. Randall, *The Misuse of the LSAT: Discrimination Against Blacks and Other Minorities in Law School Admissions*, 80 ST. JOHNS L. REV. 107, 108–36 (2006); Kenneth Walter Mack, *A Social History of Everyday Practice: Sadie T.M. Alexander and the Incorporation of Black Women into the American Legal Profession, 1925–1960*, 87 CORNELL L. REV. 1405 (2002); DANIEL MARKOVITS, THE MERITOCRACY TRAP: HOW AMERICA'S FOUNDATIONAL MYTH FEEDS INEQUALITY, DISMANTLES THE MIDDLE CLASS, AND DEVOURS THE ELITE 203–04 (2019).

91 Dorothy Atkins, *Atty's "See You Next Tuesday" Remark Prompts Bar Referral,* LAW360 PULSE (July 20, 2022), www.law360.com/pulse/articles/1513284/atty-s-see-you-next-tuesday-remark-prompts-bar-referral.

92 *See, e.g.,* Veronica Root Martinez, *Combating Silence in the Profession*, 105 VA. L. REV. 805, 805–17 (2019); Daria Roithmayr, *Barriers to Entry: A Market Lock-in Model of Discrimination*, 86 VA. L. REV. 727, 755–63, 785–87 (2000).

93 Martinez, *Combating Silence, supra* note 92, at 815–17.

94 *See, e.g.,* DERRICK BELL, SILENT COVENANTS: *Brown v. Board of Education* AND THE UNFULFILLED HOPES FOR RACIAL REFORM 134–35 (2004).

95 *See, e.g.,* Eric H. Holder, Jr., *Fifty-Third Cardozo Memorial Lecture: The Importance of Diversity in the Legal Profession*, 23 CARDOZO L. REV. 2241 (2002).

96 MEERA E. DEO, UNEQUAL PROFESSION: RACE AND GENDER IN LEGAL ACADEMIA 139–70 (2019).

97 *Id.* at 158.

98 *Id.*

99 *Id.*

100 *Id.; see also* Meera E. Deo, *Trajectory of a Law Professor*, 20 MICH. J. RACE & L. 441, 458 (2015).

101 DEO, UNEQUAL PROFESSION, *supra* note 96, at 158.

102 *See, e.g.,* Eilene Spear & Rachel Popa, *Legal Industry Updates from the National Law Review: Law Firm Moves, Hires and Response to Racial Injustice*, NAT'L L. REV. (June 29, 2020).

103 Law Deans Antiracist Clearinghouse Project, *supra* note 78.

104 Law Firm Anti-Racism Alliance, *About Us* (2022), www.lawfirmantiracismalliance.org/lfaacharter/Home.

105 *See, e.g.,* David Douglass, *Just Actions, Not Just Words*, ABA J. (Winter 2019–2020).

CHAPTER 7. A SERPENT IN THE EAR OF THE PRESIDENT

1 Paul Kane, *Inside the Assault on the Capitol: Evacuating the Senate*, WASH. POST (Jan. 6, 2021, 9:50 PM), www.washingtonpost.com/politics/reporter-senate-evacuated/2021/01/06/3e7d5456-5061-11eb-83e3-322644d82356_story.html (describing the occupation of the Capitol); Peter Baker, *A Mob and the Breach of Democracy: The Violent End of the Trump Era*, N.Y. TIMES (Jan. 6, 2021), www.nytimes.com/2021/01/06/us/politics/trump-congress.html (describing the Save America March).

2 Charlie Savage, *Incitement to Riot? What Trump Told Supporters Before Mob Stormed Capitol*, N.Y. TIMES (Jan. 12, 2021), www.nytimes.com/2021/01/10/us/trump-speech-riot.html.

3 *Id.*

4 Dan Barry & Sheera Frenkel, *'Be There. Will Be Wild!': Trump All but Circled the Date*, N.Y. TIMES (Jan. 8, 2021), www.nytimes.com/2021/01/06/us/politics/capitol-mob-trump-supporters.html?searchResultPosition=1.

5 Alan Feuer, *A State Senator Referred Rudy Giuliani for Disbarment*, N.Y. TIMES (Jan. 14, 2021), www.nytimes.com/2021/01/11/us/giuliani-disbarment.html.

6 Luke Mogelson, *Among the Insurrectionists*, NEW YORKER (Jan. 15, 2021), www.newyorker.com/magazine/2021/01/25/among-the-insurrectionists.

7 Kane, *Inside the Assault*, *supra* note 1 (describing the occupation of the Capitol).

8 *Id.*

9 *Id.*; Jenny Gross & Luke Broadwater, *Here Are the Republicans Who Objected to Certifying the Election Results.*, N.Y. TIMES: POL. (Jan. 8, 2021), www.nytimes.com/2021/01/07/us/politics/republicans-against-certification.html.

10 Richard H. Fallon, Jr., *Judicial Supremacy, Departmentalism, and the Rule of Law in a Populist Age*, 96 TEX. L. REV. 487, 549 (2018).

11 Richard E. Levy, *The Tie That Binds: Some Thoughts About the Rule of Law, Law and Economics, Collective Action Theory, Reciprocity, and Heisenberg's Uncertainty Principle*, 56 U. KAN. L. REV. 901, 903 (2008).

12 Jonathan Swan & Zachary Basu, *Episode 2: Barbarians at the Oval*, AXIOS: OFF THE RAILS (Jan. 17, 2021), www.axios.com/trump-lawyers-biden-election-victory-debf79bc-750b-457b-a736-789b501d62a7.html; Jim Rutenberg et al., *77 Days: Trump's Campaign to Subvert the Election*, N.Y. TIMES (Feb. 12, 2021), www.nytimes.com/2021/01/31/us/trump-election-lie.html.

13 Swan & Basu, *supra* note 12.

14 Maggie Haberman & Alan Feuer, *Trump Team Disavows Lawyer Who Peddled Conspiracy Theories on Voting*, N.Y. TIMES (Dec. 19, 2020), www.nytimes.com/2020/11/22/us/politics/sidney-powell-trump.html (noting the Trump campaign's statements distancing itself from Powell).

15 *Id.*

16 Swan & Basu, *supra* note 12.

17 Zach Montague & Alan Feuer, *Trump Campaign Lawyers Step Up but Are Swiftly Knocked Down*, N.Y. TIMES (Nov. 25, 2020), www.nytimes.com/2020/11/20/us/politics/trump-election-lawsuits.html.

18 Ashcroft v. Iqbal, 556 U.S. 662, 696 (2009) (Souter, J., dissenting).

19 *See* Amended Motion for Temporary Restraining Order, Latinos for Trump v. Sessions, 6:21-CV-43, 2021 WL 354970, at 2 & n. 2 (W.D. Tex. Jan. 21, 2021), www.courtlistener.com/recap/gov.uscourts.txwd.1120287/gov.uscourts.txwd.1120287.6.0_1.pdf.

20 *See, e.g.*, Trump v. Biden, No. 20–882, 2021 WL 78068, at *1 (U.S. Jan. 11, 2021) (denying a motion to expedite consideration of a petition for writ of certiorari challenging the Wisconsin election results); Trump v. Boockvar, No. 20–845, 2021 WL 78067, at *1 (U.S. Jan. 11, 2021) (denying a motion to expedite consideration of a petition for writ of certiorari for challenges to the Pennsylvania election results); Texas v. Pennsylvania, No. 155 ORIG., 2020 WL 7296814, at *1 (U.S. Dec. 11, 2020) (finding that Texas did not have standing to challenge the manner in which another state conducts its elections); Donald J. Trump for President, Inc. v. Sec'y of Pa., 830 F. App'x 377, 382 (3d Cir. 2020) (denying an injunction pending appeal that would have challenged millions of mail-in ballots).

21 *Texas*, 2020 WL 7296814, at *1.

22 Aaron Blake, *Trump Lawyers Suffer Embarrassing Rebukes from Judges Over Voter Fraud Claims*, WASH. POST (Nov. 11, 2020, 11:53 AM), www.washingtonpost.com/politics/2020/11/11/trump-lawyers-suffer-embarrassing-rebukes-judges-over-voter-fraud-claims.

23 Wis. Voters All. v. Pence, No. 20–3791, 2021 WL 23298, at *3 (D.D.C. Jan. 4, 2021).

24 Bush v. Gore, 531 U.S. 98 (2000).

25 Wis. Voters All. v. Pence, 514 F.Supp.3d 117, 121 (D.D.C. 2021).

26 *Id.*

27 *Id.*

28 Wis. Voters All. v. Pence, No. CV 20–3791 (JEB), 2021 WL 686359, at *2 (D.D.C. Feb. 19, 2021), *appeal dismissed sub nom.* Wisconsin Voters Alliance v. Harris, 28 F.4th 1282 (D.C. Cir. 2022).

29 *See Bibas, Stephanos*, FED. JUD. CTR., www.fjc.gov/history/judges/bibas-stephanos.

30 Donald J. Trump for President, Inc. v. Sec'y of Pa., 830 F. App'x 377, 381 (3d Cir. 2020).

31 In re Giuliani, 197 A.D.3d 1, 4 (1st Dep't 2021).

32 *See* Complaint Against Rudolph Giuliani at 11, Atty. Regis. No. 1080498 (Jan. 20, 2020) (on file with author). The author is a signatory to the complaint, though had no role in its drafting.

33 *Id.* at 11.

34 Annette John-Hall, Opinion, *The Capitol Insurrection Was Never About the Election. It Was About White Supremacy*, WHYY (Jan. 16, 2021), https://whyy.org/

articles/the-capitol-insurrection-was-never-about-the-election-it-was-about-white-supremacy.

35 *See* Email from Jeffrey Clark to Jeffrey Rosen et al. (December 28, 2020), www.judiciary.senate.gov/imo/media/doc/Rosen%20Ex%206%20-%20SJC-Pre-CertificationEvents-000697-702%20(December%2028,%202020%20email%20and%20attachment)1.pdf.

36 *Id.* at 2.

37 *Id.* at 2.

38 *Id.* at 3.

39 Katie Benner, *Trump and Justice Dept. Lawyer Said to Have Plotted to Oust Acting Attorney General*, N.Y. TIMES (Jan. 22, 2021), www.nytimes.com/2021/01/22/us/politics/jeffrey-clark-trump-justice-department-election.html.

40 Maggie Haberman, *In Videotaped Testimony, Barr Dismissed Trump's Claims of Fraud*, N.Y. TIMES (June 9, 2022), www.nytimes.com/2022/06/09/us/bill-bar-testimony-trump-january-6.html.

41 Memorandum from William J. Olson, attorney, to President Trump, *Preserving Constitutional Order*, at 1 (Dec. 28, 2020).

42 *Id.* (emphasis in original).

43 *Id.*

44 *Id.*

45 *Id.* at 2.

46 *Id.*

47 *Id.* at 2–3.

48 *Id.* at 3.

49 *Id.*

50 *Id.*

51 Memorandum from John Eastman, attorney, to Vice President Mike Pence, *January 6 scenario*, at 1, www.cnn.com/2021/09/21/politics/read-eastman-memo/index.html.

52 *Id.* at 2.

53 *Id.*

54 *Id.*

55 *Id.*

56 U.S. CONST. amend. XII.

57 Eastman Memorandum, *supra* note 51, at 2.

58 Collected emails between Gregory F. Jacob to John Eastman, *Subject: Pennsylvania Letter*, (Jan. 6, 2021, 12:14PM EST) (emphasis added), annexed as Exhibit N to Congressional Defendants' Brief to Plaintiff's Privilege Assertions, Eastman v. Thompson, Case No. 8:22-cv-00099-DOC-DFM (March 8, 2022).

59 *Id.*

60 *Id.*

61 *Id.*

62 *Id.*

63 Pub. L. No. 45–90, 24 Stat. 373 (1887).

64 Jack Beermann & Gary Lawson, *The Electoral Count Mess: The Electoral Count Act of 1887 Is Unconstitutional and Other Fun Facts (Plus a Few Random Speculations About Counting Electoral Votes)*, 16 FIU L. REV. 297, 314–19 (2022).

65 Eastman Memorandum, *supra* note 51, at 1.

66 Email from Jeffrey Clark, *supra* note 35, at 1.

67 Eastman Memorandum, *supra* note 51, at 1.

68 Tim Wu, Opinion, *What Really Saved the Republic from Trump?*, N.Y. TIMES (Dec. 10, 2020), www.nytimes.com/2020/12/10/opinion/trump-constitution-norms.html.

69 Benner, *Trump and Justice Dept. Lawyer*, *supra* note 39.

70 Sherrilyn A. Ifill, *Lawyers Enabled Trump's Worst Abuses*, N.Y. TIMES (Feb. 12, 2021), www.nytimes.com/2021/02/12/opinion/politics/trump-lawyers.html?referringSource=articleShare.

71 *Id.*

72 State *ex rel.* Okla. Bar Ass'n v. Andre, 957 P.2d 545, 548–49 (Okla. 1998).

73 MODEL RULES OF JUD. CONDUCT r. 2.9 (A. B. A. 2020) (prohibiting ex parte communications); MODEL RULES OF PRO. CONDUCT r. 3.5(b) (A. B. A. 2020) (prohibiting ex parte communications).

74 MODEL RULES OF PRO. CONDUCT at pmbl. ¶ 6.

75 Rule 8.4(b) renders it professional misconduct for a lawyer to "commit a criminal act that reflects adversely on the lawyer's honesty, trustworthiness or fitness as a lawyer in other respects," and 8.4(c) prohibits lawyers from "engag[ing] in conduct involving dishonesty, fraud, deceit or misrepresentation." MODEL RULES OF PRO. CONDUCT, *supra* note 73, at r. 8.4(b), (c).

76 *Id.* at r. 8.4(d).

77 *Id.* at r. 8.4(c).

78 *Id.* at r. 4.1.

79 *Id.* at r. 3.1.

80 *Id.* at r. 3.3.

81 *Id.*

82 The Model Rules' terminology section provides, "'Knowingly,' 'known,' or 'knows' denotes actual knowledge of the fact in question. A person's knowledge may be inferred from circumstances." MODEL RULES OF PRO. CONDUCT, *supra* note 73, at r. 1.0(f).

83 FED. R. CIV. P. 11(b).

84 *Id.*

85 FED. R. CIV. P. 11(b)(1).

86 FED. R. CIV. P. 11(b)(2).

87 FED. R. CIV. P. 11(b)(3).

88 556 F. Supp.3d 680 (E.D.Mich. 2021).

89 *Id.* (emphasis in original).

90 *Id.*, footnote omitted.

91 *See, e.g.,* Lawrence C. Marshall et al., *The Use and Impact of Rule 11,* 86 Nw. U.
L. REV. 943, 965–66 (1992); Melissa L. Nelken, *Sanctions Under Amended Rule
11—Some "Chilling" Problems in the Struggle Between Compensation and Pun-
ishment,* 74 GEO. L.J. 1313, 1327 (1986); Georgene M. Vairo, *Rule 11: A Critical
Analysis,* 118 F.R.D. 189, 200–02 (1988); Gerald F. Hess, *Rule 11 Practice in Federal
and State Court: An Empirical, Comparative Study,* 75 MARQ. L. REV. 313, 337–41
(1992). *But see* ELIZABETH C. WIGGINS ET AL., FED. JUD. CTR., RULE 11:
FINAL REPORT TO THE ADVISORY COMMITTEE ON CIVIL RULES OF
THE JUDICIAL CONFERENCE OF THE UNITED STATES § 1C (1991); Stephen
B. Burbank, *The Report of the Third Circuit Task Force on Federal Rule of Civil Pro-
cedure 11: An Update,* 19 SETON HALL L. REV. 511, 521–23 (1989).

CHAPTER 8. THE ACCESS-TO-JUSTICE CRISIS AND THE
RISE OF LEGAL TECHNOLOGY

1 THE HAGUE INSTITUTE FOR INNOVATION IN LAW & THE INSTITUTE
FOR THE ADVANCEMENT OF THE AMERICAN LEGAL SYSTEM, JUSTICE
NEEDS AND SATISFACTION IN THE UNITED STATES OF AMERICA 2021:
LEGAL PROBLEMS IN DAILY LIFE (2021).

2 U.S. LEGAL SERVICES CORPORATION, THE JUSTICE GAP: THE UNMET
CIVIL LEGAL NEEDS OF LOW-INCOME AMERICANS 8 (April 2022) (citations omitted).

3 *Id.*

4 *Id.*

5 *Id.* at 9.

6 *Id.*

7 *Id.*

8 REBECCA SANDEFUR, ACCESSING JUSTICE IN THE CONTEMPORARY
USA: FINDINGS FROM THE COMMUNITY NEEDS AND SERVICES STUDY
9–10 (2014).

9 *Id.* at 12–13.

10 Gillian Hadfield, *The Cost of Law: Promoting Access to Justice Through the (Un)
corporate Practice of Law,* 38 INT'L REV. L. & ECON. 43, 43 (2013).

11 GILLIAN K. HADFIELD, RULES FOR A FLAT WORLD: WHY HUMANS
INVENTED LAW AND HOW TO REINVENT IT FOR A COMPLEX GLOBAL
ECONOMY 79 (2017).

12 Rebecca Love Kourlis, *Public Trust and Confidence in the Legal System: The Way
Forward,* INSTITUTE FOR THE ADVANCEMENT OF THE AMERICAN LEGAL
SYSTEM, https://iaals.du.edu/blog/public-trust-and-confidence-legal-system-
way-forward (September 13, 2019).

13 CLAYTON M. CHRISTENSEN, THE INNOVATOR'S DILEMMA: WHEN NEW
TECHNOLOGIES CAUSE GREAT FIRMS TO FAIL (1997).

14 W. Bradley Wendel, *Foreword: The Profession's Monopoly and Its Core Values,* 82
FORDHAM L. REV. 2563, 2568–69 (2014).

15 GEORGE MARTIN, CAUSES AND CONFLICTS: THE CENTENNIAL HIS-TORY OF THE ASSOCIATION OF THE BAR OF THE CITY OF NEW YORK, 1870–1970, at 191–92 (1970).

16 BILL GATES, THE ROAD AHEAD 316 (1995).

17 CLAYTON M. CHRISTENSEN & MICHAEL E. RAYNOR, THE INNOVATOR'S SOLUTION: CREATING AND SUSTAINING SUCCESSFUL GROWTH 34–35 (2003).

18 Author Interview with James Sandman (August 4, 2022).

19 On the difference between machine learning and artificial intelligence, see Bernard Marr, *What Is the Difference Between Artificial Intelligence and Machine Learning?* FORBES (Dec. 6, 2016), www.forbes.com/sites/bernard-marr/2016/12/06/what-is-the-difference-between-artificial-intelligence-and-machine-learning/?sh=185675a22742.

20 Mark K. Osbeck, *Lawyer as Soothsayer: Exploring the Important Role of Outcome Prediction in the Practice of Law*, 123 PENN ST. L. REV. 41, 88–91 (2018).

21 MODEL RULES OF PRO. CONDUCT r. 1.1 cmt. 8 (A. B. A. 2020).

22 Deborah Kelly, *The Legal Services Corporation's Solicitation Restriction and the Unconstitutional Conditions Doctrine: Has the Death Knell Sounded for Future Challenges to the Restriction?* 29 SETON HALL LEGIS. J. 247, 256–58 (2004).

23 Author Interview with Adam Stofsky (September 13, 2022). References to comments made by Stofsky or about Briefly are drawn from this interview.

24 Author Interview with Elizabeth Tran & Marilyn Brown (January 11, 2022). References to comments by Tran or Brown are drawn from this interview unless otherwise indicated.

25 Email from Marilyn Brown to Author, dated January 11, 2022 (on file with Author).

26 RICHARD SUSSKIND, ONLINE COURTS AND THE FUTURE OF JUSTICE (2019).

27 Judith Resnik, *Fairness in Numbers: Comment on* AT&T v. Concepcion, Wal-Mart v. Dukes, *and* Turner v. Rogers, 125 HARV. L. REV. 78 (2011).

28 CAROLYN ELEFANT, KNOWING AND PROTECTING YOUR RIGHTS WHEN AN INTERSTATE GAS PIPELINE COMES TO YOUR COMMUNITY: A LEGAL AND PRACTICAL GUIDE FOR STATES, LOCAL GOVERNMENT UNITS, NON-GOVERNMENTAL ORGANIZATIONS AND LANDOWNERS ON HOW THE FERC PIPELINE CERTIFICATION PROCESS WORKS AND HOW YOU CAN PARTICIPATE (May 17, 2010), https://lawofficesofcarolynelefant.com/wp-content/uploads/2010/06/FINALTAGguide.pdf.

29 Author Interview with Carolyn Elefant (January 12, 2023). References to comments made by Elefant are drawn from this interview.

30 RICHARD SUSSKIND, THE END OF LAWYERS? RETHINKING THE NATURE OF LEGAL SERVICES 29 (2008).

31 HENRY FORD & SAMUEL CROWTHER, MY LIFE AND WORK 72 (1922).

32 Raymond H. Brescia, *Uber for Lawyers: The Transformative Potential of a Sharing Economy Approach to the Delivery of Legal Services*, 64 BUFF. L. REV. 745, 760–66 (2016).

33 Author Interview with Mark O'Brien (August 12, 2022). References to comments made by O'Brien or about Pro Bono Net are drawn from this interview.

34 Author Interview with Sateesh Nori (August 12, 2022). References to comments made by Nori or about JustFix are drawn from this interview.

35 Erica Braudy & Kim Hawkins, *Power and Possibility in the Era of Right to Counsel, Robust Rent Laws & COVID-19*, 28 GEO. J. ON POVERTY L. & POL'Y 117 (2021).

36 Consumer Financial Protection Bureau, *What Is a Qualified Mortgage?*, www.consumerfinance.gov/ask-cfpb/what-is-a-qualified-mortgage-en-1789.

37 BRUCE LARSON, FAITH FOR THE JOURNEY 32 (1986).

38 CLAYTON CHRISTENSEN, TADDY HALL, KAREN DILLON & DAVID S. DUNCAN, COMPETING AGAINST LUCK: THE STORY OF INNOVATION AND CUSTOMER CHOICE (2016).

39 Author Interview with Swapna Reddy (August 18, 2022).

40 MODEL RULES OF PRO. CONDUCT, *supra* note 21, at r. 1.5.

41 Matter of N.Y. City Lawyers' Ass'n v. Dacey, 28 A.D.2d 161 (1ˢᵗ Dep't, 1967), *rev'd*, N.Y. Cty. Lawyers' Ass'n v. Dacey, 21 N.Y.2d 694, 965 (1967).

42 *Id.* at 174.

43 *See, e.g.*, Medlock v. LegalZoom.Com, Inc. (Report on Findings of Fact and Recommendations to Approve the Settlement Agreement) 2013 S.C. LEXIS 362, at 17–18.

44 Citizenshipworks, www.citizenshipworks.org/en.

45 Tara Hughes & Joyce Reichard, *How States Are Using Limited Licensed Legal Paraprofessionals to Address the Access to Justice Gap*, A.B.A. STANDING COMMITTEE ON PARALEGALS AND APPROVAL COMMISSION BLOG, (Sept. 2, 2022), www.americanbar.org/groups/paralegals/blog/how-states-are-using-non-lawyers-to-address-the-access-to-justice-gap.

46 *Id.*

47 Fern Fisher-Brandveen & Rochelle Klempner, *Unbundled Legal Services: Untying the Bundle in New York State*, 28 FORDHAM URB. L.J. 1107 (2002).

48 Daniel J. Siegel, *Playing in the Regulatory Sandbox: A Survey of Developments*, L. PRAC. MAG. (July 1, 2021), www.americanbar.org/groups/law_practice/publications/law_practice_magazine/2021/ja21/siegel.

49 Author Interview with Deborah Enix-Ross (December 13, 2022).

50 Siegel, *supra* note 48.

51 TOM KELLEY & DAVID KELLEY, CREATIVE CONFIDENCE: UNLEASHING THE CREATIVE POTENTIAL WITHIN US ALL 24–25 (2013).

52 LEGAL SERVS. CORP., REPORT OF THE SUMMIT ON THE USE OF TECHNOLOGY TO EXPAND ACCESS TO JUSTICE 8–9 (2013), www.lsc.gov/our-impact/publications/other-publications-and-reports/report-summit-use-technology-expand-access.

53 Kevin Roose, *An A.I.-Generated Picture Won an Art Prize. Artists Aren't Happy*, N.Y. TIMES (Sept. 2, 2022), www.nytimes.com/2022/09/02/technology/ai-artificial-intelligence-artists.html.

54 Jenna Greene, *Will ChatGPT Make Lawyers Obsolete? (Hint: Be Afraid)*, Reuters (Dec. 9, 2022), www.reuters.com/legal/transactional/will-chatgpt-make-lawyers-obsolete-hint-be-afraid-2022-12-09.

55 Kevin Kelly, The Inevitable: Understanding the 12 Technological Forces That Will Shape Our Future 41 (2016).

56 Andrew McAfee & Erik Brynjolfsson, The Second Machine Age: Work, Progress, and Prosperity in a Time of Brilliant Technologies 284 (2016 ed.).

CHAPTER 9. THE PURPOSE OF THE PROFESSION

1 Patrick R. Krill, Ryan Johnson & Linda Albert, *The Prevalence of Substance Use and Other Mental Health Concerns Among American Attorneys*, 10 J. Addiction Med. 46, 47–48 (2016).

2 *Id.* at 49.

3 *Id.* at 51.

4 Cheryl Ann Krause & Jane Chong, *Lawyer Wellbeing as a Crisis of the Profession*, 71 S.C. L. Rev. 203, 207 (2019).

5 *Id.* at 206.

6 Krill, Johnson & Albert, *The Prevalence of Substance Use*, supra note 1, at 50–51.

7 Heidi Alexander et al., *The Profession: The Road to Attorney Well-Being: Past, Present, and Future*, 65 B.B.J. 22, 22 (2021).

8 Krill, Johnson & Albert, *The Prevalence of Substance Use*, supra note 1, at 50.

9 Lawrence S. Krieger and Kennon M. Sheldon, *What Makes Lawyers Happy? A Data-Driven Prescription to Redefine Professional Success*, 83 Geo. Wash. L. Rev. 554, 588–91 (2015).

10 *Id.* at 591.

11 *Id.* at 592.

12 *Id.*

13 *Id.* at 618.

14 Melissa H. Weresh, *The Chicken or the Egg? Public Service Orientation and Lawyer Well-Being*, 36 U. Ark. Little Rock L. Rev. 463, 485 (2014).

15 *Id.*

16 Krause & Chong, *Lawyer Wellbeing*, supra note 4, at 236.

17 *Id.* at 204.

18 *Id.*

19 *Id.*

20 *Id.*

21 *Id.* at 236. This recommendation is not without criticism. *See* Nicholas D. Lawson, *"To Be a Good Lawyer, One Has to Be a Healthy Lawyer": Lawyer Well-Being, Discrimination, and Discretionary Systems of Discipline*, 34 Geo. J. Legal Ethics 65, 94 (2021).

22 Krause & Chong, *Lawyer Wellbeing*, supra note 4, at 237.

23 *Id.* at 238.

24 *Id.*

25 *Id.* at 239.

26 DANIEL H. PINK, DRIVE: THE SURPRISING TRUTH ABOUT WHAT MO-
TIVATES US (2011).

27 *Id.* at 78–79.

28 VIKTOR E. FRANKL, MAN'S SEARCH FOR MEANING 110 (1992 ed.) (1946).

29 *See, e.g.*, ROBERT M. COVER, JUSTICE ACCUSED (1975); Stephen Ellman,
What Role Should Morality Play in Judging?, 19 CARDOZO L. REV. 1047 (1997).

30 Ethan S. Burger & Mary S. Holland, *Why the Private Sector Is Likely to Lead the
Next Stage in the Global Fight Against Corruption*, 30 FORDHAM INT'L. L.J. 30
(2006).

31 Bates v. State Bar of Arizona, 433 U.S. 350 (1977).

32 URBAN JUSTICE CTR., DEBT WEIGHT: THE CONSUMER CREDIT CRISIS
IN NEW YORK CITY AND ITS IMPACT ON THE WORKING POOR (2007).

33 MODEL RULES OF PRO. CONDUCT r. 1.6(b) (A. B. A. 2020).

34 *Id.* at r. 1.6, com. 17.

35 For a description of the campaign for marriage equality, see NATHANIEL
FRANK, AWAKENING: HOW GAYS AND LESBIANS BROUGHT MARRIAGE
EQUALITY TO AMERICA (2017).

36 Obergefell v. Hodges, 576 U.S. 644 (2015).

37 Respect for Marriage Act, Pub. L. No. 117–228 (2022).

38 MODEL RULES OF PRO. CONDUCT, *supra* note 33, at r. 8.3(a).

39 Weider v. Skala 80 N.Y.2d 628 (1992).

40 Mary Walsh Fitzpatrick & Rosemary Queenan, *Professional Identity Formation
and Its Pedagogy*, 89 UMKC L. REV. 539, 540 (2021).

41 Standard 311(b), A. B. A., 2022–2023 STANDARDS AND RULES OF PROCE-
DURE FOR APPROVAL OF LAW SCHOOLS (2022).

42 *Id.* at 311(d).

43 For a description of ways to make effective legal training less expensive to achieve,
both as it relates to earning a juris doctor and other degrees, see BENJAMIN H.
BARTON & STEPHANOS BIBAS, REBOOTING JUSTICE: MORE TECHNOL-
OGY, FEWER LAWYERS, AND THE FUTURE OF LAW 164–77 (2017).

44 *See* NATIONAL CONFERENCE OF BAR EXAMINERS, ABOUT THE NEXT-
GEN BAR EXAM, https://nextgenbarexam.ncbex.org.

45 Shira Feder, *Law Students Say They Avoid Therapy Because They Worry It Could
Affect Their Job Prospects*, INSIDER (Feb. 25, 2020, 11:58 AM), www.insider.com/
law-students-avoid-getting-mental-health-treatment-due-to-stigma-2020-2.

46 556 F. Supp.3d 680, 732 (E.D. Mich. 2021).

47 *Id.* (citation omitted).

48 *Id.*

49 FED. R. CIV. PROC. 11, Advisory Committee Notes to 1993 Amendments.

50 556 F. Supp.3d at 734.

51 *Id.*

52 *Id.*

53 *Id.*

54 NASCO v. Chambers, 501 U.S. 32 (1991).

55 FED. R. CIV. PROC. 11(c)(2).

56 *See* 3 U.S.C. § 5; Bush v. Palm Beach Cty. Canvassing Bd., 531 U.S. 70 (2000); Bush v. Gore, 531 U.S. 98 (2000) (concurring opinion of Renhnquist, C.J.).

57 3 U.S.C. § 15.

58 552 F. Supp.3d 1168 (D. Colo. 2021).

59 *Id.* at 1174.

60 2022 WL 17588344 (10ᵗʰ Cir. 2022).

61 *Id.* at *1.

62 Goodyear Tire & Rubber Co. v. Haeger, 581 U.S. 101, ___, 137 S. Ct. 1178, 1186 (2017).

63 Texas v. Pennsylvania, 592 U.S. ___, 141 S. Ct. 1230 (2020). Technically, the case was never filed. Rather, on December 7, 2020, the state of Texas petitioned the Supreme Court for permission to file the action. The Court denied that permission on December 11, 2020, finding Texas did not have standing to bring the action.

64 *See, e.g.,* NASCO v. Chambers, 501 U.S. 32 (1991).

65 Alan Feuer, *A Judge Wants a Bigger Role for Female Lawyers. So He Made a Rule.*, N.Y. TIMES (Aug. 23, 2017), www.nytimes.com/2017/08/23/nyregion/a-judge-wants-a-bigger-role-for-female-lawyers-so-he-made-a-rule.html.

66 For an exploration of these issues in the context of immigration matters, see Ingrid V. Eagly, *Remote Adjudication in Immigration*, 109 Nw. U. L. REV. 933 (2015).

67 Brian Baxter, *Morgan Stanley Top Lawyer Demands Law Firms Return to Office*, BLOOMBERG (July 16, 2021), https://news.bloomberglaw.com/business-and-practice/morgan-stanleys-legal-chief-wants-law-firms-back-in-the-office.

INDEX

AALS (American Association of Law
Schools), 59, 88, 132
ABA. *See* American Bar Association
Abbot, Everett V., 65
Abbott, Lyman, 92
Abel, Richard, 81
abortion rights, 113
access to justice, 3–4, 12–13, 158–99; cartelization of access to legal profession
and, 109; client advocacy of, 234–35;
commoditization of legal services
and, 167, 177–78, 183–84, 193–94; concerns about, in late nineteenth to early
twentieth centuries, 67, 75; contingency fees, criticism of, 75–77; COVID-19
pandemic and, 119, 120, 159; dispute
resolution, 174–75, 189–90; experimentation, permission for, 195–96; law
schools, role of, 219; legal information
delivery systems, 175–77, 190; legal
services technologies, 177–84, 191;
"legal tech," promises and problems
of, 162–67; as legal value, 108–9; monopolized market for delivery of legal
services and, 198; nonlawyers, services
provided by, 193–94, 196–97; professionalism concerns related to, 184–85,
186–87; remote court proceedings, 119,
120–23; remote technologies and, 170;
rise of public interest bar and, 90–93
(*See also* public interest bar); rule of
law and, 159–62, 185; statistical evidence of crisis in, 159–60; triage tech,
170–73, 178, 191–92, 193, 194; UPL rules

and, 210–14; values-based approach
to, 184–89, 198–99
access to legal profession: cartelization and
access to justice, 109; institutionalized
exclusion, 136–38; Jacksonian democracy and early nineteenth century
opening of, 40; law schools, reform
proposals for, 218–22; legal education, institutionalization of exclusion
through, 80–90, 102; racial/gender
justice and, 140–41; reform proposals,
222–24; weak barriers to entry, late
nineteenth to early twentieth century
concerns about, 6, 8, 68. *See also* bar
examinations/admission to bar; education, legal; immigrants entering legal
profession; racial and gender justice
Acemoglu, Daron, 10, 98, 100, 105
Adams, John, 2, 6, 18, 19, 20, 23, 27, 32, 65
Adams, John Quincy, 48, 253n89
Adams, Samuel, 32
adversarial nature of American law and
American democracy, 104–5, 106–7,
236
advertising by lawyers: in late nineteenth
to early twentieth century, 77–78; publicity tech, 168, 170–71, 175, 178
Advisory Committee on Civil Rules, 227,
229
African Americans. *See* racial and gender
justice
Alabama: constitution of 1901, 74; ethics
code (1887), 72, 73–74, 75, 77
Albany Law Journal, 55

institutional perspective, 6–11, 12, 94–112;
adversarial nature of American law
and American democracy, 104–5,
106–7, 236; American democratic
institutions, role of legal profession in
function of, 100–101; change, potential for, 105, 201–2; characteristics of
American legal system, 102–5; crises,
addressing, 111–12; exclusion, institutionalized, 136–38; inclusive versus
extractive institutions, 10, 98–99, 105,
109, 185–86, 198, 207; professionalism
and, 101–2, 106–8; reform proposals
and, 208–9; on rule of law, 100–101,
102–4, 266n35; theoretical approach,
95–100; values-based approach to, 101,
106–11
insurrection (January 6, 2021), 4, 142–43,
146, 148, 153, 230, 239
internet, legal use of, 164–66, 168

Jackson, Andrew, 6
Jackson, Jonathan, 22, 29–30, 32
Jacksonian democracy, 40–44, 65, 70
Jacob, Gregory, 150–51
January 6 insurrection (2021), 4, 142–43,
146, 148, 153, 230, 239
Jay, John, 17, 27, 33
Jefferson, Thomas, 2, 20, 27, 28, 29, 31–32,
81
Jews entering legal profession, 66, 74
Jim Crow, 51, 62, 74, 91, 200, 208
Johnson, Jeb, 133, 136
Jones, Thomas Goode, 74, 260n102
JustFix, 180–82, 280n34

Kasparov, Garry, 198
Kaufman, Lieb, Lebowitz & Frick, 118
Kent, James, 54
King v. Whitmer, 155–56, 227
King's College (later Columbia Univer-
sity), 25
Kourlis, Rebecca Love, 161

Krause, Cheryl Ann, 204–5
Krieger, Lawrence S., 204, 205, 206

laissez-faire economics, 61
Langston, John Mercer, 51
late nineteenth to early twentieth
century, 11, 61–93; ABA's Canons of
Professional Ethics (1908), 72–80;
crisis of legal profession in, 62–68;
early codes of ethics, 69–72; law firms,
68–69; organization of lawyers in,
68–69; profit orientation of lawyers,
concerns about, 63–65, 67, 75; public
interest bar, rise of, 90–91; social and
technological change in, 61–62, 68;
social origins and standing of lawyers
in, 63–65
law and lawyers in America. *See* American legal profession
Law Deans Antiracist Clearinghouse
Project, 132, 138
Law Firm Anti-Racism Alliance, 138–39
law firms: formal organization of, 6;
institutionalization of, 9–10; late
nineteenth to early twentieth century, 68–69; minorities and women,
limited entry for, 59; New York City
firms joining city bar association,
54; reform proposals involving,
235–36. *See also specific firms by
name*
law schools. *See under* education, legal
LawHelp, 171, 180
lawyer disaffection, 4, 12, 202–7
lawyer disaffection, problem of, 4, 12
Legal Aid Society of New York, 91, 92
Legal Design Lab, Stanford Law School,
226
legal education. *See* education, legal
legal information delivery systems, 175–
77, 190
legal profession, American. *See* American
legal profession

ABOUT THE AUTHOR

RAY BRESCIA is the Hon. Harold R. Tyler Chair in Law & Technology at Albany Law School. Previously, he represented client groups from low-income communities of color in New York City and New Haven for fourteen years. He also served as a law clerk to the Honorable Constance Baker Motley of the U.S. District Court for the Southern District of New York. He is the author of *The Future of Change: How Technology Shapes Social Revolutions* and the co-editor of *Crisis Lawyering: Effective Legal Advocacy in Emergency Situations* and *How Cities Will Save the World: Urban Innovation in the Face of Population Flows, Climate Change, and Economic Inequality.*